REALITY GLASSES:

Personal Change in a World Without Free Will

Alan Jaffe

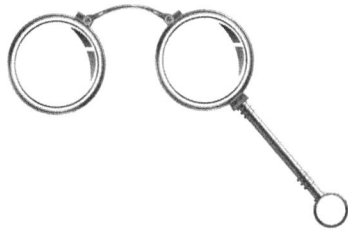

© Alan Jaffe 2020

All Rights Reserved. No part of this publication may be reproduced, distributed, or transmitted in any form or by any means, including photocopying, recording, or other electronic or mechanical methods, without the prior written permission of the author, except in the case of brief quotations embodied in critical reviews and certain other noncommercial uses permitted by copyright law.

ISBN 978-0-578-66773-7

PREFACE

Why write this book? So many great journeys begin with a question.

I remember the younger of my two very intelligent brothers telling me one day, "Alan, it isn't your job to change people." I love statements like this: They pull me out of my current mindset and make me really think my personal reality which determines how I view the world.

The hardline, deterministic answer to the question would be the following: I have no choice but to write this book. The stars have aligned in such a way, making the world the way it is. That, combined with my genetics—which I have no control over—compels me to write this book right now. But here is the answer as it appears to me: because I want to. Isn't that the answer to why we do everything? And here is some information about why I actually wanted to write this book.

The world has been saturated with the constant instant sharing of new information due to the advent of the internet. Though easy access to information is still relatively new, we are starting to see some short-term results of having a colossal amount information at our fingertips. Like shaking a snow globe, the dust hasn't completely settled, but we are finally able to peer through the storm. It is my opinion that we need a way of viewing, processing, and filtering the sheer volume of information. By having a better understanding of the information, and thus the world we live in, we can choose what to change without unknowingly being changed and live our lives without being constantly manipulated, whether or not we also consciously choose to maintain the convenient illusion that we are fully in charge of our lives and choices through the exercise of our so-called free will.

Thank you so much to everyone whom I have met along my journey, people who were willing to share freely their own viewpoints, leading me to the actualizations of which I am to share in this book. There are many whom I am unable to thank for they have already passed away, or whose books and videos on the internet I have learned from and yet have no way of thanking them directly. We truly stand on the shoulders of those who have gone before us.

WARNING

If you don't want to have your view of reality altered, then please don't continue.

TABLE OF CONTENTS

Preface i
Warning ii
Introduction ix
    A Central Question xi
    New Glasses xi

Section 1: Building New Glasses 1

    Chapter 1: Meta and Viewpoints 1
        Levels 2
        Deciding What You Want 3
        Be Wary of Fear 4
        Higher Versus Lower Meta 6
        Viewpoints 7
    Chapter 2: Bell Curves and Greyscales 9
        Terminology 9
    Chapter 3: The Human Equation and Change 19
        The Human Equation 19
        Change 19
        Reality 19
        How the Formula Works 20
        A Word on "Good" 25
        Change and Cognitive Dissonance 27
    Chapter 4: The Realities of a World Without Free Will 31
        Coping with Reality 31
        Free Will and Responsibility 32
        Fear and Freedom 33

Criminals, Extremism, and Changing the Natural Script 36

Human Outliers 38

Ego, Hate, and Bigotry Just Doesn't Make Any Sense 39

Why Is Fortune-Telling in This Book? 40

The Connection 42

Section 2: Playing with Our New Glasses 45

What Do We Know Now? 46

Humans and Computers 46

Changing Gears Between Free Will and No Free Will 47

Stay in One Gear All the Time: The One True Meta? 48

Focus Has Limits: The Power of Adaptation and the Weakness of Fixation 49

Don't Be a Jerk 51

On Autism and Categorizing States of Realization 52

The Optimistic Side of Inevitability 53

Levels of Understanding 55

The Secret Hidden Section of Ultimate Knowledge of WTF Is Going on in the World and How to Understand the Way the World Works 60

Everything is Cause and Effect (The Apex Meta for Our Universe .. 60

Cognitive Dissonance 71

A Shift 84

Phrases and Quotes That I've Heard and How I Translate or Understand Them Through the Lens of Cause and Effect, AKA Reality 85

A Word to Fiction Writers 87

Four Chapters Defined by Cause and Effect 88

Some Things to Consider from the "Fallout" of Causation 90

The Causation of Changing a Person's Reality 91

Everyone Has a Weapon, a Tool 92

Section 3: Experiences/Memories, Rules, Platforms, and Apex Platforms 95

Another Way of Viewing the Hypercube and How It Relates to Point of View 97

Learning to Reform the Platform 98

Reluctance to Perform a Task and Procrastination 99

WTF is an Apex Platform? 100

Purposely Changing the Platform and Seeking Balance in One's Life 104

It Takes Time to Build a Platform: Don't Wait for an Emergency .. 106

The Need for Rules & Cubes 107

The Pros and Cons of Rules 109

Analyzing Competency Via Memories, Rules, Cubes 116

Obsession 117

This Book: Rain, Lightning and Changing People—A Callback to Chapter 3 119

The Power of Belief 123

Do Versus Try 125

Societies 127

Many Causes, Many Effects: When Causality Gets Complicated ... 128

Time and Causation: Two Ways of Talking About the Same Thing 131

Complexity with Understanding and Learning 132

Illusory Cause and Effect that by Its Existence Produces a Real Cause and Effect 133

Personal Values from One's Platform(s) 137

Do the Ends Justify the Means? and Unintended Effects 138

Wish Fulfilment, Time Travel, Omniscience, Omnipotence, and Mistakes 143

v

Letting Go 145

Stuff About Religion and Cognitive Dissonance 146

Combining the Bell Curve with Cause and Effect; Cups Of Different Sizes 156

Questions as Stimuli (Causes) and Aggressive Interviewing......... 158

Applying Cause and Effect to Understanding Stimuli and Change . 160

Not All Experiences Are Created Equal: Using Simple Math to Understand More Complex Issues 162

My Mathematical Goblet Runneth Over....................................... 163

I Giveth and I Taketh Away.. 165

Put the Thingamajig In the Doohickey 168

Learning Difficulties Part 1: Senses.. 172

Learning Difficulties Part 2: Problems with Platforms; and Trust, Both Internal and External 174

Learning Difficulties Part 3: Belief and Keeping Ego in Check 177

Don't Fear Learning... 178

You Don't Know All of Who You Are... 179

Self-Efficacy and Becoming a Superhuman 180

False Claims About Causality and Confusion of Causality 182

It Could Be Worse—It Could Also Be *Way* Better........................ 184

False Causality 185

Moving a Knight: False Rules and Boundaries............................... 186

Ought Versus Is.. 187

Dumb Arguments: If Not Red, Then It *Must* Be Blue! 189

Arguing Past Each Other.. 191

For the Love of Arguing 192

Parenting 197

Unbalanced Relationships.. 199

Powerful Stimuli, Memories of Those Who Have Died 200

Changing Behavior 201

Causality: Does Math Always Work? (Yes); Confusion (Illusions of Randomness) 203

How Things Appear Versus the Reality of How They Actually Are Along with the Illusion of Free Will and Other Things 207

"Wants" Rule the World of Free Will 208

The Illusion of Randomness 209

Science: The Sometimes Accurate but Often Imperfect Cataloguing and Understanding of Cause and Effect 211

Science, Truth, and Belief 213

Moral Stuff 215

Consequentialism and Ignoring Reality 219

Identity Politics 223

Free Will and Accepting Cause and Effect 224

Cause and Effect with Free Will 224

Beware of Addiction: Forced Cause and Effect and Evilness 224

Beware of Artificial Intelligence 225

Levels of Absorption: My Love/Fear Relationship with Virtual Reality 226

Technology and Outsourcing: Things Get Worse 231

Virtual Reality Is Child's Play When It Comes to the True Evils ... 232

Rock the Damn Boat! 234

The Difficulty with Having to Make Decisions: The Need for Trust 236

Being Taken Advantage of 237

The Wars of Ideas 238

One of the Most Beautiful Relationships 239

Learning People: The Art of Getting to Know Someone 240

What You Realize You Didn't Realize 240

Social Situations, Autism, and Authenticity 242

The Physical Reactions to Being in a Platform
(Mindset/Meta/Viewpoint) 245

Authenticity and Memories: Becoming More Positive and Negative
.... 246

Truly Being with Someone: Sharing the Same Platform/Meta 247

Inauthentic Dating 250

Logistics 251

Rituals: Fantasy or Reality 252

New Beginnings: Building Social Platforms 253

Knowing What a Person Wants 255

Causality: The People We Meet 256

To Shortcut or Not to Shortcut 256

Opinions, Opinions, Opinions: When Platforms Collide 259

Reverse Platforming 267

Why Do I Study Martial Arts? 268

In a New Light 269

Closing Thoughts 272

INTRODUCTION

My hope is that this book will be a catalyst that will enable people to attain what they want in life. It is meant to create, not destroy. Sorry in advance for the inevitable collateral damage.

One of the feelings that I enjoy the most in life is when I realize just how much I have changed/learned/grown in various aspects of my life. At the end of the book, I hope that you will have the same feeling.

I can't give someone free will in a world without free will, but perhaps I can help steer the ship that is a human's life to help get them to where they want to go.

This book will deliver beliefs based on a foundation of logic to achieve a deep connection and solidarity with our fellow human beings and other lifeforms on this planet. By the end of the book, you should feel more secure in having an understanding of how the universe works.

Please read the next italicized section. Then, after finishing the book, return to this Introduction and reread the words. You will be able to test on your own how much your perspective has changed.

> *I don't want to change people's minds—actually, that is a lie I tell myself. I do want to change people's minds because I want to change their lives for the betterment of humanity.*
>
> *I can't force you or anyone to change. Well, I suppose I can force some of you to change, but I can't force all of my readers to change unless I do something extreme, and that would break a lot of views of morality.*
>
> *It is possible that even though I can't force anyone to change their minds, their minds still could change after reading my words. So is that forced change? If I pour water on a plant that is ready to absorb the liquid and it grows as a result of the water, then is that truly forced? If I pour water on a rock and it doesn't grow, then,*

well, what's the point? If there is no free will, then is everything we experience a forced experience? Are we all just victims of causality?

Yes, we are.

Please humor me and play along with this book. Even if you don't want to change at all, just look at this book as a mental exercise or simply pure entertainment. I just want you to see the way I view the world, even if just for a moment.

You know, the funny thing about reality is that it's a lot like a magic trick. Once you see how the trick is done, then you can never un-see it. The previous reality dissolves, and what is left is something totally new. Of course, just like waking up from a dream, you still can choose to believe that the dream is real. But even if you are able to override the logic of your own mind, the dream would still only be real for you alone. If you convince a lot of people to ignore reality, then that makes the dream only real for that group of people. The group can be wrong together. If many people convince everyone to believe in the dream, then everyone can be wrong about reality together.

There is no reward for getting more people to be wrong about reality. While sharing and believing misinformation as a collective might protect the individual from societal pressures, it doesn't actually have any effect on making the untruths real. What is so dangerous about misinformation is that, even though it doesn't directly change reality, it will still change a person's reality, and so it will change them. We have to be careful about our viewpoints.

If you believe in destiny and fate, then you are crazy. That, or you were born thousands of years ago when people were superstitious or just ignorant about the world.

At least that is what I used to believe. Now, however, I don't just believe in fate and destiny—I know that it is 100% real.

Do you?

A Central Question

I have been asked many times over the course of my life, "Alan, why do you study martial arts?" This book will explain to you my entire worldview so that I can answer this question in the most convoluted and roundabout, yet most accurate, way.

New Glasses

What we are going to do right now is build glasses from which we can see the world in a different way.

Analogy 1: The Puzzle

Imagine that you have a puzzle with extremely tiny pieces. Each piece can only be one color, but together they form a beautiful nature image. Now imagine that we take away everything that is the color green. The leaves and grass would disappear. Or perhaps we don't take away green, but we remove the color grey: Now the tree trunks would be gone.

You understand how this works. If you were to remove the puzzle pieces of any one color, then the picture wouldn't be complete. Going through life without a basic understanding of how the world works is like is like trying to see a painting with several colors removed from it. It will be stressful and confusing.

Analogy 2: The Elements

Imagine that you are on a spaceship, and you make contact with aliens. You wish to accurately describe our planet to the aliens. It would be impossible to explain how the world works without teaching them about the four elements: earth, water, fire, and air. Try to imagine our planet without earth. We wouldn't have, well, earth, rocks, or trees. The world wouldn't make a lot of sense. Now imagine the world without water. You would run into a lot of problems such as being confused about how creatures are able to live without water. You can keep going on and on with this example, but I think you get the point.

The above examples explain how difficult the world is to understand when you leave out either major or even seemingly minor components. Even small puzzle pieces missing from a puzzle can ruin the picture. In a two-dimensional puzzle, a puzzle piece is connected only to what borders it. In our world, there are far more connections because time changes the connections of each piece. The number of connections is far more complex.

Some say that everything is connected. The more common problem that exists is that people add stuff to the puzzle that doesn't belong. Imagine someone wants to put together a puzzle of a beautiful mountain and valley, and they can't let go of the belief that there should be a huge spaceship in the center of the valley. As long as they think there should be a spaceship in the center of the valley, the picture won't be accurate. This is a big problem because it is the result of misinformation and assumptions.

This fallacy—holding onto misinformation in the face of clear counter-evidence—occurs frequently in the field of education. It is a problem that crosses multiple disciplines, whether it is an athlete or musician learning a physical skill or a mathematician or writer working learning a more abstract or cognitive skill, and is reinforced by the incorrect view that the mind is distinct from the physical body.

Most people believe that, once they put on the special glasses of knowledge, they will see things in the world that they hadn't been able to see before. They want to believe that without knowledge they see an empty valley, and then by putting on glasses, suddenly a spaceship appears in the valley that they hadn't been able to see before. This is true for infants who are beginning life with a clean slate. When it comes to teenagers and adults, the opposite is often actually true. If someone wants to get to a higher level of reality, then they first have to remove all the misinformation from their current reality. Then, once the false beliefs have been removed, they can then begin to add and learn and truly get to the place they want to be at mentally.

A quick note on the placement of certain ideas within chapters: I will often explain the same concept in slightly different ways, moving from the particular to the general and back to the particular, because I want the lessons of this book to really click with different readers in different ways so that the book is a strong catalyst for change.

Section 1: Building New Glasses

CHAPTER 1: META AND VIEWPOINTS

KEY CONCEPTS: Ways of thinking about reality in both a broad general sense as well as the narrow sense for specific situations. Focusing on a particular situation versus "zooming out" and looking at how the situation pertains to the greater whole. Short-term thinking versus long-term thinking. Reality and Belief.

* * *

I chose the triple bar sign to represent the levels of *meta* for two reasons. First, a person's view at the current moment is a sum of the complex equation that makes a person who they are. One doesn't have much of an equation without an equal sign or identity sign or a similar concept. *Yes, I just reduced human beings to an equation.* Second, one line stacked upon another looks like levels to me. To my mind, it makes sense that there are different levels of cognition and thinking about situations—people are able to move between the levels with just a "decision."

Why the word *meta*? Meta is used in various contexts. While most see the concept of meta as just not taking a situation at its face value or as "gaming the system," meta in the present book refers to a different perspective on a given situation, often other than the one intended. This different perspective is brought on by a change in one's "mindset," which means that there is almost always a different set of values or morality when someone changes their meta view.

Seeing a situation at its face value is also one level of thinking. People have different "interpretations" of rules and how any given situation "should" be. Therefore, is there a "regular" meta that other metas are based around?

Here is meta as it pertains to a specific situation: thinking outside the box, not playing by the intended rules, looking beyond the game. The most common example of this is the genie in a bottle. If one uses the three wishes to ask for more wishes, then that would be gaming the system. This kind of gaming the system is not the kind of meta that this book will be dealing with—though you may end up being able to game the system of life by having a clearer picture of reality (in other words, it isn't the intent of the book, but you can benefit in such a way). Instead, the kind of meta this book refers to is more along the lines of different ways of looking at a similar situation: from the basic rules of a situation (as it is intended) to various aspects of a situation in a broader context.

Levels

Picture a wooden chair with a pad on it.

On a basic level, the chair is a chair. It is as basic as it sounds. Some concerns might be *Can it hold my weight? Is it comfortable?* But that is as interesting as the basic concept of a chair gets. On another level, the chair is the combination of materials that constitute it: pieces of wood (in this scenario) that are of specific measurements and are attached at specific angles with specific adhesives. On yet another level, the chair is a combination of atoms. As we learn more about the world, the meta changes and grows. Ultimately, everything is energy.

The takeaway from the previous paragraph is that all of the various ways of thinking about the chair are technically correct. The question is the following: What is the most useful for the situation you are in in life? Most of the time, for most people, the basic understanding of the chair is far more important than any other meta. If a person is in a survival situation, then whether a chair is made out of wood or plastic matters a lot more. If someone is an engineer and they are making a chair, then they have to know the structural integrity of the chair so that they know how much weight it can support. Otherwise, they could lose their job. Therefore, while they know they are building a chair, the second level of meta (knowing the angles and materials of the chair) is far more important. Lastly, there is the atomic composition of the chair, something that may be "more true" in actuality, but those who can take advantage of this knowledge are few and far between. In other words, there are few situations where understanding the atomic composition of the chair actually matters.

In your life, what is the "correct" level of meta that is most useful/applicable to get the things you want? The depth or level of meta will change depending on what situation you are in.

Deciding What You Want

Even more difficult than choosing a meta is deciding what you want in life. Most people will reach a point in life where they will experience a shift of meta. People who live life in the here-and-now will experience a shift in meta when they sit down and play a game with a child. When my father played a game of chess with me when I was barely able to walk, he knew that he could beat me every single time if he wanted. He knew that winning the game wasn't important but making sure his child was having fun and learning how to play the game was. He also knew that if he defeated me repeatedly that I might get frustrated and give up, and, worse than that, I might not want to play again later.

There is, however, another meta (there always is another meta). The meta of a parent sitting down with a child might be to teach them a game, but more often than not, it is to build a relationship with them. Winning the game isn't important, but creating memories and spending time together is. So when an adult sits down and plays with a child, most of the time, the child is zoomed in and their meta is at a basic level: that of playing the game and winning. The adult, however, has stepped back and is in a different meta. Then there are times where the child begins to beat the parent, who is going easy on them, and the parent's meta flips, and they realize they have to work harder and play a better game. As a child, I saw this as a major victory—and it was.

A lot of times when people talk of children as having a "child-like mind" what they really mean is that they are seeing the world at its most basic level, which is what they need in order to gain sustenance and learn the physical and mental skills that they will require later in life. The child isn't any less intelligent than the adult. The child is just in a different meta.

It is true that some adults don't have the ability to step back from the most basic of meta either. This isn't to say that the basic meta is always bad or wrong. For a human being, being able to step back and put themselves in various metas is extremely important for changing their life and getting what they want.

When a person "steps back" and "chooses" what meta they are in, then the act of doing so is similar to certain meditations. A human is capable of stepping back mentally and viewing the constant stream of thought in their mind. While humans can hop back into the passenger seat of the car, it is my current belief that many animals are not able to do the same. They are stuck in the driver's seat. I don't believe that many animals can observe their own mind. Many are stuck in a more basic/animalistic "lower" meta.

Be Wary of Fear.

Fear and anger bring us down to the most basic meta: the animal level, for that is the most useful (short-term) for survival. The brain likes to revert back to what it believes is the most useful meta. So, by making a meta more useful (mentally), your brain will accept it more and go to it more often. More about this the discussion of free will.

Is it possible to change meta without changing the focus or weight of information? No. Meta is dependent on a person's knowledge and using their focus to hone in on certain knowledge or factors. We have often heard that knowledge is power. Here is a specific example of how that works with regards to meta-cognition.

Consider the following scenario: There is a hostage-negotiator, and he is talking to the hostage-taker (the person holding the hostages). The negotiator is generally completely on a different meta than the hostage-taker. However, imagine the following scenarios and how the meta/mindsets would change in each scenario not only for the hostage-negotiator but also for the hostage-taker.

> Scenario 1: The hostage-negotiator is dealing with a hostage-taker who has taken hostages for the first time.
>
> Scenario 2: The hostage-negotiator is dealing with a group of professional hostage-takers who frequently take hostages.
>
> Scenario 3: The hostage-negotiator is dealing with a hostage-taker who was not only a former hostage-negotiator but also one of the best hostage-negotiators in the world.

Imagine how Scenario 3 would be different if the hostage-negotiator believed incorrectly that the hostage-taker was the same as the hostage-taker in Scenario 1. The meta, or being in the wrong frame of mind (generally due to not having enough information), can be catastrophic. One with more experience in a given situation generally is on a higher platform from which to view said situation and thus has an advantage. Why? Because they have more knowledge. Knowledge is power. I want you to have power.

Here is another example of how one's mindset changes with knowledge. Suppose someone enters a doctor's office and is told that they have a chronic disease with no cure, a disease that they are going to have to deal with for the rest of their life. Before going into the office, they were physically in the same body as when they left (minus whatever changes happen due to the mental changes). However, their mindset, how they might view life, and the decisions that they make with their time/energy/focus might be completely different upon leaving the doctor's office.

There is a time for a more basic meta. Sometimes having extra knowledge can slow a person down, especially if that extra knowledge doesn't directly help a situation. If one is fighting for their life, that isn't the time to think about existential situations (of course, sometimes it might be). Instead, being in an animalistic state and seeing a situation for "how it is" would generally give the best outcome for that situation. A boxer in a ring only needs to care about what is going on in that ring and perhaps the words from his coach. Any extra knowledge from outside doesn't help the boxer at all. If the boxer's meta is based on his thoughts about dinner or a date he is going on the next day, then the boxer better be way more skilled than whom they are fighting. If they aren't, then their date won't be able to recognize them the day after.

Generally speaking, having a more basic/animalistic meta makes decisions easier because the world appears more black-and-white. Less knowledge makes situations appear more black-and-white. If one has all the knowledge, then the situation is black-and-white based on an individual's morals. If one steps back from the basic meta, then all of a sudden they are applying other factors such as goals, values, and morality to the different meta. That is why a child's meta sometimes seems the purest because it is devoid of extra opinions and "stuff." One of my long-term struggles has been that I enjoy the comfort of a black-and-white world. I want to know how the world works and be able to make clear decisions. I have struggled with this. I have seen others struggle with higher meta as well, wanting to revert back to a simpler time when decisions were easier.

> I have observed a full-circle when it comes to understanding in any particular area of life. First one has no knowledge and so the world appears black and white. Then they gain some knowledge and everything gets grey and confusing. And last, they are able to see most of what influences a given situation, and things become more black-and-white again.

Higher Versus Lower Meta

Is there such a thing as a "higher" and "lower" meta? I don't believe so. More knowledge can be good, but the determining factor is the following: What will the outcome of a situation be if I'm in a particular meta? There is always a best meta for every situation in life depending on what a person wants. Everyone can see that there is a time to be in one meta versus another meta. I have this mental image of Benjamin Franklin's spectacles. He could raise and lower lenses to quickly move between various views (literally).

There is a huge advantage to being able to do this mentally as well. When confronted with a situation, it can be helpful to purposely tackle it from various cognitive levels, and thus goals or moralities, before making a decision. There is an advantage to being able to hold several different metas in one's mind and weigh and consider them together. It is difficult, but we should try to make our minds like Franklin's glasses and go through the different ways of thinking about life while still retaining all aspects of it. There is rarely an absolute meta or point of view that is always the best for all situations. Because of this, there is an advantage to adaptability and being able to change one's mindset.

By the end of this book, you may end up thinking the following way:

> *When I zoom out meta-cognitively and reflect on the process of what seems like decision-making, then I feel depressed realizing/knowing how little control I have over my own life. However, when I am zoomed in and am in the moment/living day-to-day, the realization/understanding of how the world plus the people in it work/function gives me incredible solace.*

There are fewer surprises, and things just make sense. You can look at old situations anew and see why things are the way they are. The realization is especially helpful when confronting new situations that would otherwise be confusing or difficult to explain. We'll do this together in the book's second main section, "Playing with Our New Glasses."

Viewpoints

As mentioned above, when we step back from the most basic ways of viewing situations, we tend to add in more complex morality, viewpoints, and other "stuff" to the meta. It would be very easy to mistakenly believe one is in a higher meta when in actuality one is going in the opposite direction of reality. A meta is perhaps more than just a viewpoint or a lens that people see the world through. It actually changes the person and thus the world and then the person again, and we move into a bilinear causality situation.

When you think about a situation, the lens that you view reality through is already tinted because (unless you are an infant) you have a reality-influenced meta based on your values. As human beings, I'm not sure that we can separate ourselves completely from our wants and desires, but it is a noble attempt. All meta has some basis in values. If someone says that they are above values and that their meta is the truth because it is based on science or some higher reality, then their value is "truth" and "reality" itself.

Most people don't like reality/truth as a value because they would prefer a fantasy or illusion of feeling special or being "in control of their lives." I think that having truth as one of the values that tints the lenses of an individual's reality is extremely useful. I value reality. If one doesn't start with what is true and what is reality, then how can one make rational decisions? Any decisions based on fantasy are from the start going to be flawed.

Years ago, I had a conversation with a martial arts master. I told him that I wanted to understand truth. He told me that that was impossible because everyone has a different reality based on who they are as well as their experiences (which is true). I told him, "Well, if an alien comes to our planet, then they can judge us without being marred by our viewpoints. So that would truly be a clear perspective!" He replied, "Yes, but the aliens would be coming here with their own views." I really enjoyed that conversation, even as annoying as I found it.

CHAPTER 2: BELL CURVES AND GREYSCALES

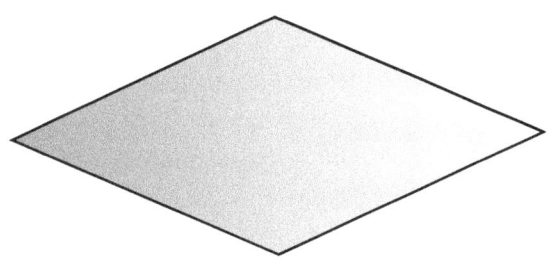

Terminology

Bell Curve: A graph of a normal (Gaussian) distribution, with a large, rounded peak tapering away at each end. When a data set has a distribution that is approximately bell-shaped, then it is referred to as a *bell curve*. There is what is known as the Empirical Rule (also known as the 68-95-99.7) for data with a bell-shaped distribution:

> About 68% of all values fall within 1 standard deviation of the mean.

> About 95% of all values fall within 2 standard deviations of the mean.

> About 99.7% of all values fall within 3 standard deviations of the mean.

Simplified explanation: Most people fall into the middle average of the population. The further you get to any extreme, then the fewer people are there. In this book, I use a squished diamond to represent the bell curve.

Outlier: A data point that is distinctly separate from the rest of the data. If you take the following set of numbers—1, 25, 27, 30, 33, 61—the 1 and the 61 are outliers. Outliers would be people who are outside the bell curve. Outliers are data or information that falls outside of the statistical norm.

The aspects of people and that of the rest of nature can usually be represented in a bell curve. If you take the entire human population in any given area from intelligence to physical strength, then you will see a bell curve. Take a group of people who are each thirty years of age. In this example, they are all attempting to do a physical exercise, the bench press. There are very few in the group who cannot lift the bar by itself. Then the numbers increase as we get to the average amount that someone of that age can lift. Once we get to the mean/average, then the numbers begin to decrease faster and faster until there are only a few who are lifting the highest amounts of weight. Imagine that after a steady climb, the three strongest thirty-year-olds of the group lifted 280 pounds, 290 pounds, and 700 pounds. The one who lifted 700 pounds would be an outlier because they are statistically outside the boundaries of the rest of the group. So, when understanding people and the world, there are individuals who are extreme and are themselves outliers, but the majority of the population is along the gradient in the middle.

The bell curve is how humans are on almost any given dimension unless there is a unique, extreme circumstance, which one could say is itself an outlier-situation relative to the possible situations that one would encounter in the world.

Strawmanning is when you take the undesirable end of the spectrum of data (one tip of the diamond) and highlight it in such a way that the data of that undesirable end of the spectrum is exaggerated to negatively represent the overall data set. Usually, highly positive aspects of the diamond are downplayed or ignored.

Steelmanning is when you take a sample of the most desirable end of the spectrum of data (one tip of the diamond) and highlight it in such a way that the data of that desirable end of the spectrum are exaggerated to positively represent the overall data set. Usually, highly negative aspects of the data are downplayed or ignored.

Everyone engages in strawmanning with things they don't like and steelmanning with things that they have an affinity towards. The reality is that whether you are strawmanning or steelmanning, you are not seeing the situation clearly. One has to account for all of the data as a whole in order to understand data accurately.

There has been tribalism with an us-versus-them mentality for about as long as there have been humans on the planet. Even today, groups of people—governments, organizations, and even families—perceive the population this way. If you don't have a tribal mentality, then the factions will try to "help" you understand their way of thinking. They are constantly fueling their specific agendas with black-and-white scenarios because such myopic views appeal to people. They do to me.

I love situations in life where the "right" decision is obvious. Everyone wants there to be an evil so that they can feel like they are a "good" person. A human doesn't have an easier time feeling like a "good" person than when there is another human being that they can label as a "bad" person. There is evil in the world, but humans are victims of evil, not evil themselves. This is equally true for outliers: those who had the misfortune of being born with a mental illness or had the warp in their minds forced upon them after birth through life experiences.

Humans have a habit of using black-and-white tribalism to legitimize their violence instead of coexisting. It was useful for humans to form groups and fight over resources when they were scarce in the past. I hope we don't get to that point in the future. I hope it doesn't get so bad that there is another world war or catastrophe.

Here is how to use the diamond to visually represent how extremism and group mentality works. Everyone is doing it these days, so why not be able to do it yourself? Below is the step-by-step guide. Have fun with it!

Step 1

Take the diamond (a bell curve set of information or data) and make sure to color one extremist viewpoint light or good (the one you want), then color the other side darker or evil. Now that you have color differentiation, the next step is to show moral superiority in another way by rotating the diamond, making sure that the extremist view that you value is facing upwards to show that you are above and superior to the other viewpoint.

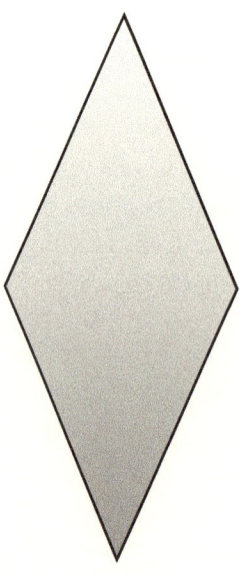

Step 2

Cut out the middle section where balance, compromise, and rational thought occur so you are left with extremes. (Delete between the horizontal lines.) If you'll remember, 95% of the population would generally be in the middle section that we are removing.

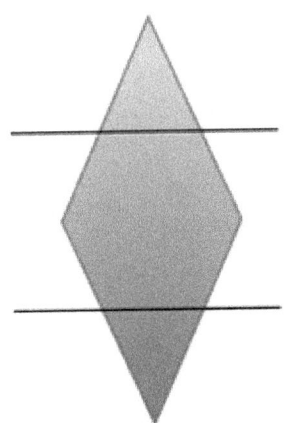

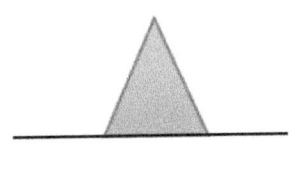

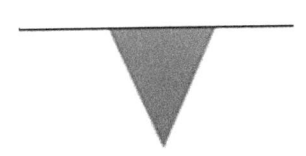

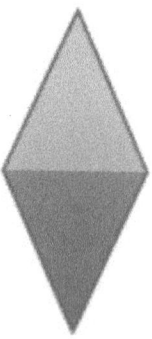

Step 3

Demonize the "other" extreme viewpoint. If you can't find enough things that are wrong with their viewpoint, then make some stuff up. That's right: You are part of the elite group who are right, so the ends justify the means, which means that you can make up lies about the "other" group as long as you are supporting the one right and true faction. Then tell the fifty plus percent of the population who normally exist in the middle area (that was conveniently removed) to pick one extreme or the other: "If you aren't with us, then you are against us."

Say whatever you can to make them feel guilty for not being an extremist with the same views that you have. Make them feel like they have no choice. Make them feel like one side is obviously morally superior to the other. The gradient triangles change to triangles that are completely black and white with a clear border between them. Also make sure to take any outliers and apply them to the various sides to further "prove" how bad the other viewpoint is with the now artificially created black-and-white viewpoints.

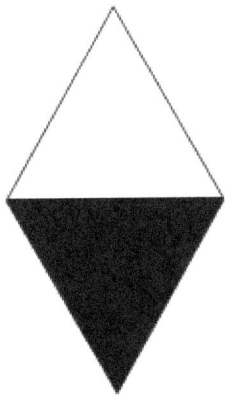

Congratulations! You know have done what so many groups and organizations have done!

The above example with the triangles is just one way that people who would normally fall in the middle of a population are taken advantage of, brainwashed, or otherwise manipulated. More on how people work and how to ~~manipulate~~ change them in the next chapter!

There is an old phrase, *the silent majority and the extreme minority*. Often, the silent majority is ruled and pushed around by the extreme minority. This is due to a variety of reasons, but one reason is that people want the world to be black-and-white. The more extreme a position, then the more black-and-white it is. It becomes "easier" for people to wrap their heads around. Often, people want the difficult decisions in life made for them. There is less mental stress with easy decisions. There is more mental stress with hard decisions. Most people would rather avoid the mental stress than make hard decisions that are based on actual knowledge.

A lot of us subscribe to a meta (*dogma* at times) as a method of self-medication (we all self-medicate to some degree) so we don't go crazy in what appears to be an overly-complex world. We often manufacture scenarios that are black and white in our minds because in reality there are few things that are black and white. That is one of the rules to understanding the world. Many people believe that it would be too much effort to look up information or gain actual knowledge about a situation for them to make a rational decision based on facts. It takes effort to gather the necessary information or knowledge in order to make ration decisions based on facts instead of being lazy and blindly trusting information given to us or simply making decisions based on insufficient information.

Factions in society try to make people seem more different than they actually are in order to push their nefarious agendas. Such diseases of the mind permeate our society to the point where people don't even realize that they are being manipulated. I remember the first time I realized this. I was six years old. A teenager in my neighborhood was babysitting me while my parents were away. We were sitting on the couch watching a movie, and she told me that she was black. I looked at her like she was crazy. I said, "You have black hair, but your skin is brown." She got very upset, and I had no idea why. She replied, "You are wrong: I am not brown—I'm black and you are white!"

I had to prove that she was obviously confused, so I pulled out my awesome collection of crayons. I held a black crayon and a brown crayon on her arm and said, "Look! You're not black, you are brown! The colors are labeled on the crayons." Then I put a peach-colored crayon and a white crayon on my arm and said, "Look, I'm way more peach than white." She was very upset, and I just didn't get it. To me, things were obvious.

Calling people black or white is just another way that the viewpoint of society tries to manipulate us. Calling people various shades of brown and combinations of white, peach, tan, or beige would be far more accurate. The reason we aren't called as such is because doing so would be less convenient for those who want to assume power over groups of people. It would make the population harder to market to, manipulate, and control.

Below is a visual representation (using the diamonds for the bell curve or variations thereof) that gives a visual of what happens when two populations or cultures or, on the micro scale, two people with different views meet each other.

Let's use capital punishment, in this case death by hanging. The greyscale gradient rectangle in the background represents how open people are to public hangings as an acceptable form of punishment. To the far right (the lighter end of the rectangle), you have people who are extremely against it, and to the far left (the darker end of the triangle) are people who are extremely for it. Suppose the diamond on the right is Europe in the year 2000, and the triangle to the left is Europe in the year 1800. An extremist against hanging might be an extremist in the other direction in the year 2000.

I like visuals.

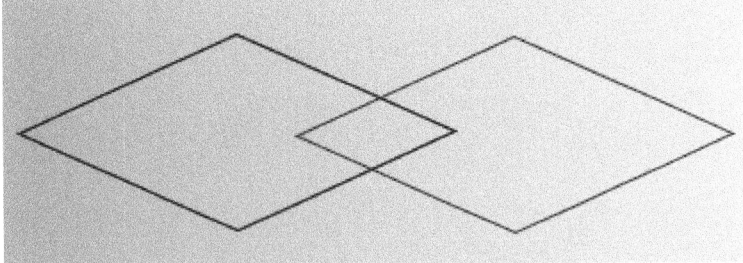

How much they overlap shows the overlap of opinions on both a macro- and a micro-level.

CHAPTER 3: THE HUMAN EQUATION AND CHANGE

The Human Equation

Everything that makes up who you are when you are born plus the life experiences that you have equals how you are at this moment.

$$\sum$$

Simplifying people as an equation, hence the $\sum$ symbol.

Change

Changing yourself. Changing people. Changing the world. Changing people. Changing yourself.

I use the Palatal Click symbol because it looks like a tree to me. The tree symbol is for people. For this book, I like the symbol of the tree for showing how to change people as explained below.

How we think at any given moment is a result of everything that made us who we were when we were born plus all of our life experiences.

> [You when you were created] + [Life experiences, which includes all of the stimuli you experience up to this very moment from the world around you] = Your current state.

Reality

There are two main components that determine how a human being behaves/who they are:

1. A base complex formula (the core of who a human being is).

2. Numbers that change various aspects of the formula (life experiences/input from the outside world).

Imagine each section of a formula representing a different aspect of who you are at birth:

$$A(a + a) + B(b + b) + C(c + c) + etc. = \text{Who you are.}$$

(It should be relatively obvious that I'm not a mathematician—just go with this example as a way of understanding the overall concept.)

The various letters are different dualities and/or dichotomies: aggressive versus passive, firm beliefs or stubbornness versus willingness to change, intelligence, health, and so on. People are on a bell curve when it comes to any of the various pieces of the core formula. There are individuals on extremes and even some outliers, but the overwhelming majority of the population is along the gradient in the middle.

How the Formula Works

The base formula is a person's nature, their intrinsic "out of the womb" self.

Adaptation is greater in youth; this is obvious in physical states but also in mental states. Imagine that you are a mathematical formula, and every experience that you have is a number that gets added to various parts of your formula, changing it. The numbers would be relatively larger when you are first born and then over time gradually become smaller.

When you are born you might be a 10. Adding 1 to 10 is 11. That is 10% of who you are. Now once a person is at 1,000, that same +1 experience is only 1/1000th and would hardly change the person at all. Of course, people do learn and change through life, so there are other factors that influence a person's rate or ability to change. Nature *or* nurture is an argument between extremes. The reality is a synthesis between the two for most, if not all, areas of a person's life

Imagine that you are building a pyramid-shaped structure with mud bricks. You slap wet mud down on the ground, and it cakes in the sun and hardens. Then you put on another layer of wet mud. When the wet mud first lands on the solid bricks, you can scrape it off easily. But once it hardens and sticks to the bricks below and around it, then it is harder to remove. The added layers are like experiences falling upon the core formula of who a person is. The easiest time to challenge new information is right when the mud of stimuli has fallen on a person.

Imagine you have someone you care about, and they went to their first cult meeting, hearing all sorts of nonsense from the cult leader. If you talk to them about it the day right after, then you would have a much easier time of preventing them from being "changed" than if you allowed those muddy ideas to harden into bricks after which more bricks would fall upon them. Also, if you wait, then they will be exposed to additional cult experiences, which will meld together and support each other. This is why cults often remove people from society for a lengthy period of time: They can build up "brainwashing" experiences before sending them back out into reality.

Let's say someone has within them a negative or undesirable belief or mindset such as *I'll never be good at sports*. Perhaps they weren't naturally talented, and they had some large numbers in their childhood that further swayed their negative beliefs about themselves. Because of this, that person may avoid pursuing sports, and so they become worse at them. Then they don't want to participate in sports, and then they become even worse, and so they further avoid sports—it is a snowball effect that doesn't end. By the time someone is an adult, it is like having an upside-down pyramid of bricks with the brick on the bottom being the core belief and the bricks stacked upon it being all the experiences that shield that belief from being challenged. You can picture a tree or an ice cream cone or a core with shielding over it, whatever works for your mind. The longer a person is alive (more accurately, the more numbers [experiences] that are added to a person's formula), the harder it is to change the base of it.

People are a lot like typical planets. The planets have a solid core and become less dense farther away from the gravitational center. This is similar to a person's own core and the addition of new information to the equation that makes them who they are. People often feel attacked. Do you think it is actually possible to attack someone (not in a physical sense) and not attack *who they are* when you attack a piece of their beliefs? In reality, you are just attacking some experiences that they have had. Attacking *the way a person looks* doesn't make sense at all, because then you may be attacking how they appear (which is determined before they were born) and so you are attacking someone for merely existing. This doesn't make any sense to me.

Attacking people themselves means attacking someone over something that they have no control over. Since there is no free will, it doesn't make sense to attack someone in general. Attacking an individual thus doesn't make any sense. Attacking stupid ideas makes sense.

While one may be able to attack damp or wet mud, it is much harder to change mud that has solidified and is now stacked upon a person's core (or at least if they think it is stacked upon their core or part of how they identify themselves). So how does one change themselves or other people, especially if their beliefs are blocked by layers of bricks or armor or whatever you want to call it? The answer itself is in *weakness*.
The core formula will only change when external stimuli (numbers from the example above) fall upon people when they are in a state of weakness. Imagine weakness as rain that falls upon the bricks and begins to turn them back into mud.
How intrinsically weak a person happens to be (how suggestable they are) is first determined by their core formula. Further mental or emotional weakness can be brought on by various factors, including age (typically adolescence). I hated hearing, "young and impressionable" when I was young and impressionable. I hated it because it was true. Try telling a teenager that they are in a state of mental weakness and are more susceptible to change and being manipulated.

When someone suffers a great loss, they are in a state of great change and should watch out lest they be manipulated by nasty people. A great loss can be different things: a divorce, breakup, losing a job, and perhaps the loss of someone close to them via moving away, ending a relationship, or death. A great loss is generally similar to someone suffering a traumatic life event. If someone survives a major accident or surgery, they are going to be in a different body: They lost their body. Have you seen this state of weakness outside of humans? Think about the ways in which you can befriend an animal that humans normally don't befriend (humans are animals): You can bond with an animal when it is an infant or in a state of suffering such as being injured or starving.

Being in a state of weakness can have positive outcomes. Sometimes it is good to be able to rewrite the script and change your own base formula or re-look at certain beliefs you have. You are changing all the time. The world is changing. Everyone you know is changing. These extreme times of our lives can shed light on who is really important to us and who really cares about us. In your time of need, who was really there for you? Maybe a person who was a close friend to you is now just a friend, or perhaps someone really stepped up when you needed help.

It is unfortunate that certain societies set such strict boundaries on children so that they see the world totally as black and white with false barriers all around them (barriers in their minds). Yet that same society that created them also expects them to do a complete 180 and be flexible adults who can think for themselves once they reach an artificial number of revolutions around the sun.

Another example of when a person is in a state of weakness is when someone is under a lot of stress, often caused by fear. The fear of loss is one of the most influential forms of fear. One should take extra time to think about their options and get outside help when they are in fear of losing a job, a marriage, or any other significant relationship. The best advice I've been given is the following: Generally, one doesn't need to make huge, life-altering decisions in the moment, or even that day. Take some time and really think things through and get the opinions of outside sources before making any big decisions.

Other times of weakness include when a person is suffering with an addiction such as drugs, depression, anxiety, and other mentally-compromised states. Love and infatuation as well can bring a person into a state of weakness.

It is interesting how people often hold the "higher" intellectual metas at a lofty level and the more animalistic/lower metas at a lower level even though it is through those more animalistic metas that we are better able to affect a person's core and cause true change. That being said, when someone makes an artificial change due to being in a lower meta, that doesn't mean it will stick and they will be changed long-term. If one can change a person's view from several different meta, then the changes will make it stick and will change them in a more profound way. There is showing someone that doing X is good, and there is letting them experience it. Then, if one follows up by rationally explaining that X is good, it will make the experience much more powerful—the resulting formula will change.

Your stimuli make you who you are. You are the culmination of everything that makes you "you." Part of who you are therefore is because of the other person. They are not just part of your life—they are part of you. We should therefore be very careful whom we spend time with: whom we let into our lives and whom we keep around us, because to some degree they will affect you. I've heard statements such as, "You are a combination of the three people that you spend the most time with" or "Your enjoyment at a job is the result of the four people whom you work the most with." These phrases have some truth to them.

What is interesting about the fact that people become part of other people is that there are certain people who end up being a large part of who you are. They are powerful *catalysts* in your life, people with opinions that you hold higher than others. They are like having lightning rods stuck into a tree. They can touch your core and change your views. These individuals or the ripple from these individuals (explained below)—if they are held with enough esteem in our own mind—have a sort of highway to access who we are at our core. They have that permanent connection to our core formula and can influence us in ways that others cannot. We experience this when someone we care about tells us something about ourselves that hurts us to our core. Their opinion is more valuable to us because we believe that they have certain great knowledge or insight into who we really are.

The opinions of people who don't know you shouldn't affect you to any meaningful extent. The thought of other people being part of your reality is continually interesting because now people whom we've never met (thanks to videos on the internet and lectures we can listen to) can have a profound impact on our lives in the same way that books and works of art had on people before the advent of electricity. The ripple effect can be renewed. I owe a lot of who I am to people whom I never have met nor ever will be able to meet. So thank you.

We can be disappointed or confused when someone who has given us good information suddenly tells us something that isn't true. Imagine a situation involving a person whom you liked or respected and you learn that they are really a scumbag (at least one of their mindsets has a strongly negative aspect to it). One has to question that if they were nasty in one way, then maybe they were nasty in other ways. Or, if some information they told you ended up being false, then what else were they lying or just ignorant about? Don't "throw the baby out with the bathwater"—just because someone is wrong in one instance doesn't necessarily mean they are wrong in another. More on that when we examine *platforms* later.

We generally know ourselves better than other people. Whether we admit to certain flaws or not is another matter. When someone says something true about us, perhaps giving us insight to our core beliefs/values/formula, then it will ring true to us.

Imagine you are in school and your teacher whom you admire comes up to you and says that they think you are very good at math. Their opinion has weight because of their profession and how you feel about them. Furthermore, the comment is reinforced if you have previous stimuli (such as high test scores) that reinforces that you are good at math. Now you have two forms of stimuli that impact and support each other. Suppose someone you don't know comes up to you and tells you that they think your hair looks like "alien hair." Well, part of you intrinsically knows this isn't true because you probably haven't seen aliens (mostly). When negative or positive comments are said to us, the ones which we already know are true end up having a stronger effect on us. They impact us whether by making us more content or hurting us.

A Word on "Good"

When I was growing up, I would often hear parents telling their children, "Be good" or "Be a good boy" or "Be a good girl." Parents often try to instill values in their children, but I have noticed that many do not. This "good" that a child is supposed to be is not well-defined. So you end up having people who want to be whatever this "good" thing is but aren't sure what it is or how to get there. It's like a special, unattainable paradise, a fountain of youth that drives people crazy in the hopeless journey to find it.

To make matters worse, children and adults haven't been taught how to think critically for themselves, and so they don't have a way of figuring out what is indeed good. This is especially problematic for people who don't spend time thinking about their past experiences and their lives in general. With much uncertainty, they end up seeking this idea of "good" from other places. Fortunately or unfortunately, there are a lot of factions and individuals who *know* what is good and are more than eager to share their *good* with those who are lost and especially those who are weak. A lot of times people will follow what dogmas say is "good" instead of deciding for themselves. Even if just part of a dogma resonates with what they were taught as a child, then they might assume that the entire dogma must be "good" or "true." People can be lazy, and it is a lot easier to accept the dogma as a whole rather than critically analyze each individual piece that comprises it.

It takes thinking to analyze ways of thinking. You can see this a lot if you are part of the population that's unfortunate enough to still be watching commercials. "Today the economy is bad" (arguably true), then "You work hard for your money" (true or not, it is a statement that a lot of people would agree with), then a commonly-agreed-upon fact or reality such as "Sleep is good for your health," and finally, after providing two or three truths, they will push whatever false product or idea they want you to buy: "So buy/try/do [whatever we are trying to sell]." I have noticed that when you do something that someone else tells you is "good" or a group or organization decides that something is "good," then most of the time that activity is only good for the person making the rules.

Thinking for yourself is good. Reflecting on your life and memories is good. You are your memories. We base who we are upon our memories, whether they are real or not. False memories and imaginings also affect our perceived past. If you falsely believe that something is real or that something has happened to you, then part of who you are is based on fantasy. It is real for you alone.

Change and Cognitive Dissonance

What else can put a person in a state of weakness? Any event that challenges their current view of reality to such a degree that it causes cognitive dissonance—particularly a cognitive dissonance with one's core formula attacking the structure from its earliest onset.

Generally speaking, the latest parts of the formula (the last bricks that were laid down that haven't completely hardened yet) are the most susceptible to change. To penetrate the core layer of mud (the base formula), one has to cause a sudden, violent action that will send a person into a state of weakness. I call it *lightning*.

Imagine a devastating lightning strike that shoots through the mud as if it wasn't there and penetrates the being to their core. This would be like skipping the supporting arguments protecting an idea and attacking the core belief itself. I also see it as a spear thrust that goes right through the armor, ignoring the defenses and stabbing the flesh beyond, that flesh being the core of a person.

There is a more subtle way to change someone. The second way of changing is what I'd like to call *rain drops*. Imagine water falling on the bricks, slowly weakening the surface. When the surface weakens and falls away, then the core can be exposed. Let's return to the armor analogy: It would be like damaging the pieces of armor until it becomes useless and falls away, exposing the body before one goes in for the kill. Mentally, if one can destroy many of the weak points of a belief or argument, then the person holding the idea might admit that the core just can't be true because all of the beliefs that stem from the core don't hold up to logic or whatever the situation is about. Even if one doesn't destroy all the armor, if you can drip enough water in an area or damage a certain area of the armor, then one can break through. Sometimes enough water can cause a mudslide. It is interesting to see this happen to someone mentally.

Here is another image: a sapling, a young, newly-formed tree with a slender trunk. One could easily chop it down with a single swing of an ax. Even if one doesn't chop it down, one can still get to the core. As the tree ages, it forms more and more rings around the core. For a fully-grown tree, it might take a very long time (if ever) to get to the core with an ax alone. People are like this.

The two ways of changing someone in the mud example were lightning and raindrops. With the tree metaphor, lightning would still work and raindrops would be replaced with an ax. Lightning can strike to a tree's core or even burn the whole tree down, whereas chopping with an ax would take longer.

The mental mimics the physical because the mind and body are intertwined. It is a lot easier to fix a physical problem if intervention begins early, such as finding a disease and beginning treatment right away. The same is true for mental diseases (dogmas or being brainwashed) as mentioned above. If someone hears a lot of false information on, say, a cult, and their friend comes to them that day and they talk about it, then the friend has a far easier time of persuading the individual than if they let the bad information metastasize.

People often become attached to their thoughts and see those thoughts as a part of *who they are*. This is because their thoughts are a part of their programming, and the longer the programming stays inside of them, the more it hardens and sinks down towards their core of how they see themselves. A person's own thoughts are part of the stimuli that makes them who they are. The thoughts and stimuli that are remembered become more *catalyst* than simple thought.

CHAPTER 4: THE REALITIES OF A WORLD WITHOUT FREE WILL

Coping with Reality

The reality is that free will doesn't exist and that it's OK that it doesn't exist. Don't worry, you've lived your entire life without free will, so nothing actually changes.

$$B + L = U$$

The equation $B + L = U$ explained: B (everything that made you who you are from conception through birth) + (plus) L (all of the stimuli and experiences of life) = (equals) U (you).

Here is another formulation: The *genes you were born with*, including everything that made you who you are at birth (feel free to include souls or energy or whatever else you believe in) *plus* the *events in your reality* will *equal* or make you *who you are*. Who you are at any given moment determines how you will act at that specific moment in time.

What does this mean? A lot of things. First, you are the result of your life experiences, shaped by everything that made you who you were when you were born, determined by all the events leading up to your birth, which was in turn a result of everything leading up to your conception, and this can be traced back and back all the way to the creation event or before then depending on what you believe in.

It actually doesn't matter what you believe. The equation that shows the reality of who you are based on the cause and effect leading up to your creation and everything in your life doesn't really change. So whether you believe in a god or many gods, fate, the Big Bang, or whatever, this equation still works.

Getting over the fact that *we don't have the free will that we think we have* has been the most difficult aspect of reality for me to accept due to my ego, of course. To be honest, I am not 100% certain that there is no free will, but I am 100% certain that our ability to actually choose to alter our lives is much more constrained than we realize. At the current moment, I am leaning towards a world with zero free will.

Determinism, fatalism, and cause and effect are all facts. Wanting to understand the world and truly see how things work while not accepting determinism and causality is like wanting to go swimming in the pool but being too afraid or unwilling to let go of the railing at the side. I'm here to let you know that there is nothing to be worried about. The world won't descend into darkness, and you won't give up all your values and morality and start doing "bad things" once you and others come to realize what part of you has known all along: the truth about free will.

Letting go of fantasy and accepting reality is part of the journey to understanding who you are. If you don't understand who you are and how the world works based on reality, then how do you expect to go where you want to go in life?

Here are some realities that, as I have, you should accept so you can see the world clearly—if that is in fact what you want. If you want there to be free will, that doesn't make it any more likely that free will exists. I have stayed away from quoting sources up until this point, but I would like to break that habit because free will seems to be such a difficult topic for those whom I have talked to. Luckily, modern neuroscience has come to the rescue in the form of many scientific studies. If you want more scientific knowledge to back up the claim that free will is an illusion, then do some online research. Hearing an idea repeatedly from just one source or person won't be enough to change most minds.

Free Will and Responsibility

Most of the time, if you tell someone that there isn't free will or if someone considers the idea of a world without free will, then the reply or counter-argument that is given overwhelmingly is, "Well, if there is no free will, then I'm not responsible for my actions, and I can do whatever I want. People can act badly, and the world will just fall apart." At that point, it is customary for humans to shut their brains off, stop thinking about free will, and just go on with life.

The second counter-argument that makes people shut their brains off is the following: "Well, if free will doesn't exist, then we are all autonomous robots with no choice or true agency. We are no different than machines. Thinking of life like that will depress me." This argument is a want, a desire, a fear. What these arguments don't provide: any evidence, proof, science, or anything that actually supported by reality and how things in our world work. At best, the fear that not having free will would make people behave worse is simply a point of view or meta that a person can be in that would make them behave better or worse.

People are afraid of reality, and many go out of their way to evade reality. I'm here to say, "Don't be afraid." Having no free will doesn't make people worse. In this book, I'm going to "exploit" the situation of a world with no free will: I am going to mine the concept of a *world-without-free-will* to discover all the possibilities instead of running away due to knee-jerk fears and impulses. Such fear only allows people to skim the surface of free will and doesn't let one explore its depths. Let's dive in.

Fear and Freedom

The first thing I can say is that you should not be afraid of a world without free will. Since our world has no free will, the thought of a world without free will is no better nor worse than the world we live in. In fact, it is exactly the same (believe it or not). Wanting something to be real has zero impact on that "thing" actually being real or not, though if you want it to be real enough, then that belief will change you and could change others and thus the world. Even if you do cause change, the false causation that the belief is trying to support doesn't become any more real. Wanting to believe that something is not true doesn't make it any less true.

The freedom one gets from reality is amazing. Since you don't believe, you don't have to put so much energy in trying to overcome cognitive dissonance or being inauthentic and lying to yourself. You don't have to turn your brain "off" because you don't like a reality that conflicts with your personal fantasy. Some people can't cope initially with a reality that conflicts with their fantasy (they can't handle the truth). But the truth is a lot easier to handle when you aren't in a fantasy world.

It is difficult to live in two separate realities at the same time. It is emotionally liberating to not have to bullshit to yourself and to others. You don't have to believe in anything without enough evidence to support a claim. There is comfort in understanding how the world works. It reduces randomness, which otherwise creates stress. Understanding how the world works reduces stress. You won't ever understand everything, so the illusion of randomness will always occur. There will always be a certain amount of stress in one's life. If you turn a blind eye to problems, you may ignore and reduce stress, but the problems still exist. So don't turn a blind eye.

If something is true, then one would expect to see repeated evidence of the cause-and-effect relationship. An aspect of this concept appears in the world of science when people talk about the reproducibility of experiments.

When one pursues knowledge, then one doesn't try to fight others intellectually or try to be "right." One simply tries to understand reality and realize that what is right or wrong is simply a matter of what is *real* or *not real*. Only from reality can one then figure out what is right or what is wrong. Trying to figure out what is right or wrong without reality is a fantasy all in itself.

Free will doesn't exist as people perceive it. Decisions are made based on past experiences plugged into the developing formula of who and what a person is. What people perceive as free will is actually the mind's ability to step back and watch its thought processes at work. This is called *mindfulness* or other names in meditation. We, as humans, are animals that are able to think on multiple levels. One of the advantages is that we can "step back" and watch the decision-making process. One might say that that means that we can make decisions, but the reality is that one's ability to step back and observe the mind's thoughts is just another piece of the core formula. How reflective a person is depends on how they are born combined with whatever stimuli/life experiences they have had that made them more or less reflective. Some people's natural formula scores higher for self-inspection, but of course like most aspects of one's reality (health, etc.), it can be improved with the right stimulus. People generally call the process of becoming more mindful *meditation*, *training*, or *practice*.

There is an incredible power that human beings have in being able to observe their mind and analyze memories (stimuli from the past). You can even recall moments when you were observing your own mind. Being able to view your reality in turn changes your reality, becoming another stimulus.

With the lack of free will, parenting becomes even more important. What a child is exposed to has a profound impact on how they will end up (see previous section about how much easier it is to change a human's core at a young age). If we are a result of our life's experiences, then can one truly be upset with parents who "shelter" (which usually has a negative connotation) or try to influence their children toward what they believe is best for them?

The argument of nature versus nurture is truly an argument about how influential a person's core formula is and how much it can change. The ability of the core formula to change (how "elastic" a person's core formula is) is one of the various aspects of the formula itself. The good and bad of a person are already predetermined. One of the most interesting aspects of humans is how much we can change physically, mentally, and so on.

Humans tend to do better with gradual change, on analogy with water droplets versus lightning. When a person has their reality changed drastically—"lightning"—they can experience negative effects. In "modern" times, we call such drastic changes with regard to viewing conflicts as post-traumatic stress. A person's ability to hold their reality together and maintain "control" of themselves while large parts of their reality are changing is called *mental toughness*.

When the concept of free will falls apart, you start to see more and more *causation* (*causality*, more generally)—thus, I slowly am weaving more discussion of causation into succeeding chapters.

Criminals, Extremism, and Changing the Natural Script

Understanding that there is a "lack of free will" in itself will affect how individuals perceive those who behave in violent or bad ways. It will also change one's mindset of how react to them. To a certain extent, we already realize this.

Consider the following exchange: Person 1 says, "I hate you, I hate you, I hate you!" Person 2 replies, "You did X, so I will respond with Y." We can see that the first example is spoken by a child, while the second is probably spoken by an adult with a little more life experience. Cause and effect are at the core of everything—that is how the world works. Unfortunately, adults "F it up." When an adult, feeling overly confident and smart, says to a child, "You *chose* to do X, so I'm going to *punish* you with Y," the "choice" is supposedly a cause, and the "punish[ment]" is the effect. The connection between the two isn't true causation because the human has to interject and "make" it causation. This is a self-fulfilling prophecy.

While it might seem that there is no direct causation, if you believe that there is no free will, then you will see that there is causation because the human had no actual choice but to interject, and so you are stuck. What is actually happening in the example above? The adult is saying, "I'm using free will as an excuse to punish you and not feel guilty about it." The same effect as above can be used but in a more logical way (assuming the child is old enough, mentally or chronologically, to be reasoned with): "You did X action. As a human being living in this world, we don't like it when people do X. As a way to change you to keep you from doing X again, we are going to Y." If a punishment won't change a person, then why give it? If they are going to repeat the undesirable action, then we don't need them in our society.

Why do we punish criminals? Is it for retribution, revenge, rehabilitation, or some other reason? Considering the previous paragraph, we realize that there are new complications with regard to punishment when you add in the consideration of an individual not having free will. How should we change human behavior? Let's take the example of criminals in changing behavior: Outliers and those at the far end of "good behavior" and "bad behavior" won't change. The main battle in changing behavior exists in the grey middle. Most people are on the fence when it comes to murder. It just takes the "right" or "wrong" situation and almost anyone can kill. Without such an extreme situation that would make most people kill, there are still those who see it as a possible solution for something they don't like.

Luckily, we have good forensics and a judicial system, and so many would-be murderers understand the punishments if they are caught for murdering someone or committing a crime of another nature. That realization is enough to stop them from engaging in the negative behavior that they would engage in otherwise. It is for this exact reason that the human mind rates negative things happening to us much higher than we rate positive things happening to us. Imagine if you had the option to eat the best chocolate cake that you could ever possibly eat but in doing so the penalty would be the same amount of time (it took to eat the cake) bent over a toilet violently throwing up. Most people just wouldn't eat the cake.

The penalties often outweigh the reward, even if they are both relatively similar. I'm extremely happy that human beings are in fact wired this way. If we weren't, then people would continue to do nasty things to one another and wouldn't care what happens to them. It is extremely difficult to stop someone who doesn't care about what happens to them. One aspect of the warrior or "samurai mindset" is about overriding this natural wiring.

The samurai is going to kill the enemy and doesn't care what happens to them. Imagine that there are two assassins coming to kill you. Hopefully, this is just a mental exercise for you and not something you'd actually have to worry about in real life. The first assassin wants to kill you but also wants to be 100% sure that they can't possibly be caught. The second assassin who is coming after you doesn't care if they are caught, killed, tortured, or anything else. The only thing that they care about is killing you. The second assassin would be infinitely more difficult to survive than the first.

It is extremely difficult to stop brainwashed suicide bombers. *Brainwashed* and *suicide bomber* are redundant terms because in this case brainwashing involves having their wiring re-done by religious beliefs (or other fake realities) so that their natural "I care what happens to me if I do X" is no longer in effect. They simply don't care if they die as a result of blowing themselves up. The dogma has changed their natural defensive and self-protection script. Some beliefs go further and tell the one who is about to blow themselves up or die for a cause that they will even go to a magical place like Valhalla or heaven where they will be rewarded for ending life in the real world (the only one that exists).

There, I'm very proud of myself. After taking you on a long stream of consciousness, I was able to come full circle back to people who are extremely gullible and are brainwashed to the extreme.

Human Outliers

There are people who are at the extreme end of the spectrum—and not only because of their genetics. Take into account those who are extremely gullible. The people in cults (religious or not) are zealots simply because they had unfortunate life circumstances. Their personalities may be extremely elastic, which could have contributed to their extremist mindset. That extreme elasticity from their core formula can also make them elastic enough to change their mental state with the right stimulus. The right stimulus changes depending on their current formula, which is of course a combination of the base formula and external stimuli. It is possible to bring them back from the edge or from their extreme state of being. In short, some of those who seem beyond help (who are at one end of the spectrum) may in fact be able to be saved because the same elasticity that allowed their mind to be corrupted can very well be used to bring them back. In general, the mind has far more adaptability than does the body.

There are certain personalities that are "highly addictive." People who get interested in a new sport or game may go "all in." They spend all their time on the new fixation. A person like that could put all that energy into something negative like drinking, drugs, a cult, or other activities that might not help them become who they truly wish to be. However, just like a knife or a tool, what can be used for bad could also be used for good. A gun can be a tool to murder or a tool to prevent oneself from being murdered. So too can a person who is highly addictive be steered towards putting all that energy, focus, and obsession into something that will be more fulfilling. Don't scratch an itch when you can apply a lotion to remedy that which causes the itch in the first place.

Ego, Hate, and Bigotry Just Doesn't Make Any Sense

How much weight should we put on our accomplishments or the bad things we have done? How much pride should we feel when we accomplish something great? Isn't it inevitable that we would? How upset should we get at ourselves if we try hard to accomplish a goal and don't succeed? How upset should we get with others? No one chooses their core formula. No one chooses the state of the world. This is true on a mental, physical, and, well, any level.

Free will doesn't lead to stress and frustration. It leads to respite and ease of regrets. Ask yourself this question: Did you pick the hair you were born with? The color of your skin? The color of your eyes? Your intelligence? Your health? Did you pick your parents? Did you pick the state of the world when you were born? Did you really have a say in anything? The answer is no. No one chooses any of this stuff. Stop giving yourself and others too much credit for things that would have inevitably happened. It would make a lot more sense to look at an accomplishment and say, "Wow, that's cool that I ended up being the kind of person who could accomplish this." It is cool to notice and see outliers and those at the positive extremes. Does it make sense to wish to be anyone else but yourself? You can't be anyone but yourself, so thinking otherwise doesn't make any sense.

Does it make sense at all for someone to be racist? As previously mentioned, you don't get to pick how you look, your genetics, or really anything that makes you who you are. No one else does, either. If you look at the events of a person's life, then you only see part of the equation. Without knowing their base formula, you can't truly understand how they were influenced by each individual experience because a person's identity is a combination of their base and their life experiences.

Why Is Fortune-Telling in This Book?

A futurist is someone who believes that they know the future. This is like someone who understands some causation and thinks they will know how the future will play out based on just seeing part of the equation of reality. It is kind of stupid if you think about it that way. Guessing the future is just that. It is always a gamble. Only in extreme situations or situations with confined causation (like a game) can one see the future with a very high probability. The more shorter-term the prediction is, generally the easier it is. The better someone is at understanding cause and effect, the more likely they are to understand what will happen. This is what makes knowing what will happen in the future so difficult. Simply put, there are too many factors for a human mind to simultaneously account for. That is another reason we should be careful of AI that can see an almost infinite number of moves ahead. Such an AI could make minor adjustments over time in order to take over and control us against our desires.

Fortune-telling is a joke because people who analyze a person's experience in order to understand or guess what is going to happen in the future are doing so without the complete set of data. Usually, a fortune-teller doesn't even know the person they are analyzing. At best you can say general things that cover "most people" on the bell curve. The rest is illusion. If a person is not typical (meaning they don't fall into the 95% of those within 1-2 standard deviations of the mean on a bell curve), then fortune-telling is pretty much useless. It is harder to understand those on the fringes. If someone can do true fortune-telling, then they would have to be able to know all of the variables in existence that would impact you. At best they can guess based on incomplete information. It is simply speculation.

Sometimes strangers will attempt to give you advice. Imagine that I'm making lemonade. There are three components to lemonade: lemons, water, and sugar. Suppose that I have all three components in an industrial blender. It happens to be a blender that is not transparent. Imagine that a person walks up to me after I have placed all the ingredients into a blender, and this individual doesn't have any knowledge of the prep. If this person comes up to me and says that I should put in more sugar, then I would be confused because they have no effing idea how much sugar is already in the blender, nor do they have any idea what the ratio of sugar to water and lemons is inside the blender.

If someone comes up to me and tells me something specific like, "You need to do X," then it is almost always bad advice. Now if the stranger were to come up to me and say, "Do you have an X ratio of sugar to water and lemons in your lemonade?" then that would make a lot more sense. Only after a person gets to know you (the time it takes to gain experience and form memories that become the foundation for rules and platforms) can they hope to give you advice in general about what you should or shouldn't do in your life. When it comes to a certain discipline of learning, the person who is giving advice must first ascertain where along the path you are. If they don't know where you are, then how can they help you get to where you want to go?

In the same "rulebook" of thoughts is the illogical thing that happens when people idolize someone. They will say things like, "I want to be with so and so" or "I wish I was that person." When someone is idolizing, they generally have a very limited view of a person. They may be analyzing the person by only a single mode (platform) that the person is operating in. For example: a star's "mental platform" when performing on stage. Idolizing has to be more of an "emotional thing" because one logical look at it and one quickly realizes that they are making an extreme judgement based on less than 5% of the information about that individual. In the year 2019, you can follow people on various social platforms, and so you might develop a more informed view of who they are. Congratulations, you now see like 7% of who they are instead of like 1-5%. You might not realize that someone with the fancy car or a lot of money could be dealing with a severe health problem or the tragedy of someone they loved. You have no idea what is going on inside people (generally speaking). It just takes time to get to know people.

The Connection

Once I finally came to accept the realization that free will is an illusion, I began to think about all the implications that flow from this fact. One of the biggest of these implications is the realization that stimuli have a more powerful impact on me and everyone around me. Since we do not have free will, the events in our lives, the state of the world, and everything around us has a far more profound impact on us than if we did truly have free will.

> Endless implications occur when one learns a truth because that truth will ripple across one's reality and touch many areas of one's understanding. Reality repeats.

There are more major realizations one comes to when the illusion of free will dissolves from one's reality. Not only is there more weight to the understanding that we are part of the stimuli of everyone else (and they us) but also that we become stimuli for ourselves. We impact ourselves because we are part of the reality that we are observing. This goes beyond and is separate from the fact that we take in the world through our senses. Those you spend time with end up changing your environment because they *are* part of the environment—your environment. They are stimuli by their very existence. The people you engage with have a powerful impact on your formula, on who you are. Knowing that others have an impact on who you are also means that you have an impact on who other people are. We should definitely be wary of whom we spend time with, as well as the multiple environments that we place ourselves into. What are the various activities that you are engaged in? How are they impacting you, your reality, who you are? Your reality determines who you are.

Perhaps we should be careful of how we impact others since they don't have free will. Perhaps a certain morality can be derived from this fact, the fact of no free will. In what situations should you have the right to impact other people's lives? Doing nothing lets others be impacted by other things than you. So are there certain times where it is immoral to not impact another person? This is something we already consider in our lives without the notion of free will, but how does it change with the knowledge of not having free will?

Imagine a different version of the Trolley Car Dilemma where you have a raft going down a river and unless you take action to throw a rope to the raft, that raft and all those who are in it will go over the edge of the waterfall and die. Life is like this. We are all rafting along the continual river of time or change—or fate.

What is the impact of your actions and inactions? What is the impact of what you do and don't do? What do you spend your time doing every day? Since there is no free will and statistically you are probably not an outlier, everything you do will affect you to a certain degree. How do you spend your time?

Imagine you see someone offering drugs to children. If you try to interject, a friend might say, "It isn't your place to change people or influence them." People are in a constant state of being influenced. When do you think it is right for you to influence other people or the world? What kind of morality can be derived from such thinking?

Your meta and point of view will change with knowledge. At this moment, that knowledge is the fact that *free will is an illusion*. What then would be a good meta for going through life?

Do you believe that all fantasy is bad? Maybe a good strategy is to view yourself as having free will and view others as people without free will. If you do this, you'll be more critical of yourself and try to improve while at the same time be more forgiving of others. Of course, view yourself with free will at times to keep reality in check. Does a little bit of fantasy make things better? Will there be other negative consequences of adding fantasy on purpose to your life? Can you truly live a life with free will once the illusion has been dispelled?

Sometimes there's just no going back. That raft has already passed.

Section 2: Playing with Our New Glasses

Wherein we view familiar situations through the lenses of our new glasses and perhaps see old situations in a new way.

This section won't be broken into chapters, but will instead pose a series of common situations and thoughts that may be familiar to you. The chapters from Section 1 can help us navigate the landmines in a "mindfield" of taboo subjects.

CHAPTER 1: META AND VIEWPOINTS

CHAPTER 2: BELL CURVES AND GREYSCALES

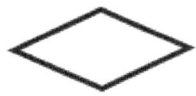

CHAPTER 3: THE HUMAN EQUATION AND CHANGE

$$\Sigma \neq$$

CHAPTER 4: THE REALITIES OF A WORLD WITHOUT FREE WILL

$$B + L = U$$

So now that you have your toys, let's play with them:

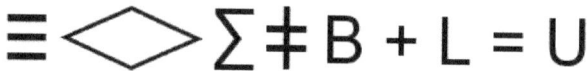

What Do We Know Now?

How unrealistic would it be for me to give a weapon to the reader, to you, to help you view everything, including this book, differently, and then think that you might not use it against the very ideas that I'm giving you? On the contrary, I love this game, the game of using the book against itself. I hope you will use the logic through this book to challenge the knowledge of the book itself.

I love this aspect of reality, even if my love of it is only derived from myself, and there is nothing truly intrinsic about it. Or perhaps there is—if I have no free will, then don't I have to find my own meaning? Doesn't this mean that the meaning I get out of life is also equally part of reality because it was meant to happen? It is very easy to confuse oneself. This paragraph in itself is an example of how to use the different concepts in this book to view reality. Now, let the fun begin.

Wait, Wait—one minute! Isn't it a bit *presumptuous*, Alan, to word that question the way you did? "What do we *know*…?" How about "What do we *think* we know now?" But inserting the word *think* makes it less impactful, less of a stimulus. So I'll just keep it as is.

Humans and Computers

To the average person, the reality of seeing humans as more like computers or robots can be seem quite dismal: Without free will there is no actual agency, and we are just automatons. So why don't I get depressed all the time?

People are interesting, very interesting, just as they are. One doesn't have to add superficial things like free will to a person to make them more interesting. The reality of how people are is plenty interesting enough. Try not to get too depressed when you come to accept that free will is just an illusion. Just because you realize that there is no free will doesn't mean that anything has changed. It has only changed in your mind.

The reality that nothing has really changed is like having a computer and understanding that everything it does it does because of the hardware and software that makes it what it is. A computer's state at any given time amounts to the hardware plus all the software and all the changes to the computer that have happened since it was created. This should sound analogous to the human formula. Humans are a baseline plus experiences that equals how a human being is at any given time. In both, hardware tends to degrade over time. I know that I could personally use some upgraded hardware—and software.

Changing Gears Between Free Will and No Free Will

During the electrical/chemical process where I am under an illusion and it seems like I am making a decision, I can zoom out meta-cognitively and reflect on the process of what seems like decision-making. When I first started doing this, I would sometimes feel depressed or disheartened because I came to the realization of how little control I have over my own life. Later on, I was able to look at myself in more of a scientific way and became very interested in how "I" work. It is amazingly sad how little knowledge the average human being has about the human body. It is equally as disappointing how little the average person understands about themselves. How much time do people spend trying to understand themselves?

When I first began viewing the world without free will, it wasn't a 100% of the time kind of thing. I was mostly viewing the world as if there was free will. I was "zoomed in" and living "in the moment," "day-to-day." Then something confusing would happen. All I would have to do is take out the false input of free will, and in doing so there would be a comforting realization that came with actual reality. The fantasy world of free will was preventing me from growing and understanding how things work. By losing free will, I was able to gain solace because I was then able to understand how things in the world work or function. The realization is especially helpful when I confront things that would otherwise be confusing or difficult to explain.

Fantasy isn't limited to free will alone. False information confuses reality. Free will is false. Free will confuses reality. Free will is another dogma like religion that can prevent people from understanding the world. Going through life with free will and fantasy is like walking with blinders. You'll constantly trip and stumble and be confused when events just "appear" out of nowhere. Giving up free will and certain other beliefs is a great tradeoff.

I am standing on a moving, changing platform. The blocks that make up this platform sometimes shift, and I view the world through the lens of free will; however, that occurs less and less frequently the more I understand about how things work.

The next time you find something in the world that seems confusing, try to step back and view the situation without free will. This will lead to a closer picture of reality. You'll lose the concept of free will and all the confusion comes with it. When I go through this mental process, then much of what was confusing isn't. Imagine going through life and having way less confusion. It is awesome.

Stay in One Gear All the Time: The One True Meta?

When I listen to religious organizations and those propounding how great their particular beliefs are, it seems that they want me and everyone else to be in their meta. A true believer or one who is devout in a particular religion is one who seems to be in the religious meta all the time. They put weight on that "knowledge" or "information" that puts them in that mindset or level of meta. It seems to me that regardless of whether the knowledge is fake or real, being stuck in one meta is detrimental to an individual and to society. For a religion to claim that the knowledge of their particular beliefs is the proper meta for every conceivable situation doesn't seem to make a lot of sense in my experience. Has it made sense in yours? There are some who believe that if a person doesn't subscribe to *their* special brand of meta, then they must be doing evil. More on this in the "If Not Red, Then It *Must* Be Blue" section later on.

Focus Has Limits: The Power of Adaptation and the Weakness of Fixation

As human beings, we have a limited amount of focus. This is true both for time and intensity. The more you increase a flashlight's area of effect, then the more diffused the light becomes and the less focused it is. To shine a flashlight at one object is to put other objects in the dark. Luckily, our flashlight of focus is moveable. We are able to move the light from one area of thought and interest to another.

One thing that makes our flashlights more interesting is that it is a two-way light beam. When we focus on things externally, we are interacting with the world using all of our available senses. At the same time, that beam of light is shooting into ourselves. When it enters us, it doesn't do so randomly but rather shines upon the associated parts of our mind and highlights the memories and all the knowledge we have accrued and combines that with our external focus. This is simultaneously external and internal. The external is the present (what we are feeling/sensing in the moment). The internal is our memories and experiences (that we draw on because of the relativity of the moment).

The flashlight is a metaphor for our mind and focus. One of the things I find convenient with regards to having the kind of mind that we have as human beings is that we can switch meta (put weight on different knowledge or turn a blind eye toward certain aspects of reality) in order to maximize our effectiveness in any given situation. When you are in a meta, you are putting weight on the knowledge that is part of that meta.

The human mind isn't aware simultaneously of all knowledge, which is good because this lets us focus on a specific situation without having to worry about extraneous information (knowledge of other meta that doesn't help a situation). Our brains have to change meta to view different "files." This is referred to as "putting on a different hat" or "switching gears," and I'm sure you've heard other phrases for it. When I sit down to write, I'm in a different mindset than when I'm cooking dinner. This is obvious and simple, yet the implications are profound. This is a cool ability that almost every human has. When you focus on a task, you will block out other information that doesn't help you with said task. When I'm playing the violin, almost all of my knowledge and abilities about the culinary arts are useless. The converse is also true. When I'm making soup, my violin skills are not only not helpful in the situation, but thinking about the violin (or viola) will perhaps cause me to burn or cut myself. Being able to focus and shift focus is critical to life.

Adaptability is awesome. Imagine if I went through life with a fixed flashlight where I couldn't pull my head away from playing the violin. This "fixed" flashlight is called fixation of the mind. It severely limits a person's ability to function and deal with new tasks. It's like having gears that won't fully shift. Does it make sense at all to keep your flashlight on just one thing even as you do different activities? Religious ideology is an attempt to keep one's mental flashlight upon one file while switching gears physically with the other. Staying in one meta isn't useful in all situations. The real advantage is adaptation of one's meta. When you are in the wrong meta for a given situation, then you are putting weight on a lot of information that has no causal effect on what is occurring in the moment.

Just as staying in one meta all the time is bad, so too is refusing to switch to a meta that is appropriate for a situation. Imagine if I said, "Technically I know that the human body is comprised of muscles, veins, arteries, and all sorts of organs. However, I think it is gross to think about someone like that. So, I refuse to ever think of a person as anything but their personality and how they look as a whole on the outside." That might actually work when just "hanging out" or having a conversation with someone. In fact, that mindset might work most of the time, but is it wise to lock one's mind into a fixation and be unable or unwilling to change?

Suppose I hold that mindset when my friend is having a medical emergency right in front of me. What if I decide that I'm just going to look at my friend and just see them as a whole? I'm going to be confused why their personality is so different, and I'll probably be even more confused as to why red stuff is coming out of them or why they can't breathe.

Cults and religious ideology will sometimes block a person from switching to an appropriate meta. In such a situation, a human won't be able to take advantage of the medical knowledge and benefits that are right before them. Take a medical emergency or decision where medical knowledge is useful because it is a *medical situation*. Suppose a person decides that the religion file is more important than their medical file and so they refuse to shift the light from religion to medicine. I've seen this happen—a person might need to have surgery, and the first thing they do is consult a cult leader instead of a doctor. I've seen members of a cult refuse to take medicine that their body needed because the medicine wasn't allowed in their faith. It sounds like insanity.

It is.

Don't Be a Jerk

My hope is that you'll feel more empowered by reading this book. Please don't be a jerk to others because you have the experience of this book that has suddenly put you in what may feel like a superior meta.

Some people believe that they are superior to others because they have stumbled upon a different point of view from what is common. Also, sometimes people are under the illusion that they are superior to other people because their meta is simply something that they specifically value while not understanding that those values are for them alone, and to everyone else, it is just nonsense. Being in a different meta doesn't mean one is more intelligent than one who is in a more basic "lower" meta. More intelligence allows one to gain more platforms that they can switch between.

Imagine a person who can hold the various platforms in their mind and then switch between them at will. Having many platforms and being able to move between them at will would be an example of someone's intelligence. If the person is wise, then they would know how to pick the most useful meta or viewpoint for any given situation.

On Autism and Categorizing States of Realization

When one views all of the cause-and-effect relationships and then weighs them according to their morality (how their meta is at the moment), then they come up with pros and cons. For the majority of people on the autism spectrum, the negative aspects of having autism outweigh the positive benefits. This is true even for an individual who is high-functioning. However, when it comes to a society as a whole, the collective ends up benefiting from people who are different. Those individuals who suffer from autism are thus of great use—at least until whatever benefits derived from that population are outsourced to artificial intelligence or Vulcans, whichever one comes first.

The hidden advantage of autism is that there are individuals who don't follow all of the same cause-and-effect rules as other human beings. This gives them a unique view of the world. In many cases, they do not have as many emotional or social connections, which can lead to them seeing a lot of situations in the world more clearly. Their view of cause and effect is a little different, which leads to different rules, which in turn leads to a different platform, which is the mind and how it determines how one sees the world.

There is a fear that I've heard from neurologically-typical people who are in relationships of some kind with those with autism. Their fear about the individual who is on the spectrum is that they do not care or love them because they don't show feelings and emotions in the same way as other people. This fear is understandable but luckily isn't true. When one sees human beings with far less or no emotion, then that doesn't necessarily lead to less compassion or caring about them.

I can't speak for others, but for myself I do feel a lot of emotions—they just go away a lot faster. It is a lot like depressing a key on a piano. Someone who is neurologically-typical is similar to holding down the sustain pedal on a piano. When you depress a key, the hammer strikes the string inside the piano and that sound is able to sustain. When I depress a key on the proverbial piano that is me with autism, the sustain pedal is not engaged, and so the sound ends almost right after it was created.

I often thought that that is one reason why people on the spectrum connect to music and objects: They are a more constant source of stimuli. It is like continually striking a key on the keyboard. If you combine this rapid fading of emotions with the fact that those on the spectrum don't quite sense that someone likes them through subtle emotional stimuli, then those together often create an imbalance of emotions between the individual with autism and the individual who is spending time with them. I can tell you that, even with all of those hindrances to relationships, I have cared. I have loved. I can also tell you that when someone is toxic and nasty to be around, then I don't have a lot of the emotional weaknesses that a neurologically-typical person has, and so I find it easier to end those kinds of relationships and get those people out of my life. So you can see there are pros and cons.

The Optimistic Side of Inevitability

I've heard people who believe that the strongest moral argument—and the most common—against the absence of free will and the presence of determinism and fatalism is that such meta/viewpoints actually make people behave worse. On the contrary, I feel that realizing one doesn't have free will as well as understanding determinism and fatalism actually makes people behave better. I am going to walk you through a step-by-step process that will show you how a logical and unemotional "Vulcan" approach to humanity can result in compassion and love. Some could argue it is a way of obtaining morality through science, but I feel that might be going too far.

Please take a moment to think about other human beings, creatures, and life in general on the planet. How does realizing that we don't have free will change how we feel about other creatures who are just as trapped in this world as we are? You don't need to use belief to find love for other creatures. Instead, let's use logic to achieve a deep connection and solidarity with our fellow human beings and other lifeforms on the planet Earth.

We should all have compassion for other living creatures because we are all at the mercy of this world. Think about a bug that enters your home. It entered your home through no choice or free will of its own. Furthermore, that bug probably has no concept of what your home is to you and who you are. What about a tree that happened to grow where it grew or just life in general on this planet? If we can understand the situation of other lifeforms, then how much more compassion should we have for each other?

Remember, just as you didn't pick where you started in this world, so too did no one else. If you were born as they were, a baby with their genes, in their exact place in the world, with their parents (or not), in their society at the time the world was in the very state it was in, then you would be them exactly. You would have made every single decision that they made. You would be them. So too with any other animal, creature, or plant.

One cannot have true compassion while simultaneously holding on to dogmas that espouse wish-fulfilling fantasies. Try not to fall victim to believing things that make you feel artificially special

Once you realize that it doesn't make sense to hate animals, trees, bugs, or other things for existing just the way they are, then you come full circle and realize that it doesn't make sense to hate yourself for who you are.

or magical. I know it is much more appealing to believe that you are a special, magical being rather than just another human. But realize that it isn't so bad being a human. Humans are special. Human beings are awesome.

To want to make yourself artificially more special is a desire to separate oneself. If you are part of a cult or if you believe in fantasy, then you believe in something that would make you separate from the very world that you are part of: something that doesn't make sense; something that doesn't follow all the rules of cause and effect—something like free will.

Levels of Understanding

Here is another way to think of meta. This relates to people and the world we live in, as most stuff does. People like labels and numbers, so here we go.

Level 0:

A person who can't see outside of themselves. Some people call this egotistical. For many, it is just solipsism. Solipsism isn't as crazy as one might think because we do in fact experience everything through our senses. Everyone around you is a stimulus (a cause that affects you), and that's why it seems like the world revolves around you. The perception of stimuli doesn't make the world revolve around you, but it builds your platform that determines how you see the world. This creates a cyclical situation. It ends up being very close to bi-linear causation. Specific cause and effect stimuli from the world change your platform, which changes how you see the world, which changes your platform again, which changes how you see the world, and so on.

The world impacts you → your platform is changed → you see the world differently → the world impacts you → your platform is changed, and it goes on and on. Through this process, you change, grow, and evolve.

The world as you know it is tempered completely through your senses and your mind. If there was a "full dive" virtual reality like in *The Matrix*, then you really wouldn't know the difference between reality and fantasy. You wouldn't know that you are in a simulation. This can be dangerous because the reality is that we all don't experience the world evenly. This is true in subtle ways such as the fact that people eating the same meal won't taste the food *exactly* the same way because they are all in different bodies.

For a more drastic example, let's examine sight. There are many differences in how people see: Some people are colorblind, some need glasses, some do not need glasses. Those who need glasses might need them for a multitude of reasons: far-sighted, near-sighted, astigmatism, and of course different magnitudes of correction. A person would be just flat out wrong to think that their other senses are any different. If you were a professional musician and were attending a wedding, then when the guy playing a trombone cracks a note, you might actually be the only one to notice. Or one of two as it happened when I was at a wedding.

The reality is that we don't experience the world nearly as similarly as we may believe, not only because of variations in our senses, but the state of our minds as well. All of which are based on—*drum roll*—B + L = U.

Level 1:

A person who is able to extend oneself to include their family. The basic people who have taken care of us or the immediate support group.

Level 2:

A person who is able to extend oneself to include their friends. This goes beyond biological family to other relationships. This is the ability of someone to take a friend who isn't of their blood or immediate tribe and still consider them family.

Level 3:

A person who is able to extend oneself to include people who are like them on superficial levels that are easily determined by the common senses.

> Sight: They look like them.
>
> Sound: They sound like them.
>
> Meta: They have similar values.
>
> (So on and so on.)

Level 4:

A person who is able to extend oneself to include people who are like them on perhaps a "deeper" level. Look, I understand there can be some confusion or even discrepancy over what is "superficial" and what has "weight." That's cool. Think about why that is.

These are the things that someone doesn't usually realize unless they are intuitive. A person "feels" like them, like one of their "group."

There are certain vibes that people of a cult (who are true followers) give off. These vibes are hard to fake for outsiders. Most people aren't aware of the vibes, but to those who are aware of this other "sense," it makes the world a lot clearer.

There is a lot more to this.

Level 5:

People are able to extend themselves to others who have had similar life experiences—same school, home town, upbringing, etc.—as long as they again "feel right."

Level 6:

A person who is able to extend oneself to include others who had similar life experiences even though they are a bit different now.

Level 7:

A person who is able to extend oneself to include their local community.

Level 8:

A person who is able to extend oneself to include their broader community (for example, the state level).

Level 9:

A person who is able to extend oneself to include their country. This would include a lot of people who don't think like them. This seems hard for many people.

Level 10:

A person who is able to extend oneself to include other countries that are similar to their own, countries with similar values.

Level 11:

A person who is able to extend oneself to include other countries and all the people of the world.

Level 12:

A person who is able to extend oneself past humanity and appreciate other living creatures that society has come to appreciate depending on the region (dogs, cats, cows, whatever). The easiest are other mammals.

Level 13:

A person who is able to extend oneself to include other living creatures such as birds, fish, and other things that one's society doesn't normally value.

Level 14:

A person who is able to extend oneself to include all manner of creatures, bugs included.

Level 15:

A person who is able to extend oneself to include all forms of life including plants.

Level 16:

A person who is able to extend oneself to include all things that impact life, things that themselves are not alive. The sun or the moon. That rock that you sit on when you are tired. The mountain that helps you determine your location. A true appreciation for nature as a whole.

Level 17:

One who is able to extend themselves to the planet that they live on as a whole—even the rocks.

Level 18:

A person who is able to extend oneself to include things that are perhaps beyond the physical or the boundaries of their planet, plane, whatever.

Feel free to continue the list as you wish. This should be enough to help you understand what I'm talking about, whether you agree or not. I want to be understood—only then can someone agree or disagree.

The short, abridged version: You can condense levels 0-12 to just finding the shared humanity between all people. Levels 13-15 cover non-human living things. Levels 16 and on cover other physical things as well as beyond the physical.

Sometimes you get to what appears to be the top of a mountain and realize that it is just a ledge. This is a good feeling because it means that you have the opportunity to climb higher and understand everything in a deeper and more profound way.

Sometimes an event in your life occurs. and you realize that your past experiences were just a dream, and now you have real insight into how the world works.

The Secret Hidden Section of Ultimate Knowledge of WTF Is Going on in the World and How to Understand the Way the World Works

AKA *TSHSOUKOWTFIGOITWAHTUTWTWW* for a short and easy way to memorize it.

A few years ago, one of my close friends gave me one of the funniest birthday cards. On the front it read, "Within is the secret to life." Inside was a bunch of illegible symbols. Needless to say, my hopes were dashed. Many people are looking for that "secret" to life to understand how the world works. Well, I have good news for you. In this section of the book, I'm not going to tease you. I'm not going to give you some bullshit answer or riddle or say something obscure just to lead you on. Here is actually how the world, the universe, and everything else works.

Everything is Cause and Effect (The Apex Meta For Our Universe)

Cause and effect is the answer to every question. Just let that sink in a little.

Cause and effect is both the key to everything and the key to nothing. What I mean is that while it technically is the answer to every question, just saying, "cause and effect" isn't enough. It explains how everything works and yet isn't specific enough to be completely useful in a complex situation. One needs specific examples of cause and effect to truly understand a given situation. The path of understanding the world through cause and effect is like understanding the complex via the simple.

Reality is complicated, but don't worry, it isn't *that* complicated. Below are definitions of things through the lens of reality (AKA cause and effect).

Note that these are grouped based on commonalities but are not in alphabetical order. This is meant just as a mental exercise. I refer a lot to memories and experiences as well as rules and platforms. Feel free to skip ahead and see the charts and read further about them, then come back to the definitions.

The list of definitions and phrases below is purposely "all over the map." The seeming randomness further accents how causation permeates everything. Just remember that all words are in fact made up.

Cause and Effect

1. The relationship of how everything works.

2. The relationship between all aspects of reality.

Causes happen before effects. An effect can be a cause for something else but not for the cause that preceded it. It describes change through time, and time is a way of calculating the rate of change between the initial cause and when the effect is fully actualized. Without time there is no cause and effect. Without cause and effect there is no time. Time is relative and so is causality.

Newton's 1st Law of Motion

Nothing changes or is affected without a cause.

When something changes or is affected, then there is always a cause that triggered the effect.

Newton's 2nd Law of Motion (Part of It)

The way something is affected is directly related to the specific nature or details of the cause.

Reality

A series of linked cause-and-effect events that continues on until it doesn't.

Non-Fiction/Realistic

If a setting is nonfiction or realistic, then it is one where the cause and effect that one can observe in the real world is identical to the cause and effect that one observes in the story.

Fiction/Fantasy

A story or setting does not follow the cause and effect of the real word. Often, stories will make their own rules of cause and effect, and sometimes the stories will even follow their own rules—if you are lucky.

Truth

1. Actual cause and effect.

2. What really happened.

Fake

1. Not the actual cause and effect.

2. Anything other than what really happened.

3. An event that didn't happen.

Omnipotent

The ability to cause any effect.

Omniscient

The ability to completely know and understand all causality.

Causality is dependent on time, so without someone being able to extrapolate cause and effect to infinity, they cannot be considered omniscient.

Obfuscation

A misrepresentation of a cause or effect.

Generally exaggerated but often just a false statement.

Believable

A situation usually absorbed secondhand that describes a cause-and-effect event where the effect is one that would logically follow the cause.

Often, something is believable when a human being of sufficient age and awareness would be able to look at their life and see many examples of cause-and-effect relationships (memories) and have multiple examples that are directly related to the one that is labelled as "believable." The term *believable* is different from what appears to be the root word *belief*.

Belief

1. A platform without a base.

2. Rules without experience or memories to support them.

    a. A belief is something that one holds without the memories/examples mentioned in the believable definition above. In belief, one doesn't need to have any supporting memories/rules; that is why it is called belief.

    b. Technically anything and everything that isn't true can be a belief because a belief is not based on reality.

True Belief

When a person has accepted a belief as part of their reality.

This acceptance of a belief as being part of a person's platform is done regardless of the fact that the belief has no basis in reality.

That's Unbelievable

1. A phrase used to describe a situation where the cause-and-effect relationship is uncommon.

2. A phrase used to describe a rare effect created by uncommon causes working in conjunction with one another.

Pros/Cons

Prescribing morality to cause and effect through the lens of a meta (a specific value system based on highlighting certain cause-and-effect situations and experiences). Memories of experiences can be true or not true. If something is partially true, then part of it is true and part of it is false.

Learning

1. *Mental.* Realizing the cause-and-effect relationships in various disciplines.

2. *Physical.* The way one's body is affected by various causes.

   Remember, the brain is part of the body.

Memory

The ability for a human to recall past cause-and-effect situations/events.

1. Whether accurately or not.

2. There is incredible power in reflecting and learning the causes and effects that have impacted oneself. We should reflect on our past. Humanity should reflect on history.

Meta Cognition

Putting one's mind in a different situation (or point of view) due to having certain knowledge of various cause-and-effect situations, often by putting weight or value on a different set of cause-and-effect relationships.

Comedy

Humor derived from a situation where the effect is not what one would expect.

1. Usually exaggerated or opposite of one would expect.

   Generally, the effect ends up being an exaggerated form of the expected effect, or it is an effect that is totally different from the expected effect. A lot of times, by learning the effect, one realizes that the implied or hinted-at cause is the actual cause.

2. Sometimes people mention effects (or the way things are) in such a way to point out that the cause is unknown (to many). This is done to point out that there is a mutual confusion among people about the cause(s) of such an effect.

3. Often a type of storytelling that begins with a cause and ends with an unexpected effect.

Confusion

Not understanding the cause-and-effect relationship in any given aspect of reality.

Confused

When one experiences causation in such a way that the cause or the effect or both don't coincide with the memories and rules that make up a person's platform (view/mindset/meta).

These experiences may be truly what happened or warped by their senses and/or misunderstanding from their platform or other variables.

Random(ness)

1. A human's inability to see or understand a given cause-and-effect relationship.

    a. Often used as an "excuse" for why humans don't understand something.

    b. It is also often used (like other made-up dogmas) to protect a human's ego.

    c. Usually refers to an event that occurs over a specific time.

2. An illusion created by a person's inability to see all the cause-and-effect relationships in a given situation.

    The illusion of randomness is created when a person doesn't see or fully understand all the variables leading to an outcome.

Complexity

A situation where a typical human being would have trouble keeping track of all of the cause-and-effect relationships (variables).

This is usually because there are many variables whose change occurs over the same time though situations can be complex if a human being's ability to sense what is going on is limited and/or the cause-and-effect relationship of an individual component of the many variables is not well known.

Ambiguity

A situation where the effect isn't easy to predict because the causation is not clear.

Uncertain

A situation where a human being doesn't have a grasp of the causes that are occurring at a given time and thus is not able to determine how those causes will affect the future.

Dogmatism

A human's made-up causation to describe a situation where the reality is not easily understood.

    a. Many humans do this to make themselves feel more confident about their understanding of the world.

    b. Many humans do this to make themselves less fearful of just how much they don't comprehend.

    While a short-term solution to fear, it actually creates more fear and unknown in the future (as is the case with false understandings about reality).

    c. This often forces a person to lie to oneself.

d. This creates future cognitive dissonance when the false beliefs of the dogma conflict with true experiences in reality.

Lie and Lying

When a person gives an explanation of cause or effect that is false when they know that a different causation happened with reference to a piece of their platform (including experiences, memories, and rules).

    a. A plague on humanity.

    b. Lies ruin our perception of cause and effect, making history and news less reliable. Makes everything, people included, less reliable.

Making a Decision

1. An action (mental or physical or otherwise taken by a living entity) taken as a result of one or more cause-and-effect stimuli.

2. It generally is the cause of another effect (as most everything tends to be).

Aggressive

The act of creating cause-and-effect relationships.

Passivity

Allowing current cause-and-effect relationships to continue on as if you don't exist.

The reality is that you do exist. Sorry, you are already part of most equations.

I love noticing how many definitions start with the word *when* and how often we use it. This word *when* denotes time and causation. That's just cool. We think about time and causation all the time, whether we are cognizant of it or not.

"Doesn't Matter"

1. When there is a cause with no effect.

    Is there anything that doesn't have any effect? Or rather, there always an effect, but sometimes it is so inconsequential that it has no effect on our goals in life.

2. A phrase usually used by an individual when the effect doesn't matter to the mental state/values of that particular individual.

Perfect or "Perfect Timing"

1. When an effect cannot be improved by additional causation.

2. Timing is *perfect* when the causes occur in such a way to form a desired effect in such a way that the addition of other causes could not improve upon the effect.

3. The phrase *perfect timing* is redundant because everything is cause and effect, and cause and effect always denotes a sense of time. Thus, it refers to a specific moment in time, a specific moment of change.

Science

The discipline of systematically isolating cause-and-effect relationships to understand various aspects of our reality.

Superstitions

When people put weight on an object or activity that they believe is a cause without any evidence of causation.

1. Actually, the superstition has little to no impact on the effect. If it has an impact, it is only on people and not on the actual object or ritual.

2. Very similar to many dogmatisms. Superstitions are hard to reproduce because the effect of said superstition comes from the individual.

Knowledge and Wisdom

1. The understanding of causation in any given discipline or area.

2. Congruent/compatible information derived oftentimes from multiple cause-and-effect relationships where the effect is extremely likely to happen from a given cause or causes.

   Many times, when referring to a person or persons, the knowledge/wisdom is from memories of past cause-and-effect relationships that as a whole have created a platform so significant that it becomes a catalyst/"cause" that affect life in a significant way, that is, many of the things people think or do, so much to the point where they see the knowledge/wisdom (whether actually true or not) as part of who they are, because the knowledge/wisdom *is* part of who they are, at least at that moment in time.

Resonate With

When a person draws a connection (conscious or not) between one or more former cause-and-effect relationships and an experience occurring in the moment.

    a. Can also be with the memory of an experience.

    b. The stronger the resonance, then generally the more cause-and-effect relationships one has had in the past that relate to it. The stronger the resonance, the deeper into one's platform of self-identity the cause and effect extends.

    c. One can have a *reverse resonation*. This happens when a person gains new knowledge then goes back in their memories and draws the connections. It is the reverse of *to resonate with*.

    d. *Antonym*. The opposite of Cognitive Dissonance.

Cognitive Dissonance

1. *General*. The mental stress someone feels when a piece of their identity, generally knowledge/wisdom, is in conflict with cause-and-effect relationships that a person is witnessing.

2. *Memories and Experiences*. When the memories of old cause-and-effect relationships don't match the experiences of new cause-and-effect relationships.

    A lot of times people will believe that because they have seen a lot of cause-and-effect relationships, then that means that all causes would equal the effects that they have seen.

3. *Rules and Building Blocks*. When the experiences of reality seem in direct conflict with rules that a person has formed.

4. *Platform(s)*. The "shaking" of a person's platform.

   Rules act as building blocks for platforms. So, when these rules are "attacked" by the different stimuli, then the platform that the rules support shakes.

In Denial

A situation in which an individual refuses to remove previous examples of cause and effect from their past (that are currently acting as memories/experience in support of rules and through rules platforms) even though they experience a lot of cognitive dissonance (examples in the present/current reality that are in conflict with those previous cause-and-effect examples).

1. Usually, when one is in denial, it's because of an overwhelming conflict between whatever cause and effect that makes up part of their rules/platform and reality.

2. The individual in denial is unable to reconcile the conflict. 1+1 cannot equal both 2 and another number.

3. Being in denial is one effect of fear. The person in denial refuses to change their platform or pieces of their platform despite what they are realizing.

   This is often due to a fear that comes with the realization that more things that they once believed to be true (part of their platform) are also untrue.

4. When someone is unwilling to change their platform, then they will simply ignore the current cause and effect. They tend to numb their senses and ignore reality. This can lead to full mental meltdowns and other problems.

5. Often when a person is the victim of a dogma/religion/cult or other belief system that doesn't have reality as part of its "education," then members of said discipline will constantly come into conflict with reality that disproves the fantasy that is now part of their platform (of reality). They will often try to remedy this cognitive dissonance when they are in denial by talking to other people who also believe in the fantasy as a way of adding in more memories or experiences to try to increase the balance of memories towards the fantasy so there won't be as much of a cognitive dissonance. This is a yo-yo of disaster in the making. Try as people might to escape reality, reality will always catch up.

6. When people ignore much of reality, they are also said to be in denial. Changing can be difficult because one has to let go of pieces that made them who they were.

Just as we should not judge another person by any singular platform, we should realize too that who we are isn't determined by a single platform either. This understanding can help weaken the ego-formed glue that tends to hold false beliefs within a platform.

Epiphany (A Moment of Clarity of Thought)

1. When a person's mind finally draws the connections between various cause-and-effect situations in such a way that it forms a new worldview (knowledge/wisdom).

2. When memories or experiences come together to form a rule.

3. When rules come together to form a platform.

Many times, epiphanies will become catalysts that will have powerful effects on future decisions, because a person's reality is based on their perception of cause and effect. It is based on their platform.

Wise

1. An attribute ascribed to a person who is able to take advantage of the cause-and-effect relationships that they have experienced.

2. One who is able to extrapolate cause-and-effect relationships to new and other scenarios.

   Someone who is wise has enough knowledge of causality to be able to predict effects based on causes with a much higher accuracy than the average person.

3. When someone is able to take advantage of their knowledge and wisdom.

    a. Wisdom is based on experiences. Humans have neither the minds nor lifespan to be wise about everything. Therefore, being wise is often a situational, disciplinary experience.

    b. The further one stretches the disciplines, the less a person will appear "wise." To be wise means that one has to have a solid platform in a certain area of knowledge. To say that someone is wise in everything would mean that they would have to have a solid platform in everything. That is stupid. Such a notion is not very wise.

    c. There is a concept of true wisdom and someone being truly wise. This is when a person has an apex platform that gives them insight into causation among various disciplines. This is not a complete understanding of every discipline, but someone with this kind of wisdom does have a strong platform from which to learn from. They should learn faster when it comes to almost anything.

      i. The swordsman and philosopher Miyamoto Musashi wrote about this in his *Book of Five Rings*.

      ii. An apex platform or true wisdom of causation is like the way grammar works across different kinds of literature and disciplines of writing. More in the apex platform section of the book.

Insanity

1. When one believes that a different effect will occur even if repeated causes are identical.

2. A person experiences that 1+1 = 2, and then believes that if they add 1+1 again, it will equal anything other than 2.

    a. When one is insane, their platforms are warped and so their mind cannot understand cause and effect in many platforms.

    b. They may often have memories of events that never happened.

3. What people might say about me after reading this book.

Having Control Over One's Life

1. When someone is able to create causes that will affect their life, typically moving it in the direction that they want to go.

2. When an individual is able to obtain goals and get what they want.

> I want to change you but not so much that I would have to manipulate you to do so. Is this book a manipulation or have I stated my intent enough to feel less guilty about it? Or perhaps I just don't feel guilty about it because I don't have free will and have to write this book and you didn't have any choice but to read the book, and so this was all just meant to happen. That's the way my brain works.

Manipulate

Changing someone without them knowing.

1. Often in a negative context but can just as well be positive.

    Parents often change their children without them knowing in order to improve them (based on the morality their platform determines are positive changes at the specific time).

2. Generally changing the affected person in a way that makes them more like how the manipulator (one doing the causation) wants them to be.

Influence Someone (Control Over Another's Life)

When you are able to make causes that will affect someone's life

Influence means change.

One should thus be careful of their own moralities with regards to their platform and the platform of the one they are influencing.

Teaching

A relationship where one entity creates causes that affect another entity generally in a way that empowers the other with knowledge and abilities (learning mental and learning physical).

Unfortunately, you can teach someone things that are not true as well. One has to be careful when influencing or "educating" others.

Fluke

A cause-and-effect relationship that occurs so infrequently in nature that it is a statistical outlier.

1. Most people are surprised by flukes because their perception of the causes was not great enough to realize that it would occur.

2. Flukes don't exist when enough knowledge exists.

    a. If one knew all of the causation of a situation, then they would realize that it would happen 100% of the time when it happens.

    b. If one has more knowledge, then they wouldn't ever see a fluke. it would just be a rare occurrence.

    c. A full solar eclipse would have seemed like a miracle or fluke in the past. However, now we have more knowledge, and so it is no longer a fluke or miracle or anything else but a rare occurrence.

    Eclipses are cool.

Miracle

1. A belief about a cause-and-effect relationship. Generally, a belief is the cause part of the cause-and-effect relationship

2. A belief used in place of a cause where one doesn't have the knowledge/rationality to understand the specific causality.

3. Sometimes a miracle is a belief that explains the entire causality. In these examples, not only is the cause a belief but so is the effect.

Intoxication

The effect from the cause, which is generally alcohol.

Medicine (Western)

Using chemistry (chemicals) as a cause to change the human body towards a desired effect.

Unfortunately, many causes can have multiple effects.

1. Do you think it is "not right" for someone to give medicine and not be honest with the individual about all of the effects that such a cause (of taking the medicine) would have?

2. What about a drug company or doctor who uses obfuscation to manipulate someone into changing themselves?

3. How do you feel about a society that you may be part of that allows the above to occur without consequences to their actions?

Gifted/Talented

When someone's base (how they are when they are formed) is in such a state that it allows the person to naturally excel in a given area with less than normal stimuli or cause-and-effect changes upon them.

1. Children are often labelled as talented because they haven't had a very long time to gain skills because there haven't been many cause-and-effect experiences that would indicate that their base would have more weight for their current situation. Being gifted or talented is thus related to one's base.

   > Sometimes I've been labelled as talented in, say, music, where in reality I had to experience many cause-and-effect situations both mentally and physically to get to where I am.

2. An adult who is good at a skill may still be talented even if they aren't talented in the area of the skill. Their talent may be perseverance.

Bad luck

Someone who happens to be the victim of negative effects due to external cause-and-effect relationships going on in the world around them.

1. Generally, the one with bad luck doesn't seem to be creating causes that would lead to negative effects

2. The phrase "You have bad luck" generally refers to someone who has repeated experiences of bad things happening to them outside their control.

Trustworthy

A label or rule placed upon a person or entity who is known for their consistent, positive cause-and-effect relationship with others over time.

Like other "rules," it is formed from multiple, related memories.

Consistent

A person or situation with predictable cause-and-effect relationships.

Explanation

Describing what specific cause lead to an effect.

Making an "Informed Decision"

A situation where one can reasonably presume what the cause-and-effect situation will be based on having many examples of similar cause and effect.

Can often be combined with general rules or "laws" derived from an apex platform.

Something Doesn't "Make Sense"

Often, one can look back at numerous cause-and-effect events that they have witnessed and see that a certain cause-and-effect situation doesn't line up with anything they have in their memories.

Miracles are a good example of something not "making any sense."

1. Not only do they not fit into any grouping of other experiences that can support them, but such causation is often in direct opposition or contradiction to the very memories that one has experienced.

2. People have what I call "laws": They are part of a person's apex platform. These laws are like gravity on Earth. When you are on Earth, then gravity generally applies to you in everything that you do. Often when something "doesn't make sense," then it is violating a law. Something you know to be true and is so basic and part of our reality that no one in their right mind could refute it.

Example: Fire will burn your hand.

"Related to Each Other"

Non-biological. Two events that have a direct cause-and-effect relationship with one another.

Advice

An attempt to use past knowledge to help someone navigate the cause-and-effect nature of our world.

This is often done in two ways:

1. Telling someone what causation to employ to achieve a desired effect.

2. Telling someone to avoid a certain causation because it will lead to a negative effect.

Knowing the Difference Between "Good" Advice and "Bad" Advice

The difference between knowing and understanding the cause-and-effect relationships in a given situation or not knowing and not understanding the cause-and-effect relationships in a given situation.

    1. Unfortunately, someone needs some experience (or trust) to know whether advice is good or bad.

    2. When one is giving good advice, they are doing so from a platform that is built on rules and thus specific cause-and-effect situations that relate to the given topic of which the advice is about.

A Moment in Time

Pausing time and thus cause-and-effect relationships to see how things are (the current state of causation).

    1. It is often used to analyze causes or cause-and-effect relationships that lead to the moment, AKA understanding the past.

    2. Or it is used to analyze the current situation to try to predict what will happen in the future.

Acting Selfishly

An action when someone is the catalyst for a cause-and-effect relationship with multiple effects where one effect or more are positive for the catalyst, and the other effects are negative for other people.

Someone Is a Selfish Person

A mindset/meta where the person in the mindset will repeatedly cause effects that are positive for themselves while showing a total disregard for the collateral negative effects on others.

Paranoid/Paranoia

When a person doesn't understand cause and effect in such a way that they over-inflate a cause, making it seem as though the causation has a greater impact on an undesirable effect than it actually does.

1. The cause may actually not have any impact on the feared effect.

2. Often, a person may believe that the cause would make the effect extremely likely to occur when in reality the event has little to no chance of occurring. In any case, it is a person's inability to understand causation.

This is just another example of how education can lead to a saner and happier life.

Sadly, simply having an understanding doesn't always help people who are unfortunate enough to have a paranoia. Something has to be done to help them, something that can help change their platform.

Can't Remember

1. A failure of a person to change their platform to the exact configuration needed to draw upon the memory from that platform.

2. When a person shifts their platform then attempts to accesses rules that are related to the specific memory that they are trying to remember, but they can't find that memory in the specific "rule drawer" where the memories that support said rule are kept.

Matrix Conversations

Conversations that bounce between topics of fluff and substance with little or no segue in between the changing of said topics.

I'm making up this term. *Obviously*. The movie *The Matrix* would change back and forth from teenage-entertaining combat straight to philosophy for adults (much like an anime).

1. Many of the conversations I have with my close friends seem like this because we'll go from talking about fluff such as the latest movie or something funny that we saw straight into politics, religion, philosophy, and other topics that tend to have a greater influence on humanity.

2. Changing topics like this makes one change their platform. It is interesting to feel this.

A Shift

You know that moment in a conversation where your mental platform starts shifting and you are about to say this great thing that "came into your head," but someone else says something, and because you are a good listener, you actually process what they say, and your brain shifts to the platform associated with what they are saying? After they are done speaking, it is your turn to speak again, and you want to go back to the platform that you were in the process of going to before they started speaking.

But you can't. You can't because you already shifted to a new platform. You realize that you aren't going through the process of morphing into the correct platform and are instead in a totally unrelated platform: the platform of *confusion*. You then tell the other person, "I forgot what I was going to say." I hate it when that happens.

Sometimes you will tighten your head and earlobes and get frustrated because the "gears" that change one platform to another (metaphorically) grind. This is one of the many forms of fixation. Having a relaxed and clear mind is the way to be free. Don't abide.

Often, people will try to morph their platform into a specific platform in order to access a memory. It is hard to will it to change because will is a bit of an illusion. If one instead tries to insert the appropriate causes to change the platform (effect), then they will have a much easier time remembering. Causation works in the mind too.

Are there words, phrases, ideas, or concepts that don't fit into cause and effect? If so, then they are probably bullshit because they don't exist in any reality. This is another way of saying, "Are there things you've been taught that don't seem to fit into reality? If so, then they are probably not true."

Phrases and Quotes That I've Heard and How I Translate or Understand Them Through the Lens of Cause and Effect, AKA Reality

Through the Lens: From a specific platform configuration.

Everything happens for a reason: Everything happens *because* of a reason. Consider a religious person who says, "God is in control of everything" versus someone who isn't religious at all and says, "Everything is random." Now if you remember the chapter on greyscales and bell curves, then you will realize that these two statements might be outliers and not representative of the majority of said groups. But when I hear phrases like this, I smirk to myself because the reality is that the religious person who says that "God is in control of everything and there's an order and purpose in the world" is far more accurate than someone who believes in randomness. They might not understand the causality behind the effects that they witness, but they do realize that there are patterns in the natural world and can tell that much of it isn't just random. Caveat: Someone who is labelled an atheist (generally by a religious person or organization) just means they don't believe in a god. That doesn't mean that they in any way shape or form have to believe in something else like randomness.

Be the change you want to see in the world: If you want a certain effect, then be the cause. If you want to see the world change in a certain way, then be the cause that will affect the world and make it change in the desired way.

It was meant to be or *It wasn't meant to be*: A kind of superstition, where someone believes in luck or ascribes luck or fate (incorrectly and in place of the actual causation) to a situation. The reality is that everything that happens, whether big or small, was "meant to be." How do we know? Because it happened.

Often, people use this statement to mean that something wasn't meant to be for the long term. In reality, this situation is likely to be attainable or unattainable (meant to be or not meant to be) just for that given moment.

That makes sense: What you are telling me is something that I believe to be true due to my memory of related past cause-and-effect relationships.

I can feel the gears changing/working; *I can smell rubber burning*: These statements are often used to describe a person who is thinking.

How I view it: I can feel—part of me can sense—a platform shifting, trying to rearrange information (cause-and-effect situations) into the rules that form the platform. Sometimes, this is feeling the platform shifting to view the world in a different meta through which a new viewpoint is actualized.

Follow your dreams: Let's dissect this.

Dreams are goals (often lofty). They manifest often as images in one's mind. The reason why they are powerful is that dreams often rule out an infinite number of possible outcomes. Imagine your dream is to live in a beautiful, wooden cabin in the woods. For this example, assume that it is the only home you plan on owning. As you go through life, you will accumulate different furniture and items. If you think about the end-goal, in this case the cabin, then it can help you decide what to keep and get rid of. Can you picture that modern coffee table in your forest cabin? Probably not. Throw it out.

The same can be true in a lot of areas—for example, having a dream or goal of the kind of person you want to be. Would that person act in a certain way? Would they treat others a certain way? What would *that kind of person* spend their time doing? How about imagining the kind of parent you wish to be? How would they act? In summary, having a dream/goal/endgame in mind helps to reverse-engineer and help change one's life to accomplish the dream. The dream becomes a catalyst for itself.

Losing one's focus: When someone has a platform whose focus is directly related to a physical or mental task that they are working on and they lose the platform or change platforms while doing said task.

They don't know any better: The subject that the phrase refers to doesn't have enough experience or memories (or lacks the capacity) to form the appropriate rules in order to understand a given situation.

I love this game, and I hope that you will try this on your own: Think of several words or phrases and redefine them using cause and effect. Even though you haven't played this "game," you'll find that it isn't that hard. Why? Because the game is based in reality, and luckily most of your experiences have been in it.

A Word to Fiction Writers

I enjoy good stories, especially ones that have fantasy and sci-fi aspects to them. In these situations, the creator of the story changes causation from what we experience in the natural world to a different causation for the world or setting of their story. Sometimes I feel that a story is ruined or part of it is ruined when there is a break in continuity within a world that was created in the story. This often occurs when a story (regardless of medium) breaks its own rules of cause and effect! The current causation in a story (current experience) has to coincide with previous causation (memories) that was established earlier.

If you have money and decide to purchase a franchise or story, then please do everyone a favor and understand the causation (or lack thereof) in the story that you are now the owner of so you don't "F" it up!

Four Chapters Defined by Cause and Effect

What kind of person would I be if I didn't use my own reasoning against myself? Here are the previous chapters defined by cause and effect.

The four chapters are part of my own platform, the knowledge/wisdom that I have gathered from my memory of previous cause-and-effect relationships over the course of my life thus far. They make up part of my meta/mindset/viewpoint and thus impact what I do. These rules are not a complete picture of my mind and certainly are not the only knowledge or causes that affect me. They are, however, ones that I feel could have a positive impact on the lives of others.

1. META AND VIEWPOINTS:

The current orientation and formation of an individual's platform, which determines the mindset of the individual. It is through this mindset/point of view that a value system/reality becomes the basis or "glasses" through which they interact through the world (causation).

2. BELL CURVES AND GREYSCALES:

A knowledge about human beings and reality derived from many cause-and-effect experiences/relationships. The greyscale portion shows that while everything is technically black and white (cause and effect/one outcome/going to happen or not happen), the way it is perceived by humans is as variety or a gray scale. The bell curve portion (variety) is due to the slight nuances of causes that don't create an exact effect (similar to what was stated in the definition of Newton's Law). Causes often create a predictable variation of effects related to human beings and other aspects in nature and can be graphed mathematically in a bell-curve shape.

A bell shape occurs due to the differences inherent in any population of human beings.

3. THE HUMAN EQUATION AND CHANGE:

Everything about a human being is a cause-and-effect relationship. A person changes or is affected, which causes them to be different, which affects how they see and interact with the world and everything about them, which affects how they perceive and interact with the world, which changes everything about them. A person is constantly changing through cause and effect.

4. THE REALITIES OF A WORLD WITHOUT FREE WILL:

Everything is cause and effect. When you see something like free will in the world, something that seems to be just random or to just appear or come into existence through magic or other supernatural means, then it is breaking the rules of cause and effect. A red flag should go off in your mind, warning that you are not seeing a situation in its entirety and that what you are seeing is in fact not real. It is an illusion. That in of itself doesn't prove that free will doesn't exist. To experience life as a human is to live in a reality filled with illusions. Visual illusions are obvious, but there are many more. Simply recall any day of your life and think about how time appears to speed up and slow down.

The burden of proof is, in my opinion, on the one who says or believes that something exists to prove it exists. Show the memories and experiences that form the rules and platform for the idea that you are propounding. Show the causation of this belief so I can move it to the reality category of my own mind. If you believe that leprechauns exist, then prove it to me. It is a colossal waste of time to disprove leprechauns, free will, and other stupid ideas. Just because something appears to be true doesn't make it so.

This book is my own attempt to do exactly the following: Give examples/memories that you can relate to and build rules and then a platform of reality. That is why I go into so much detail with my examples and explanations of each concept. I don't want you to believe anything in this book but to truly know and understand that it is reality.

Some Things to Consider from the "Fallout" of Causation

Does it make sense to make up or assume a cause to a known effect if one doesn't really understand or know what the actual cause is?

Does it make sense to make up or assume an effect from a known cause if one doesn't really understand or know what the actual effect is?

Suppose your computer doesn't work correctly one day. Is the computer's non-functionality just random? Or merely a chance that it would happen? Is there perhaps a reason why it isn't working?

People are like computers. Can we assign free will to computers when we ourselves don't have it? A better question would be the following: Can we give computers the illusion of free will? Like us?

If your car breaks down or something doesn't work in it, then is that random or is there a cause behind it?

If a leaf falls, is that totally random? (Hint: No.)

Given that all knowledge is simply understanding the cause and effect of various situations, disciplines, and reality, do you believe that all knowledge is good? Knowledge itself is neither good nor bad. Knowledge is simply a precursor to determining what is good and bad.

If everything is cause and effect, does good or evil exist, or are things just the way they are?

Can you think of anything that is not a cause-and-effect relationship?

If so, might it be a misunderstanding (incomplete information of causation) about the subject at hand? Perhaps that "knowledge" or "information" is just flat-out wrong.

Having true free will seems to "break the rules" of causation. Be wary of things that break the rules of cause and effect, especially the ones that you have personally witnessed.

The Causation of Changing a Person's Reality

A person's reality and how it changes is based on a few elements and simple steps.

Who They Are:

A person's body (everything that makes them who they are at a given time).

This includes non-physical things such as memory. People have certain rules or processes that they follow based on their memory of past experiences. It would be highly inefficient for a person to have to go through endless memories every time a new experience occurs, so past experiences or the cause-and-effect relationships between past experiences are often condensed into rules or a platform off of which a person operates. The reason why we are wrong a lot of times is because the way we take in information or view cause-and-effect situations is imperfect as well as our memories of them later on.

How They Interface with the World:

Their senses such as sight, hearing, etc. How a person experiences the cause and effect stimuli around them.

Without senses, one doesn't experience anything outside of themselves. Everything we absorb is through our senses.

Comparing Current Cause and Effect to Previous Cause and Effect:

The reaction between previous cause-and-effect experiences (or how they are perceived)—"memory"—and the current or new cause-and-effect experiences that are perceived with said person's interface.

Past cause-and-effect experiences form a platform off of which a person's reality is based. This reality determines the actions they take in reality. When a person takes in new stimuli, they first go to one of the rules that forms the platform of their reality. Then if there is conflict, they may take that rule (a piece of that platform) and find a specific memory related to that rule. Arguments often play out this way when someone questions one of the rules of your platform, and so you would respond by picking a specific cause-and-effect memory (one of many) that had been used to form that rule in your mind.

Stimuli or Not?

The new cause-and-effect information is "weighed" or "compared" to the past cause-and-effect information that already existed.

The new stimuli either affects your platform or it doesn't. All experience affects who you are. For example, if one stimulus (cause-and-effect experience) does not change you, then it could still have weight when you encounter another experience that shows a similar cause-and-effect outcome. When enough similar cause-and-effect situations are experienced, they form a rule. The combination of rules forms your platform. Your platform is how you make decisions.

Everyone Has a Weapon, a Tool

The human resources you have are the following.

Time:

The speed between a cause and effect.

This is a method for determining the speed of one or more cause-and-effect relationships and is the third aspect of cause and effect. Humans tend to have an easier time understanding cause-and-effect relationships that happen within a shorter amount of time and a more difficult time understanding cause-and-effect relationships that happen over a longer period of time. Time is the rate of change. It is how long it takes for memories to form rules, and rules to form platforms. It is also how long it takes from one platform to morph into another platform.

The human construct of time appears relative because the rate of change is relative.

Energy:

How much activity you can endure; based on focus and duration.

Focus:

How narrow or spread out your mind is; dependent on time and energy. It is determined by the current state of your platform. This was the flashlight example.

Unlike bullshit lectures, conversations, books, and other "informational" books that skim the surface of ideas but don't actually give you any real knowledge (which I can't stand), this book is different. This book offers knowledge that will totally change you in a good way. Because all real knowledge is good.

This is the place in the book where things continue to change for the better.

Someone told me recently that if I were to debate someone, then I would be at a disadvantage because they could have read my book and could use that knowledge against me. I have to rely on the advantage I have in reality. This book is based on causation and extrapolations thereof. I hope that reality prevails over fantasy and that my view of reality is not warped by errors in my platform. I see such a situation as a debate as a win-win as long as both parties are being honest. If they find flaws in my book, then they are finding flaws in my own platform and so I can improve. If real knowledge (real education) comes from an interaction, then it is good.

Knowledge and reality are good.

Section 3: Experiences/Memories, Rules, Platforms, and Apex Platforms

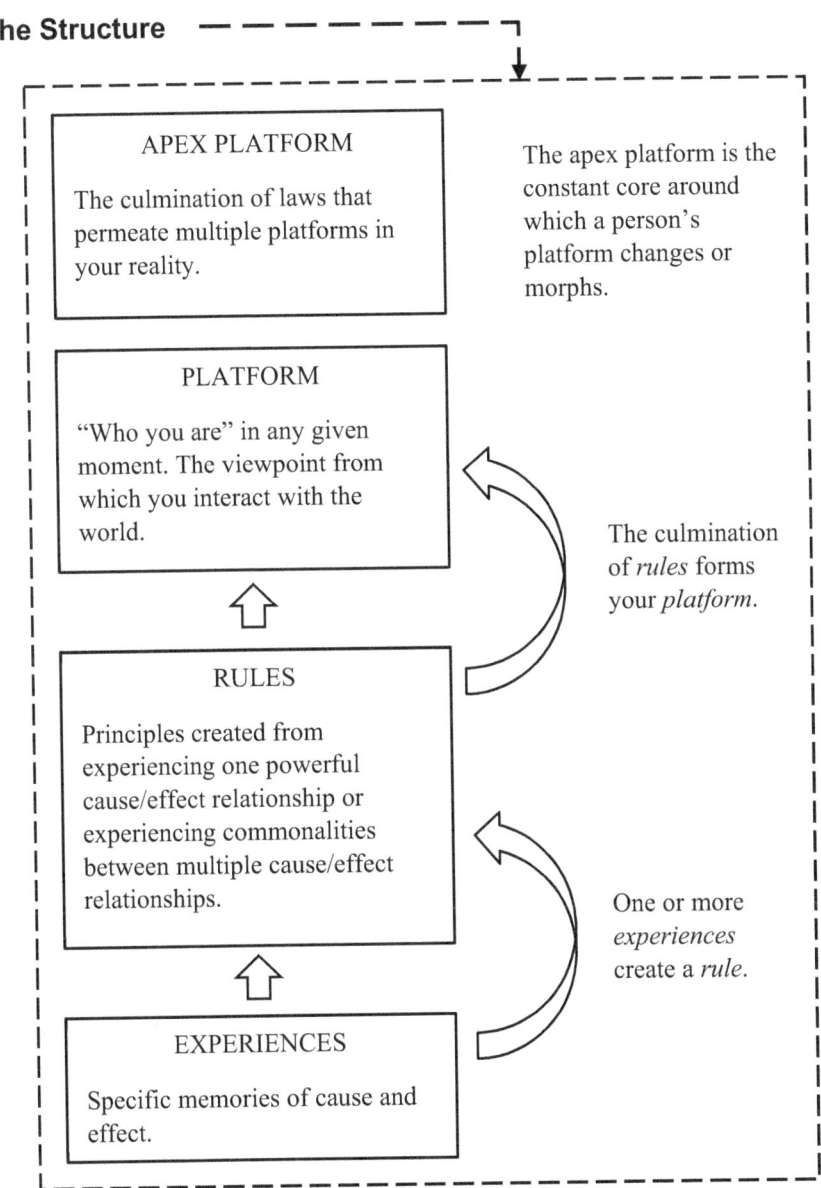

A Graphical Representation of Memory

Each memory (cause and effect experience) is like a plane.

When you have enough "similar memories" (experiences that attest to the similar/identical cause-and-effect relationships), then those memories link together.

The combined result of those memories or experiences aggregate to form a rule "box." The more similar the cause and effects are to one another, the more solid the box.

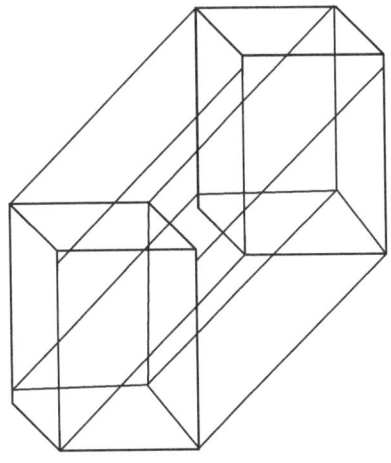

These blocks of rules make up your *platform*.

Perhaps the mind exists in the fourth dimension, analogous to a hypercube.

When examining your own mind, it is easier to look at the object from the outside and see one of the walls, perhaps a memory, or see several memories that make up a rule. It is more difficult to see one's platform.

Another Way of Viewing the Hypercube and How It Relates to Point of View

Changing a meta is like the following: Think of the platform in your mind as being a moving set of blocks that reforms into different platforms showing different sides of the blocks. Each side is like highlighting a different set of rules or memories. The level or state of metacognition at a given time lets the mind (the glass through which a person perceives the world) see the world in different ways. This change of blocks (highlighting different values/rules/memories) influences the mind and thus determines how the world looks. It changes one's specific point of view on various topics.

When someone shifts the blocks and looks through the spyglass that is created and realizes they can't see what someone is talking about, one might give them a cause or catalyst to change their viewpoint/mindset, and the blocks rearrange, letting them see through the glass in a different way. A slight shift of one's mind can make the difference between completely understanding a situation or completely not understanding a situation.

Learning to Reform the Platform

To me, it seems like the platform rearranges every time someone thinks about a different subject—in other words, places emphasis on different memories or moralities. If one were to measure or take a snapshot of a platform at any given time, then it would be the platform at that time.

Consider musicians: They are like every other person in most instances (even though they may have better hearing or auditory awareness than others). When you put a violin or guitar in their hands or sit them down at a piano, they seem to transform. They are not different people, but they go into a different "mode." This "shifting gears," "going into a different mode," "changing channels," or whatever you want to call it is what I mean by the blocks rearranging in someone's head to form a different platform that puts the focus or emphasis of reality in a different point of view. The individual is in a different state of being.

I feel different inside when I pick up an instrument. I feel different when I pick up a knife and I'm going to chop vegetables. I feel different when I sit down to watch a movie. It isn't just a physical difference (though the mental can be derived from physical changes in the brain and nervous system). It seems like the structure of the mind changes.

Imagine being able to feel the change happening in someone else's mind. There is a lag between a mind rearranging in order to put a person in a different mindset so they will take an action or have their body act differently and the action itself.

I like to think about *murmurations*—flocking—and people being in sync with one another such as a medical team performing surgery and the collective phenomenon.

The mind changes—a rearranging of blocks—then there is a lag (time for the cause and effect to happen, shifting from one mindset to another), then the action is taken once the blocks are in a new state.

Do you think it is possible, after knowing someone long enough, to sense this shift in mindset before they do? One could potentially anticipate the cause and effect in another's actions before they realize they are changing. It is something to think about.

When someone is struggling to learn whatever it is that they are trying to learn, then one strategy is to totally leave the subject or project and break from the current platform. Generally, when one releases that platform, they will rarely go back to the exact same platform. It is like stepping off of a train and then stepping back onto the "same" train, yet the train is a little different. They are in a different train car and sometimes it is nicer, sometimes it isn't, but hopefully they have a better "view" out of the window. Every time one returns to the platform, it is a little different.

What are some platforms that you haven't stepped onto in a while? Try to revisit them and see how they have changed.

This sounds a lot like evolution. It sounds a lot like cause and effect. It sounds like reality.

I see sleep as resetting all the platforms. Sleep allows for the time needed in cause and effect to learn, heal, grow, and give the platforms the chance to change. Dreams to me are like "stepping back" and watching one's own platform morph and reform to adjust and accommodate all the new causation that it has witnessed.

Right now, my head is getting "full" and my mind "strained" from working on this book. I'm going to take a break and do something completely different and give my brain time to relax and change before I come back to the book renewed and with an improved platform.

Reluctance to Perform a Task and Procrastination

Sometimes there are things that we don't want to do. We may "try" to do something, but then we feel this tension inside us. To me this tension is a "grinding of the gears" that changes one's mind from one platform to another. There can be resistance when trying to move one's mind into certain platforms. Perhaps the last time you were there it was painful or difficult. I personally have difficulty switching gears when I wish to think about someone close to me who has passed away. When I go to that platform, then I'm suddenly filled with the memories that supported the platform of that person. I remember them deeply, and it affects me.

It is because of this that I often don't switch to certain platforms unless I have some time to myself to fully be in them. Sometimes it doesn't "feel right" to go into a certain platform. While I'm in the physical platform of being in the restroom, it wouldn't "feel right" to be—at the same time—in the mental platform of talking to someone who is important to me.

When one shifts to the platform that they are reluctant to be in, then the feeling of procrastination (that tension) leaves because the procrastination (tension/grinding of the gears) is the stress one feels when struggling to change platforms. I find it interesting that we can feel resistance to change mindsets such as a project we know we should be working on. However, once we change platforms and are in that platform, we don't feel the same kind of procrastination or grinding of the gears. I feel that this shows that our focus or platform does in fact change. This also further proves that our current platform dictates our mental state and determines our decisions.

WTF is an Apex Platform?

A platform is the way a person views the world based on rules that in turn are based on memories. The basic platform changes as a person changes what they are doing (thinking *is* doing).

An apex platform is a false summit. It is one of the ledges one reaches. An apex platform is a continuity of the progressive system of memories, rules, and platforms. This fractal-like structure can continue ad infinitum. Fractals appear throughout nature so we shouldn't be surprised that our minds are built in a fractal-like way.

How can this apex platform change? The apex platform is both the alpha and the omega. It is the beginning of one's journey and the end of it.

Before we talk about how the apex platform is the beginning and the end, we first have to understand how it functions relative to the ever-shifting platforms that make up our reality.

Think of the apex platform as a person's core. It is the core knowledge of what a human being knows is completely 100% true in almost all situations. These truths that make up the core (apex platform) has a root-like system (called laws) that permeates whatever one's platform is in the moment (because it changes). This apex platform is the axis from which a person's regular platform rotates. When the platform mutates and shifts into different arrangements, it does so around the core, much like a Rubik's Cube.

How is the Apex platform formed? In the same way that similar memories/experiences form rules, so to do rules form laws. Laws are rules that exist through every single one of a person's platforms. One could call them "apex rules." The culmination of these ever-present laws forms a person's core.

Not only is gravity a law in science, but it is a law in the core of my reality as well. No matter what I am doing, I am constantly being influenced by gravity. There is a lot about life that changes from one platform to another. It is because of this that people will often say that whatever you know is just your opinion. This argument is just wrong. To say that there is no truth or no reality is to say that all laws are false. If someone comes up to you and says that gravity isn't real, then I don't know what they are talking about. Laws are such a great place to start understanding reality. From there, maybe we can find some sort of morality.

Laws act the same way rules do in support of a person's specific platform. They are different, however, from rules because they carry with them more weight. This weight is due to the cause and effect being consistent between all of the other platforms that a person holds.

This section refers to laws involving a person's core. It is possible that rules can permeate several different platforms within an individual. If these rules do not permeate all of the platforms that a human operates in then they are still considered rules and not laws with respect to a person's reality—the core.

How is the core or apex platform the ending? This core/apex platform is at the very core of who a person is. Therefore, it is hard to change. In earlier sections of the book, I talk about how to change someone's rules: They would have to attack the rule itself or the memories. The more memories, the harder it is to change the rule. The memories act as a logical barrier around the rule.

If one wishes to change someone's core, then they would have to go through the barrier of nearly every single platform, because the laws that make up a core permeate not just one platform but rather many platforms. This is why it is very hard for a person to truly grow and change. Sometimes a person has a belief that unfortunately makes its way into their apex platform. This is a serious disease in their mind and can be hard if not impossible to remove without serious intervention. The apex platform seems like an ending and sometimes negative because the realization of such means that an individual reaches a point of stagnation. But this is positive because there are core realities (actual knowledge) that help an individual understand the rest of the world (assuming that they are actually rooted in true cause and effect).

The apex platform is the beginning because one realizes that it uses platforms in the same way that platforms use rules. What if the process can be repeated ad infinitum? What if there is a platform superior to the apex and a form superior to that? So in reality an "apex platform" is a misnomer because it changes and adapts (hopefully). What may be an apex platform to a child will later become a regular platform to an adult.

A very young child has a small world. Their parents, a few friends of their parents, and relatives are all the human interaction they will have. Then they have the home they live in. That is their world, their reality. As their reality changes and they move to different areas and locations, they will learn that what seemed like laws when their reality was their home are now just rules of the platform, which is their home. They now have a different platform for being a school with different rules for such a platform.

Once they have a new platform, many of the laws, such as *Never do X at home*, become rules for the platform of home, while other rules that are true in all platforms, such as not sticking things in electric sockets (that aren't intended to be stuck in them), become laws because they provide true information across all platforms

For the overwhelming majority of humans, space travel and being in a weightless environment is simply an experience that isn't part of our reality. We are all operating under the platform that is the planet Earth. So for most of us, something like the specific nature of gravity on our planet is a law because there is no platform that we operate in that doesn't have to take gravity into account. When humans do go to other planets, the law of gravity on Earth (acceleration at 9.8 meters per second per second) will instead become a rule for everything that falls under the platform of being on Earth.

One would have a different platform for other planets where the overall concept of gravity would still apply. If you are someone who travels between Mars and Earth, then the existence of gravity itself would be a law, but the specific nature of 9.8 meters per second squared would be a rule when on Earth. When on Mars, it would be 3.711 meters per second squared.

If we could expand our reality beyond our universe, then it may be possible that there are other constants or laws that exist in other universes. Something we may believe to be a "law" in our universe may just in fact be a rule here, while part of it may still be a law if verified by the cause and effect in another universe. This concept is what I mean by one's "core" apex platform being a false summit.

To answer the question: Yes, the core/apex platform does actually change.

This is how combining platforms works. Platforms become blocks for superior platforms. I consider rules and memories different from platforms because of their very limited and specific nature even though they build upon each other the same way.

Imagine causality as being the apex platform in our universe. What if causality is different in different universes? The rules, platforms, and laws that make up our apex causality platform are all based on memories from our universe. It is possible that another set of experiences from another universe might end up forming different rules, and thus there could be a different platform for that universe and a new apex platform would form.

Now suppose you can travel to multiple universes. You could have several platforms for each universe. If those platforms have commonalities between them, then you would have a new apex platform with laws. This process can be continued ad infinitum. Fractal-like constructs appear often in our reality.

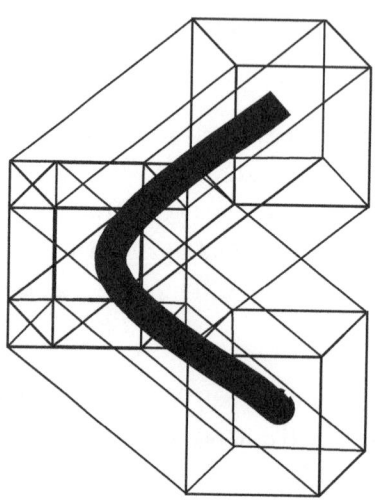

Laws are rules that exist through all platforms in a person's reality. These are rules that, as far as the person is concerned, are always active in as far as the person's causality is concerned.

Purposely Changing the Platform and Seeking Balance in One's Life

The brief version: Focusing on the bad parts of one's life is a way to help bring change to those negative areas and change the platform as a whole for the better.

The verbose version: Reforming the platform of one's mind in such a way that one looks at memories with negative effects or outcomes is a way to change oneself in a way by not engaging the same causes that lead to those negative effects. One can focus on different causes that have more desirable effects.

This is great for improving oneself. However, one can also become depressed, anxious, and stressed out if they only view their life and reality via the negative cause-and-effect relationships that have happened in their life. They may even anticipate more and more negative events to come.

The opposite is also true. If someone doesn't ever look at the negative causality in one's life, then they may become happy. *Wait a minute:* That doesn't sound so bad. But this is actually a bad thing to someone with experience and multiple platforms from which to view the world through. Why? What is wrong with being a member of a cult if you just feel good, and it's all about love?

You've probably seen the look: glassy-eyed and not-really-there. The "Everything is great and awesome and I'm just so happy and excited to be breathing this magical air around me" look. You can make a list of obvious good and bad effects that can be derived from such causation. The main problem with this mentality is that you are constantly ignoring parts of reality. Ignoring part of reality is the same as ignoring part of yourself: your life, your experiences that make up who you are. Living in a perpetual state of ordained ignorance isn't that great.

If you choose to ignore the negative sides of another person, then it will lead to relationships that are abusive. If they are not abusive then they will probably be fake relationships. The relationship isn't real because it isn't based on reality. I'm not saying to mention all the negative qualities of one's friends and family. Just be aware of them and have a full picture of who someone is.

It is easy to value and care for someone who is perfect. A human being's flaws are just as much a part of who they are as their positive attributes. We are an amalgamation of everything that makes us who we are. To truly care about someone is to care about all of them. I find something beautiful in realizing a person's faults and still caring about them and loving them. To me, that is more powerful than putting on blinders and pretending that a person is superhuman and flawless. This is just another example of how reality trumps fantasy.

We can see that being at either extreme of viewing ourselves as all positive or all negative is probably not a good idea. Being in a mindset of either extreme for long enough can have negative effects on an individual, just as it can on a government or society.

It would be a lot healthier for the individual, in my opinion, to change meta and have a balance between improving oneself as well as taking time to enjoy one's accomplishments. Viewing the negative helps one change and improve their life, which will lead to long-term happiness. The complacency of enjoying the moment allows one to relax. If someone doesn't allow themselves to relax, then they can end up in a state of only wanting to change and improve themselves, and then one day they die without ever enjoying life. Stress can lead to a shorter life. Finding the right balance is challenging because the ideal balance point changes for each individual.

Why does the balance point change? The balance point has to change for each person because each person is different. You are part of the equation that makes you who you will be.

It Takes Time to Build a Platform: Don't Wait for an Emergency

Platforms take time to form and build because they require memories and experiences. Even if someone with knowledge is spoon-feeding you rules, it still takes time for those rules to meld into the platform. What is it like if someone needs to be in a platform and they have no rules or experiences? *Panic and confusion.*

Remember the situation about medical emergencies. If one has no plan nor training, and a real need arises then they won't be able to act. They may get "stuck" mentally and not be able to function. It takes time to form platforms of how to act in various emergencies. This is why it makes so much sense to take preventive measures and ensure you are prepared for various scenarios.

There is a platform of self-defense. This is the platform one shifts into when they need to protect themselves and those that they care about when presented with a dangerous situation. There are many people that I've heard speak online or in person who are under the delusion that if a threat were to occur, then they could defend themselves effectively regardless of not having any training (experiences or memories). Here is why this doesn't make any sense: If a person doesn't have experience or memories and rules, then a person *doesn't have a platform to go to* when a real danger arises. They will be caught like a deer in the headlights, or will panic or simply be confused. This is because the dangerous situation simply isn't part of their reality. They simply won't know what to do.

The "stuck" feeling occurs when a person doesn't know where to go or what to do in a situation because they haven't put in the time to develop the platform. In the moment, one cannot amass experience and rules and platforms to deal with a situation, so there is simply nothing to do but fail.

Imagine someone who owns a firearm for the purpose of self-protection. They don't train, so they don't have knowledge/rules that one would get from experiences and memories. How then would such a person hope to suddenly go into a platform of combat and be skilled with the firearm? This is delusion. Now you have another way of understanding why.

It is because of the reasoning above that a person should begin to train and get the experience required to form rules and then have those rules form a platform so they will have a place to go to mentally and physically when shit hits the fan. This is why having some training is better than having no training. People who are well-trained are able to shift into the platform of self-defense/combat extremely easily and don't get that "stuck" feeling. Those who are extremely well-trained are not only able to enter these platforms easily, but they can also easily leave these platforms and get back to their "normal" state of being, even after an intense situation.

The Need for Rules and Cubes

Most humans are incapable of remembering every single cause-and-effect experience that they have, and so it is extremely useful to combine the lessons/values or overall themes of cause-and-effect experiences (memories) into rules that are manageable and can be called upon to aid said human when a new situation arises. The human mind simply cannot handle numerous specific cause-and-effect events at one time. It has to switch between them. It is hard if not impossible to think about more than one memory at any given time. Because of this, it is helpful to combine the values or commonalities between individual events to form rules. From enough rules you get a person's mindset/meta that in turn is how they view the world.

While this is true mentally (which is a series of physical processes), it is also true in other physical processes such as learning how to do things with your body. To illustrate this example, I'm going to explain something that is relatively simple. Take an adult who puts on a jacket and buttons or zips it up without thinking. Now go back to a time when the adult was an infant. The infant had to gain experience of how to move its limbs and how to understand what is near and what is far from it (range). It had to learn how to move its arms and how to open and close its hands at will. When one first learns how to use buttons or a zipper, they don't need to relearn how to move their arms. The use of their arms and hands is a rule (possibly a law) that is part of their apex platform, and definitely part of the "how does my body move and work" platform. Soon buttons and zippers will be rules under the "how to get dressed" platform of one's mind.

Here is a philosophical question: Would the buttons and zippers be part of the same platform or not? I feel that the answer lies in whether or not a person has to "change meta" or file cabinets when switching from one task to another. Perhaps they are first totally different platforms and then through time they become part of the same platform. Using buttons and zippers is part of the platform of clothing and putting on jackets. The mind doesn't have to consciously think about all the memories and rules and all the details in order for it to function. In fact, when a person does try to think about the details of a task that they have done many times, then they actually lose competency in said task. Eventually, the child will grow older. They will get to the Unconscious Competence stage of the *Hierarchy of Competence* where dressing oneself becomes one thought, one action, or no thought.

One thing I find really interesting—though I am not sure that I completely understand it—is when the swordsman and philosopher Miyamoto Musashi talks about being in a state of void or having the mind on an open plane. The closest I have come would be having a mind that is not in any one platform but instead is in a constant state of morphing and change. Through that fluidly, it can easily adopt the most appropriate platform for any given situation. This is a mental state of reaction. Perhaps being in no state is a platform. The platform of the void. I don't know.

The Pros and Cons of Rules

Some rules are useful enough and are better than memories because they can be applied to more situations. I have struggled with autism. One way I have struggled with learning social things would be in the realm of generalities. There have been times when I would learn what was supposed to be a general "social rule" to be taken broadly across similar situations. However, in my mind it got filed as a memory and not a general rule. Or the filing was wrong in another way and the information became a rule, but the platform I put that rule into was too narrow, and so it became a limited rule for only the particular situation in which I learned the behavior.

An example of such a specific situation is how one should behave in a restaurant. I wouldn't extrapolate and make it into a rule that would be applied to other similar situations. Instead of learning "how I should behave in a restaurant," I learned "how I should behave in *this* restaurant."

Another problem with organization also occurred when I didn't realize that a situation was different. I had a rule that was too broad and was placed in a platform where it wasn't necessary. Any time I make a mistake with the placement of a memory, then it is due to my inability to understand cause and effect. Here is a brief story of how I almost got removed from a steakhouse by the people I was with.

When I grew up, there would be occasions when my brothers and I would be served "steak" at the dinner table. For the life of me I could never understand why one kid in my middle school told me that steak was their favorite meal. To me, it was awful. First, the steak my brothers and I had was cooked to past extremely-well-done. It was this grey, rubbery "stuff." Then came the hard part, which was eating it. I had a dull knife to try to cut it apart. It was so tough that, even as a teenager, I had to struggle to pierce the rubbery stuff with a fork.

Jump to my mid-twenties, and it was my first time at an actual steakhouse. I was excited. The food smelled great. I started by ordering my steak well-done, and the people I was with stopped me. They said I could order it "medium" at the most (now I order it medium-rare). A rule I now have is this: If I don't feel comfortable eating meat at medium-rare, then why would I feel comfortable eating the food? I should go to another restaurant.

Back to the story. After ordering my steak medium, I then asked to have ketchup with it (as was customary in my household). The group I was with again stopped me. Soon the steak was brought out, and so I did what I normally did when I had steak. I grabbed the fork and placed it prongs-down on the top of the steak, then used my other hand to palm-heel the back of the fork with ferocity so that it would go through the rubber, only this time it wasn't rubber but tender, wonderful meat. The prongs of the fork shoved through the ribeye and stabbed the plate with a loud *crack*. I then grabbed the steak knife and began the arduous task of sawing through the steak before trying to saw the table in half after that. I remember pausing and looking up at everyone at the table who just looked back at me in complete shock. They asked me, "Alan, what are you doing?" I replied, "Huh? I'm eating steak." It was an unpleasant experience.

Rules are more useful in various situations even if they need "fine tuning." Some rules are perfect, meaning they are generally always right (within every aspect of a human's experience and effective cause and effect). We call these rules *laws*. Unfortunately, when a rule is right *most* of the time, it is often not specific enough to be helpful *a lot* of the time. Well, it is helpful for acquiring the basics of a new discipline; however, one still has to put in the time to gain the experience to learn the subtleties of each science. For example, yes, gravity *is* working also when I learn a new sport. That knowledge, while always important, only helps me go so far.

There is an argument that I want to make for learning enough laws. Doing so won't make you instantly a master in the disciplines and sciences that are truly important, because truly important disciplines and sciences take years of experience to master. However, even if having such knowledge of laws doesn't make you a master overnight, these persistent rules will in fact make you appear superhuman in many ways. Laws can sometimes be tailored to an individual. This is because you are perceiving the world from your body. If you take the time to truly understand your body and work on your basic movements and competencies, then how much easier would it be to pick up a new physical skill or ability? This is why the synthesis of knowledge and experience equals true power. What if you have a lot of persistent rules and laws in your mind? Will things surprise you often? This is what we are going for.

Isn't cause and effect the answer to all questions? But it isn't specific enough to be helpful. Consider these two phrases: "Things are the way they are" and "That's the way things were back then." They both describe a moment in time, and yes that is true. Things are, well, the way they are. However, that is not helpful. Why are things the way they are? *Cause and effect*. What is the specific cause of the effect? Now that is a better question. I hope you understand cause and effect because that's just the way it is.

When one combines many experiences/memories in one's mind, they should be careful of the fact that while specifics can lend to generalizations, generalizations don't always transfer directly back to specifics. Memories make rules, but rules don't always apply to all memories. There is some error that occurs, something similar to a bell curve many times. A rule is good if it can be applied to the overwhelming majority of statistics. Rules can be a good way of going through life, but one should still check new situations for statistical outliers that might not be accounted for by the rules of one's own platform—something like a steak cooked to perfection.

We know that there are many, many cause-and-effect relationships that are required to form a rainforest. We also know that there are many cause-and-effect relationships that are required to form a tundra, and so on and so on.

It is useful to combine common cause-and-effect situations into some classification (rules/cubes) so that we can talk about them and how they affect the world. One should be careful because, when one combines cause and effect, there is room for error. Not every rainforest is like every other rainforest. Some species that exist in one do not exist in another and vice versa.

Combining cause and effect in various situations is useful when one wants to talk about rainforests in general, but doing so should come with a caveat: Laws and persistent rules decrease in number the more one generalizes. This makes a lot of sense, right? Given having enough knowledge, if you are asked about a specific situation, then you know what to do in that situation. This is because you can account for all the variables/causality. The moment you pull back and talk about general situations, then you can't give specific and exact advice. Cause and effect leads to specific understanding. When one generalizes, one loses a bit of cause and effect. Speculation is therefore weak.

When anyone dives into a particular discipline such as economics, music, law, finance, combat, or construction, they will realize that when they get deep enough into said discipline, they will have to form a different language in order to talk about even simple concepts without becoming extremely verbose—like the present sentence.

Some disciplines create and use new words for their art/system as a means of being briefer. This way you can have a conversation without defining every word. When one tries to define every single word during a conversation, then it can be easy to lose the meaning of the sentence or the overall message. It also saves a lot of time. However, one needs to be careful of disciplines that make up a bunch of words because extra made-up words can be used just to confuse people and manipulate them. Sometimes extra made-up terminology is used to make a discipline seem like what they are doing is different or more complex than it is.

We need some sort of system to help us sort out words that are unique to a specific discipline. Beware of words unique to a specific discipline, because while they may be there to help you, they may also be there to take advantage of you. Behold what I call the *break-down-cause-effect-rule-to-detect-bullshit*. Here's how it works. Ask yourself, "Why was the word changed from its basic meaning?" Is the word being replaced for simplicity or brevity, or is it being changed to obfuscate reality and control and manipulate people? Can you replace the word with just one or two words without changing the meaning? If you can replace the word with just one other word, then why make up another word for it? You aren't saving time by doing so. What is the benefit?

Does that particular word really need to be there in order to explain a much larger concept that would take longer to explain? Sometimes the word that is used to replace the common word is another common word just used in a different context in order to confuse people. Take, for example, the word "learn." Learning is what one does in school to gain knowledge (with any luck). Suppose a cult uses the word "learn" to describe ritual whipping—that may be too extreme of an example.

Here is a good example where words are replaced by a discipline. The term *zenkutsu dachi* is Japanese/Nihongo. The English basic translation would be "forward leaning stance." Here, the term in Japanese is five syllables and in English it is five syllables. Both are then valid. I feel that one should know the translation regardless. Why not know both? What does it mean to be in a *zenkutsu dachi* or a forward leaning stance?

Here are the parts broken down into brief and verbose descriptions of each part of being in a proper *zenkutsu dachi*.

Piece 1:

> Brief: Stand with good posture.
>
> Verbose: Stand with the torso from the hips up being vertical with the head stacked upon the shoulders, the shoulders above the hips.

Let's pause right there. One can see that the verbose description has more cause and effect in it. What if someone doesn't exactly know what good posture is? I didn't.

Piece 2:

> Brief: Position the legs so one is forward and bent at the knee while the rear leg is straight.
>
> Verbose: The front leg is extended out with the knee bent so that the shin is vertical. The rear leg is fully extended so that the bones of the leg are straight. Do not lock the leg. The weight distribution is seventy percent on the front foot and thirty percent on the rear foot.

Piece 3:

> Brief: The movement getting into the stance is required for the stance to be correct.
>
> Verbose: You need to move correctly into the stance in order to fire the correct muscles required to optimize the stance.

Even the full, brief description is a bit verbose. So what is easier? Typing all that out? Or saying, *zenkutsu dachi* or *forward leaning stance*? Easy.

If one were to give the verbose description of *zenkutsu dachi*/forward leaning stance every time it is used instead of the name itself, then it would take a long time to just describe the position, and in the context of a sentence, one would lose the meaning of the sentence itself. Having words that mean a complexity is the same as having rules that support a variety of memories. It is the same as the human body remembering how to do things without the constant conscious input from the mind. The same thing can be said about other disciplines.

Now take another word or phrase such as "Money." Groups have long changed just one word not for brevity's or simplicity's sake but rather to soften the word and manipulate others. Money is sometimes called "offering/tithe/corban/donation/gift." I'm sure you can give another example from your own catalogue of memories. But wait, doesn't that happen for good reasons? Consider how you feel after hearing the two sentences. Sentence #1: *Please give money to charity*. Sentence #2: *Please give money to my organization*. Do the sentences feel different? You can go on and on, adding more cause and effect to get a better understanding of what you should do: Which charity? How is the charity going to use the money I give them? What is the effect that my money (cause) will have if I give it to one group versus another? This is a more honest way of speaking.

I have found that in cults and other bullshit organizations that one of the many ways they manipulate people is by interchanging words for other words or making up random words to confuse and obfuscate their intentions. Why would a group or organization change a word like *money*? The answer is obvious: because they want to get more money or convince someone to give them more money. If the organization is honest, then why would it need to change the meaning of words to manipulate people? If someone is giving money for a good reason, then the focus should be on the *reason* and not the *word*. If you are given reasoning, then also check the reasoning for more BS words and try to write them out. If something is honest and good, then why is there a need to confuse the words?

Try this exercise: Consider an organization or group that you are currently part of. First, make a list of some of the common words or phrases used specifically in that organization. See if you can break them down into their basic cause-and-effect form. Next, write out exactly what the word means (just as I did with *zenkutsu dachi*). Then, see if the meanings of the words change. Lastly, ask yourself why the words are changed.

Am I trying to use fancy words such as cubes/rules/cause/effect/meta/viewpoint to manipulate you? I feel that going back to cause and effect (the most basic way of viewing the world for what it is) is the only way I can be completely honest. I have tried to go out of my way to be extra descriptive to avoid bullshit words, and that is why a lot of paragraphs are more verbose than one might expect.

Will reading this book be a cause that will affect your life? I hope so—if it helps you in a positive way.

Analyzing Competency Via Memories, Rules, Cubes

Yet another list.

Stage 1 of Competency: Gathering Cause-and-Effect Data

The novice is someone who is in the realm of developing memories (specific examples of cause and effect) yet doesn't have enough memories to make rules (and thus doesn't have a platform for said subject). If a person doesn't have rules and yet still believes that they have a platform, then their view of the topic is warped because the "platform" that exists in their mind isn't based on enough cause and effect (not based in reality). This misconception happens all the time across not just specific disciplines but also in understanding life in general.

Stage 2 of Competency: Forming Some Rules. The Incomplete Platform

While not a complete beginner, they still don't have a grasp of the basic concepts (rules) of a discipline. They might have just enough experiences of cause and effect to form a few rules. Here they are starting to build their first platform, but there isn't enough of a foundation for it to be complete.

Stage 3 of Competency (Basic): Having Enough Rules to Form a Single Platform

At this point, a person who is studying/training in said discipline has enough experience/knowledge/memories of cause and effect to have all the basic rules that make up a discipline. For the first time, they have a true platform from which to be effective. To relate this level to something else, it would be similar to someone achieving a black belt in traditional karate. To relate this level to the bell curve, it would be like understanding the examples of people who fall within one standard deviation of the median of the curve.

Stage 4 of Competency: Having a Platform that Can Make Minor Shifts to Account for Some Variation

At this point, the individual has had more experience on a given topic, and the platform that was created by understanding the basic rules of a discipline is then expanded upon to include more in-depth application. They begin to understand variations and complications of the discipline beyond the basic rules. They can't quite shift meta, for they don't have more than one complete platform orientation to work off of, but it is more malleable than Stage 3.

Stage 5 of Competency: Multiple Platforms

At this point, a person is an expert in the subject matter. They have enough cause and effect and rules to shift their platform into other platforms, thus changing meta and point of view within the discipline and are able to look at problems (variations on cause/effect) from various angles that put more weight on some values rather than others.

Stage 6 of Competency: Adaptable Multiple Platforms

I see this as having mastery in a discipline. One has all the rules of cause and effect of a given situation and can predict outcomes with high probability. They usually only get surprised by statistical outliers. Not only do they have multiple platforms, but the platforms are malleable in such a way that they can tackle "mutations" and cause and effect that deviate from the norm. Not only do the rules form *a* platform, but the platforms together form an apex platform. The apex platform views the other platforms in the same way that platforms view multiple rules.

Obsession

There are certain personalities who will discover an area of knowledge (cause and effect) and will want to learn more. They will spend a lot of time wanting to learn how causality works in many examples. This is oftentimes bad but not always. A person who gets obsessed is like a tool. It can be used for bad or for good (like anything else). It takes time to learn because it takes many memories to form all the rules regarding an area of interest and then many rules to make up a solid platform. We need people who become obsessed, and then we need to channel them to become obsessed with things that can benefit humanity such as science and health.

If I am going to go under the knife and have a major surgery, then I want my surgeon to be absolutely obsessive when it comes to knowing everything one can know about the human body and know every variable when it comes to performing the surgery on me. A person who is obsessed wants to know all of the possible cause-and-effect relationships in a given area. When does obsession cross the line into craziness? An obsessive doctor will want to know everything there is to know about the surgery. The crazy doctor will want to experiment on you to learn even more. For *science*! That whole bit about the crazy doctor was intended to be funny.

Moving right along.

A doctor can't be too knowledgeable on all the cause-and-effect relationships involving the human body. An engineer can't be too good at understanding all of the variables when it comes to building a building or bridge. A single human being may be out-of-balance or appear addicted or different because they are obsessed with a certain area of knowledge. They are making a huge sacrifice of their time, their life for the society. This out-of-balance situation for the individual is an actual benefit to everyone else—that is, unless they are making weapons of mass destruction. Don't worry though, that example is probably a statistical outlier.

Being obsessed isn't the natural way for the average human being. Unless we are talking about sex. Around where I live, the average person doesn't have a great depth of knowledge in any one area. They are more balanced and able to function in more situations. They have a general knowledge.

Humans can only focus on one thing at a time. When a person focuses all their time and energy in one area they will, as a negative result, also be limited in other areas. We should be grateful for the people who sacrifice so much of their lives to go into depth and understand all the factors/variables/causality in an area of knowledge. Next time you see someone who is weird, don't be nasty to them. The weird improve humanity as a whole!

Well, some of them do. Others are just being weird.

This Book: Rain, Lightning and Changing People—A Callback to Chapter 3

This is my continued attempt to let you know that I'm trying to change you and others. By being honest about changing you and others, I feel like that instinctively helps people lower their guard so they can really think about the concepts and realize that I want to change them but not to manipulate them.

People react differently to lightning and rain. Lightning is a strong, instant attempt to change someone (like an intervention). Rain gradually changes someone over a greater length of time, like a friend suggesting "randomly" over the course of time that they should leave the person they are dating because they are "not a good person."

Some people are more easily changed through one method or the other, the gradual approach versus getting hit in the head with a hammer. So, if I wanted to use both approaches to change you with this book, the big sections or chapters that go into detail on a specific subject for many sentences would be like trying to strike you with lightning, whereas my careful sprinkling of an idea throughout the entirety of the book would be like rain falling.

There may even be some power in spreading out stimuli of a couple different concepts through the book, because people will absorb the stimuli as different cause-and-effect relations that build and support one another. When the ideas are too closely grouped, then they are immediately formed into one idea and mindset and thus can be dismissed all together, whereas multiple experiences are harder to refute, without help. I hope this book helps you refute multiple BS ideas when you see them. The repetition of something gives validity to itself, whether or not it is true. Think about that concept now in a new way.

Another aspect to consider about this section: Pulling you out of the meta of reading the book (by saying that I'm trying to manipulate you) might in itself be another form of changing your perspective of reality. Does it make it truer for you? Is this a greater stimulus? Maybe when you read a book you are in the platform of "reading a book," and then when I pull you mentally out of the book, I'm also hoping to pull the concepts of the book out of the pages and into your reality. I'm wanting to change your platform while trying to get you to change your platform. Maybe I should add this to my list of ways to change someone. Or is it just another form of lightning? What do you think?

When I ask you what you think, isn't that just another way of pulling you out of one meta and into another? Into your mind? Questions have power.

Maybe we should all be careful when someone tries to control us by asking what we think. Unless, of course, they are actually wanting us to have more illusions about the amount of agency we have in our lives.

Recall Chapter 3: It was the one about lightning and rain. Let's look at it through the lens of cause and effect, memories, rules and platforms and see if things still make any sense. Rain would be like adding in many more memories to the memories that a person already has. Memories are specific examples of cause and effect that form rules. One can add memories and tip the balance of a rule (sometimes a little, sometimes a lot). New experiences may confirm an existing rule, support a new rule, or contradict the current rule.

Sometimes new experiences can tip the balance between two contradicting rules that a person may hold. If this happens, the weaker rule will dissolve. Sometimes one gets enough information through experiences to replace a rule with a new one. When this happens, the former rule will begin to crack (cognitive dissonance) or may just dissolve, depending on the situation/person. Essentially, if you break enough memories, then the rule that is supported by that particular group of memories will then fall. If you make enough rules fall, then you make a significant change to a person's platform in that area. Change the platform, change the person. That is the method of rain.

The method of lightning would involve striking at the rules. This is more difficult because a person often has memories supporting the rule. In fact, people will often bring up said memories in defense of this rule that you are "attacking." One may still find that they will have to give counter-memories (or specific cause-and effect-examples) to counter the memories defending the rule that is being attacked.

It can be challenging to understand oneself because a person's platform is the lens through which they are seeing themselves. A person is a combination of all their platforms (and a little more). What this means is that they are using their own rules to analyze and judge their own rules. Of course, a rule will validate itself. This leads to personal bias: when we put an artificial weight on the supporting rules. When this happens, people will sometimes ignore good arguments against their own rules or put less weight on information/experiences if the new information contradicts one's own set of rules. A person will even put less value on their own memories if their own memories don't support the rule in question.

I've heard people say, "I feel like you are attacking me," while the attacker will say, "I'm not attacking you; I'm talking about the subject at hand (rule and supporting memories)." Rules make up a person's platform. That is why it can feel like a person is attacking another person even when they are just talking about the subject matter. Shit gets personal. This emotion also proves that their view of said topic is part of one of the platforms that makes them who they are. When a person feels personally attacked during a discussion about a given topic, then that is a sign that they have a very narrow view of who they are as an individual. The reality is that they aren't attacking the other person; they are just attacking one of the many rules that make up the other person's platform. I'd like to think that we are more than any one rule or several rules that are part of our platform. In truth, we are more than the platform itself because the platform continually changes. We change.

People often argue incorrectly by saying, "You are wrong," or "You don't know what you are talking about." It would be more accurate to keep the conversation to what it is about: the subject. If someone gives a false example of causality, don't tell them that they are wrong or bad or evil. That isn't true, anyway. They are just giving information that they believe to be true from one of their many platforms. It is that piece of information that should be argued about.

Is it possible to truly attack someone? From this mindset, "attacking someone" mentally just doesn't make a lot of sense. Someone may be wrong in just one of their memories, or rules, or platforms. If someone is wrong with laws and apex platform, then things get more complicated. While there are some people who reject that the world is round or that gravity exists, these individuals are for the most part outliers. There is no point in wasting energy arguing about such things with them because they will just ignore the information if it doesn't support their already pre-conceived rules that they wish to be true because they have a strong aversion to changing their platform to another.

If you can change a false law that exists within a person, then you can truly help them. This is hard because the law permeates an individual's mind on several platforms. It can be difficult to change laws because you need to show that it is then false across multiple platforms.

There are three components to my handy memories/rules/platforms system. It would make sense that you can change someone through their memories, rules, or platforms. So you can change someone on at least three different levels. You can try to change someone's platform. However, I feel that there is a difficulty in doing so. It would be easy to throw out a platform because several rules are wrong; however, the platform (with the exception of extremes/outliers) is probably based on some cause and effect or it wouldn't have survived in their mind.

Most arguments against an entire platform are not entirely true because that would mean that everything in that platform is false. Even if much of a person's artificial platform is false that doesn't make it 100% false. It just makes the platform false by whatever percentage it is actually false. Don't worry, though, if you have a friend with a truly false platform. Odds are that they have a lot of memories that they have suppressed in order to keep the platform real to them. If you can tip the balance and give them more experiences that enhance the suppressed memories, then you can tip the scale and the platform will fall or change.

What do you think about this third section? Do you believe you can attack someone's platform in a legitimate way? Does lightning strike the same place twice? If you change a person's platform, then how is it possible to *not* change them? One can argue on multiple levels: specific memories, rules, platforms, and laws. When one changes the rules that support a platform, then ones changes the platform because it has to settle and will often change when part of its support structure is gone. Maybe, then, it isn't necessary to attack the platform itself—maybe, then, you don't have to attack the rules, and you can just go after the memories. Maybe I'm going in circles and I need sleep.

The Power of Belief

As a species, we are on the verge of a jump in our capabilities through the power of power of stimuli (causes). Let's explore three scenarios.

In the first scenario, a father and son are at a park, and there is a stretch of flat ground that is over one hundred meters long. The son knows that his father has been "letting him win" when they have raced in the past. On this particular day at the park, he begs his dad for once to run as fast as he possibly can for one hundred meters. The father decides that he is going to do exactly that. They mark off one hundred meters precisely. Then the son gets out a stopwatch (or just his phone with the app) and starts the timer right as the father moves. The father honestly tries to run as fast as he can from start to finish.

The second scenario is a high school athlete at a track meet. This isn't just any ordinary track meet. At this particular track meet, he is qualifying to get an athletic scholarship. The only way he will qualify is if he runs as fast as he can possibly run. Only then will he will get into the college of his dreams. It is a one-hundred-meter race.

The third scenario is an unarmed man who is travelling through the forest, and suddenly a giant grizzly bear charges at him. The man has to run one hundred meters as fast as he can to get to safety.

In all three scenarios, the general intent is the same: Run as fast as you can for one hundred meters. However, the specific nature of the causes is different. If we were to assume that all three individuals had the same exact body and all the possible causes (factors/variables) are the same, then we would expect the same exact outcome. I know in reality they wouldn't be.

The high schooler is probably not a father. The track the high school athlete is running on is going to be different in real life than the terrain of the forest where the man is fleeing the bear. In all scenarios, their shoes are probably going to be different. For argument's sake, let's say that all the running conditions are the same and the only difference is in the stimuli/causes. I would argue that they wouldn't run at the same speed. In fact, I would argue that even if they all were intent on running as fast as they could, the reality is that the difference in causation will cause a difference in their running ability. The causes are different, so then also the effects have to be different.

Even if you were to argue that their running speed (one effect) wouldn't change, which I suppose is a possibility, then I would argue that there would have to be another effect such as their adrenaline or breathing that would have to change. Of course, their mental states would be different as well. Something would have to change with regard to the effect. The equation between cause and effect has to be balanced.

Here is the interesting thing about the examples above. The individual is completely influenced by their ability to perceive their reality. The reality of the bear charging at the man in the third example is taken in by the man's senses. Theoretically, the reality happens within the person. This is another example of how a person, if they believe something enough, can change the way they act and virtually everything about themselves. Belief equals change. Our intent matters.

There is an immense power that we have through the internet. At this very moment, we are all linked in ways that we haven't been in the past. The first time a person did a 1080 on a skateboard it was seen as something that was "impossible." Once people witnessed the first 1080, it went from being impossible for a human to do to being very hard to do.

People have been able to do very hard things with enough training. That specific event/stimuli/cause-and-effect enters the platform of a person's mind and becomes a memory and part of their reality. They truly know that the 1080 is possible. Now many other skateboarders have been able to accomplish the feat and many more will in the future. This is not a rare phenomenon related to skateboarding. This reality is proven time and time again in various disciplines. We as a species owe so much to the trailblazers, the first people to figure out how to do things: inventions, technology, athletics, physics, and so on, the first people to figure out the cause and effect in everything.

Not too long ago, a person could tell a story about a seemingly impossible human feat of strength, speed, or just about anything that a human could do. What was once impossible is now very much possible, and you can absorb it at the very least through your senses of sight and sound. You'll have that experience as part of the memories of cause and effect that make up your rules and thus platform of who you are. Such is the power of the internet and shared information. Such was the power of shared stories from times of old, assuming a person could believe them. Perhaps the positive side of being gullible and a believer is that you are capable of absorbing things that others dismiss as not being possible, and so you become more likely to do great things.

As a species we are on the verge of a jump in our capabilities.

Do Versus Try

Do or do not—there is no try. Belief is a sword that cuts both ways. The previous section describes how belief can be a catalyst of changing someone for the positive. It can also do the exact opposite. Belief is part of a human's equation that can be either positive or negative. You can take literally every example from the previous section and see it as negative.

When a person says they are going to "do" something, then they are making it part of their reality. They are accepting it into their formula (memories/rules/platform) in a positive way that will take them in the direction of accomplishing the said task that they set out to "do." When a person says that they are going to "try" or "attempt" something, then they are not fully committing to the act. They have put up a false barrier within their own platform and are not open to fully absorbing the experience.

If the experience does get absorbed into them, then they become surprised. I've seen this, and I am sure you have. Not fully committing means that the stimuli they are putting into their equation isn't positive. At best it is just neutral, but more likely than not it is going to be negative. Neutral doesn't sound that bad until you compare it with positive stimuli—then it seems really bad. Trying is going in the opposite direction of that which a person claims that they are wanting to go. Trying is dishonest towards others, but mostly to oneself.

Your platform determines how you view the world. You become your own reality. Your perception of the world determines your perception of the world which causes a bilinear causality. Let me explain this in a way that people who are not yet sold on the memories/rules/platform might be more likely to absorb into their reality: In other words, a large part of your environment goes with you, because most of the time, you have the greatest impact on your environment and your experience of your environment. Who you are affects how you see the environment, which in turn affects who you are.

You impact yourself. You can't help but influence yourself. This is why a person's childhood and initial platform are so critical to how they end up and why it is so hard to change people as they get older. You are constantly being influenced by your past.

Let's end on a positive note. This loop helps explain why we learn so well.

Societies

Societies are themselves platforms that impact people who are within the platform/society's sphere of influence/causality. People are impacted by the platform of a society by as much as they adopt that platform into their own platform. Even if a person doesn't see themselves as part of a society, the society will still influence them because it is part of their reality. Such is the way of causality. If someone hates society and goes against all societal norms, then they will still be changed profoundly by the society. When a platform is shared between people, it becomes a major part of each individual's platform.

When one travels to a foreign country, they soon realize that they do not understand the platform. How does one assimilate? First, they have to gain experience and learn specific rules of how to behave in the society. From enough of those specific cause-and-effect instances, they can then understand both the written and unwritten "rules" of society.

When one learns all of the rules and they become habit, then one is then part of said society. On a superficial level, to be part of a society, one accepts and adopts the rules and laws that together make up the platform of said society. On a deeper level, the change truly happens when their personal platform adopts or merges with the platform of society. If someone enters a society and not only doesn't want to adopt the platform of the society but seeks to destroy the society, then that individual is a saboteur. If they claim to be a citizen, then they are a spy.

Think about how American law relates to the formula of this book with regards to memories, rules, platforms. If someone goes to court, then there are legal laws "rules" that should determine the verdict. When lawyers argue with regards to "Law A" (which is a rule), they might pull up specific court cases (memories) pertaining to said law. The resolution of what happened in the previous court case is the resolution (causality). These previous cases act as a support structure for the legal law in question and thus the verdict of the case. They, depending on what happened, affect the ruling of the law. The laws together make up the platform from which the judicial system operates. The legal system mirrors the causality and structure of memories, rules and platforms.

> Specific court cases = memories/experiences.
>
> Rules = legal laws.
>
> The judge's mind = the platform.
>
> The ruling = action taken based on the platform's point of view.

The systems of cases support the legal law that determines how the judge views the law (or interprets the law) before giving a verdict. We also talked about how generalities don't lead to specific actions. Finding a specific memory or court case that most directly relates to the current court case (experience) helps the judge know how to proceed. This is how the mind works in general.

My dad would have enjoyed reading this section.

If I was reading this book, then this would have been the most boring section.

Many Causes, Many Effects: When Causality Gets Complicated

Complexity can be caused in various ways, but all of the ways are related to a human being's inability to understand all of causality in a given situation. It is hard to think about complexity without analyzing a human's current state of understanding. Several aspects can make a situation complex.

Multiple Causes to an Effect:

If you are baking a certain food dish, there are multiple causes: the exactness of the ingredients, the size of the ingredients after chopping them up (or not chopping them up), the exact spices (quantity/quality). Imagine gathering ingredients to put in a baking pan after which you are going to put that baking pan in the oven. If any of the ingredients are incorrect before the baking process, then your overall dish will not come out exactly how you want it to. The fact that there is room for error in any one of the preparatory steps makes the situation complex. Processes become more complex when there are more ways it can be messed up—when there is more causality.

Multiple Effects to a Cause:

You hit the cue ball in billiards, and it in turn hits the 1-ball, which hits other balls, causing a chain reaction. The billiards balls are shooting around the table and bouncing off of the sides. In this scenario, the person moved the cue stick, and yet causality impacted multiple things.

The aspect of one person using the cue stick to hit the cue ball, which then hits another ball, is one of the simplest examples that I can think of for a human to understand linear causality.

A Chain Reaction of Linear Causality Where One Is Trying to Understand How Something "Works":

My apologies to those who actually play golf. This is just an example. Please consider the following list of cause and effect that happens over a relatively short period of time. The effect: A golf ball landed in a sand trap. Why did it land in the sand trap? The golf ball "hooked" (in this case to the left because the golfer is right-handed), and there was a strong westward wind which added (another cause) to the ball going to the left (relative to the line that the golfer's heels are on). The golfer "hooked" the ball because the face of the club didn't make contact with the ball at the intended angle.

Why didn't the club face not make contact at the correct angle? Because the golfer was leaning with their right side forward. Why was their right side forward? Their right side was forward because they were trying to muscle the swing with their right arm and shoulder. Why? They were upset with their previous swing, or trying to impress someone with their "strength," or something else. You can take this back ad infinitum. The ball could have landed in the wrong location for many reasons. There is room for error/change (causality) at almost any part (step) of the process of hitting the golf ball and the golf ball's flight. Some causes could be due to the golfer but also due to wind or other things that are directly outside of the golfer's ability to influence the ball (inability to have a causal relationship with the ball). A pro golfer could hit the golf ball exactly the same twice in a row, and yet the ball can land in two different locations due to factors that are beyond the athlete's causality.

Overlapping of Causality:

When I mention overlapping causality, I am really talking about what is occurring (all of causality that happens) during a specific period of time. Let's say that for some reason you are measuring the path an arrow travels through the air. There are certain factors that appear constant such as the structure of the arrow and how it is released from the bow, which determines how much of the archer's paradox you have to deal with. Next you try to account for windage. The windage can change (along with gusts of wind) if you are shooting that bow for a far distance. This situation can appear to be like the "multiple causes to an effect."

The reason why I differentiate between them is because in the baking example one gathers the causes (ingredients) then bakes them all together at the same time to create the effect. In overlapping causality, there are different factors that influence the arrow's flight over time. It may be one wind gust, or another, or there may be a constant wind stream and wind gusts within it. There is always gravity affecting the arrow (and everything else), so because of these reasons, I call it "overlapping." Time is relative so when there are more cause-and-effect relationships happening in a short amount of time, things appear more complex. One can stretch time or slow it down to make it appear like things are not as complex. When food is heated up, it seems like time is speeding up because causality is increasing and becoming more complex. One then has to wonder if time actually exists or if it is just a way of viewing causality.

Multiple Causality Happening at One Time:

Imagine a line-battle: two armies that are each in a line and aiming their muskets at one another. The commands are given: *Ready, aim, fire,* and suddenly smoke and bullets fill the air. With all the bullets in the air at the same apparent time, the situation becomes extremely complex, and it is difficult to discern what will happen until bodies start to fall.

- This is different from "multiple causes creating an effect" because this describes many cause-and-effect relationships happening at one time.

- This is different (sometimes) from "overlapping causality" because this occurs during a shorter relative span of time.

Time Variation on Causality:

Time variation on causality is causality itself. When a human tries to understand the causality of an event, it can be more difficult when one cause takes a longer time to take effect and another cause is more sudden. Picture a boxer who is going to deliver a straight punch. Their body rotates during the entire duration of the moment, but they might not extend their arm until partway through the body's rotation. The causes overlap and meet at the exact moment to maximize the effect (impact) of the punch.

Time and Causation: Two Ways of Talking About the Same Thing

Sometimes I view time as an illusion, a mental construct we form to try to understand causality. Is there any constant? If you view a situation in a very short amount of time, then it appears constant. If you slow a camera down enough, it will appear that a bullet, shot out of a firearm, is standing still. However, if you "speed up time," then you may not see the bullet at all. Time is not a *thing*. When I refer to "speeding up time," I really mean: "increase the rate of change." At the current moment, it appears that the Earth revolves around the Sun at a constant pace. If we were to draw time out, would the rate of the Sun's revolution not change? The further the construct of time is "stretched," the more causality one witnesses.

At this moment, there is a bird taking off and landing on the other side of the world from where you are. It seems that there is no causality between you and the bird. Given enough time, it is possible that the causality of what you are doing now and that flying bird could in fact cross and have a direct causal relation between one another.

Right now, as you are reading this book, there could be an epic intergalactic war several universes away. One could reasonably argue that such a war has no impact on one's life right now. However, it is possible that the outcome of such a war could affect, if not you in the future, your descendants.

Time is not a thing. Time doesn't change. It is always now. It has always been now, and will always be now. When it appears that time is changing, what people really mean is that rate between a cause and the effect (or the rate of change) is increasing or decreasing. Among scientists there exists some confusion about time actually speeding up or slowing down. If two people are travelling in space and one approaches a black hole, then the false idea is that time actually slows down. It doesn't. The rate of change slows down. This is similar to the way a piece of fruit would rot faster in heat and slower in the cold. Time isn't changing between the pieces of fruit; the rate of change between a cause and effect is changing.

Complexity with Understanding and Learning

It is impossible to really talk about complexity without talking about human understanding and learning. Imagine that you are trying to read a teenage-level-of-difficulty book. That doesn't sound too complex. Now imagine the book is in another language. The book may not be any more complex than reading the book in your native language. The book simply feels more complex because you lack the understanding of another alphabet, vocabulary, and grammar.

When one has a good grasp of an alphabet, then the alphabet doesn't seem that complex. When one is able to make small words, then slightly larger words aren't that difficult.

It's easy to take just one more step:

> Understanding the alphabet → forming words → forming sentences → grammar rules (which apply to all sentences).

This process is similar to

> Memories/experiences → rules → platform → apex platform(s).

The laws that form the apex platform are valid through the multiple platform mutations in the same way that grammar filters down through the various kinds of writing. Some of the rules of grammar only apply to some kinds of writings, and those would be like persistent rules, while other rules of grammar apply to almost all forms of writing. The latter would be the same as laws. A specific style of writing like a screenplay that may break many common grammar rules would itself be an outlier. Such an outlier doesn't break the validity of the laws of grammar.

One might believe that laws which make up the apex platform are weak because the apex platform is broader (because it affects so many platforms). This, however, is not true. Laws are not weak like one would expect from a generalization, but, rather, they are potent because they are specific, and their specific nature works through various specific instances/platforms. When specific rules work in various platforms, then it is incredibly powerful both in the validation of itself and its ability to be consistent.

Illusory Cause and Effect that by Its Existence Produces a Real Cause and Effect

The Brief Version:

If you believe that something is true, then you have accepted it as a cause and effect into your larger rules/platform that makes up your reality. The fact that you believe it to be true makes it solidly part of your reality. Everything that is solidly part of your reality (or makes up your rules/cube/platform) *will* change you. Belief makes belief real. The caveat is that it is real to you alone. If many hold a belief, then it is true to the specific group alone.

Just because it is true to you in your mind does not mean that it is real in reality or true.

> Def. *True/real in reality*: That it has an actual cause and effect in and of itself.

This concept is also applicable to the idea that humans are creative and intelligent, so much so that we can derive meaning and create meaning and purpose where there is none. Belief can create causality so that it has a true effect. However, it is a misrepresentation of actual causality. We should be careful of unintended effects of the misrepresentation of actual causality.

The Verbose Version:

Our interpretation of *something* without intrinsic meaning and purpose can give the illusion that *something* has meaning and purpose. While that deeper meaning/purpose etc. of that *something* (whatever it is) is an illusion, what isn't an illusion is how we ourselves are changed by that *something*. Thus, that meaningless *something* gives us actual reality.

The illusion of "something that isn't true" and our endowing "meaning and purpose" to that illusion—even if not intrinsically real (meaning a clear and accurate description of causality)—will still change us. If we then believe the illusion to be true, then our interpretation makes it real. We are believing the interpretation about something to be real. The aspect of believing it is real will make our own interpretation true, at least to us, and it thus affects and changes us. Our interpretation will become a solid part of our reality regardless of the intrinsic nature of the item we are seeing.

When we listen/read/accept or otherwise absorb into our reality another person(s) deep interpretation of something, then we benefit from the deeper, human-forged meaning. It doesn't mean that the core something (subject being talked about/item itself) has any real value.

This *something* I refer to isn't one particular aspect of one's life. It can be thought of as many things or in many ways. It could be an idea—whatever a person happens to find meaning in, such as a purpose for their lives. I would suggest that we shouldn't "poo-poo" something just because it doesn't have intrinsic value. This is another way of looking at meta cognition, or rather, how a mindset can change things.

People's egos shine greatly when talking about their own unique and special "purpose in life," whereas when the same people think of life's purpose in another, then their mindset changes drastically. Imagine you are walking through a grocery store and you look at a random person. Have you ever asked yourself, "What is the secret, greater meaning in that person's life?" No, you haven't. What is the greater purpose and hidden meaning in ant's life? Why do people believe they would have a special meaning and not the ant, a cow, or a whale? It is interesting seeing how people's views of a "purpose in life" change when they think about others as opposed to themselves.

In life, we can easily argue that there is no deeper meaning, especially with an understanding of the way the world works (causality). However, we as a species are able on a macro- and micro-level to create meaning and purpose where there is none. I could argue that all meaning and values that humans hold are derived from nothing (this would be the *ought versus is* argument). This is true regardless of the size of the population, from one individual to a large multitude.

Sometimes people create meaning where there is none. We ourselves create meaning where there is none (intrinsically in the world). This entire concept, to me, has a double impact. First, one person's fake interpretation of something shouldn't necessarily be held at a higher value then another's fake interpretation of something, including the made-up values and meaning of this book.

Why are the beliefs or opinions of this book any different? This book is based on *actual causation*. Actual causation is more important than belief. When a person has in their reality that there isn't any ultimate meaning or purpose, then it gives one a clear head in accepting others as well as protecting oneself in not being persuaded by their individual beliefs. When someone propounds their interpretation of something, claiming that it is more important than your interpretation of something, then you should try to figure out which interpretation has more of a basis in causality (reality). If neither interpretation has any basis in reality, then both interpretations are equally unimportant. None of it matters.

When I hear people propounding their beliefs to one another, and they are arguing about how great or not great something is, then I just remember that the reality is that they are arguing over the imaginations of people. In reality, there is no meaning.

One could then draw the conclusion that all arguments are pointless if they are about beliefs (fantasy) and not causality. Not so—unfortunately. We have to fight against fantasy and bad beliefs. Why? because a human's understanding, acceptance, and interpretations do have some value. Here is how it works with this small "chart" below.

> Believing something is true → changes us → change others → change the world.

Ideas, real or not, that are part of the stimuli of one person can spread and change others. Belief doesn't actually make the belief itself true. It still has the power to change the world. We should be careful about what effects result from beliefs.

I find the nature of bi-causality interesting where it pertains to people absorbing information and accepting it into their reality. Once an individual believes something to be true, then that something becomes part of who they are. They might not even realize that something is part of who they are. This is because they have absorbed it so much over time that it is part of their memories that make up their platform. Their platform is who they are, and so the causality of their memories will be normal for them.

How many times have you seen a leaf fall and been totally surprised? Remember the reaction of surprise when the world of a child changes by the realization of seeing something for the first time. It could be the human's first time seeing leaves fall in any great amount, or the first time seeing the ocean. How about waking up and realizing the world is covered with snow? The world looked one way when they went to bed and different when they woke up.

It is different. I hope this book will be a snowfall in your life.

Personal Values from One's Platform(s)

I have found, from my catalogue of cause and effect, that people tend to value two things. The first one is what they are really good at (sometimes gained by experiences but more often what they happen to be born with). These are typically things like looks and money. The second group of things that a person tends to value are things that they are lacking in for whatever reason—whether they are lacking it from their base or due to the changes in their life. These are the same type of things: looks, intelligence, money, whatever.

With the second, they see the negatives of being out of balance with it (usually due to lacking said aspect). When a person greatly values what they are already good at, then it doesn't always fit with the values from other platforms, whether individual or societal. The individual appreciation for one's own abilities is how ego works.

It is important to remember that values are derived from some kind of platform. It can be a platform from a society or from one person who is influencing someone and telling them what they "know" is important. With luck, the platform will be based on some sort of causality. Unfortunately, someone's point of view (their platform which determines their values and arguments) are unimportant if it is based on something other than actual causality.

If someone happens to value strawberries more than mangoes because they taste better, then that makes sense for them and that's great—for them. If someone thinks *Star Wars* is better than *Star Trek* or vice versa, then that's great. *Star Wars* and *Star Trek* are not real (sorry), and so they are not based on cause and effect. Episode VIII of *Star Wars* didn't even keep with the cause-and-effect rules that were created within the other canon movies.

When one realizes that cause and effect have no role in the reality of an argument, then there is no point in even arguing about it. No *cause and effect* means *no reality*. It's like finding out that a friend has been lying to you. One then doubts other parts of the reality that was the platform you built up in your mind of said friend.

So that explains how believing in something makes it true to us and changes/impacts reality. The question is the following: Do you believe that believing in something truly changes the world, or, after belief, is the world still just as meaningless? Does your belief right now about this very subject even matter? It's fun to think about.

The reality is that there is no value/meaning beyond cause and effect. Fantasy is simply a tool that is employed to make us feel better about a world that we can't control.

Do the Ends Justify the Means? and Unintended Effects

Brief:

Should someone believe something that isn't true, even if that something helps them in some way? Let's break this down.

Verbose:

Should a person take into their reality a false representation of cause and effect because their intention is that it will change them in a way that they wish to be changed? This want to change is a moral judgement based upon their current state of mind (meta). Their current moral state can and will change as their platforms change with the addition of new experiences. Will an untrue cause and effect only affect one area of their life? Will it affect them in other ways that they may not be anticipating?

One ~~must~~ should take into account all of the other repercussions or the other effects. A lot of times, a cause doesn't lead to just one effect, otherwise life would be much simpler. Many times, an effect becomes a cause for another effect, and so the initial cause creates a chain reaction.

Human beings aren't good at seeing the future and preparing for the future. Therefore, many actions that people take will have unintended consequences (undesired effects). This is especially true when it comes to long chain reactions. People have a myopic view of causality, especially when the rate of causality is slow (takes a longer amount of time).

Many people make decisions that seem like a great idea from their current point of view, and then when they are older, they realize that they are in a different platform, and so their point of view with all the values that comes with the new platform is different. They then have regrets over previous actions that they made from an older platform with different values. This book is about giving people a sneak peek at platforms they might hold in the future to help them make decisions in the present that they won't end up having to regret.

Another way people make decisions that they will later regret is through being myopic not just in the short term but also when they view one area of causality. When viewing just the immediate causality or solution to an immediate problem in one's life, a person might make a decision that they will later regret. A person might feel lonely, and so they might join a group of people because it gives them security, and they want a place to belong. They might turn a blind eye to some of the other unsavory aspects of a group.

A lonely person might also be in a relationship with someone to fill a part of their stimuli that they feel they are lacking and, in doing so, might ignore the negative causality of such a relationship. In either situation, the person doesn't realize what all of the other effects are.

One should be careful of entering new situations. Try to gain as much knowledge of causality before making a decision. This applies not only to social instances like the ones above but also to other areas of one's life like finances, fitness, medical decisions, and everything else.

The lesson to be learned is this: When a person has a myopic view of reality by either

1. A myopic view of a short period of time (short-term causation), or

2. A myopic view by focusing on just one aspect of reality (one causation),

then they are far more likely to act in bad ways. The overall problem is that they are lacking knowledge. They don't see enough of causality to make a decision that they will be comfortable with as their platform changes in the future.

Suppose we could know all the side effects of a medicine: not just what side effects could potentially affect you but in actuality which ones will in fact affect you personally. Imagine if we had the technology and could tell you that, if you take a certain medicine, the doctors could tell you with 100% certainty what would happen. This could be because the doctors know your genome and your current state of being and will know how your body would react in every way. Imagine if doctors could tell you not only how this will affect you in the short-term but also the long-term as well with 100% accuracy. You can see that with all of the causality you could make a better decision.

Imagine if the doctors could tell you what would happen over the long-term if you do not take the medicine. With such full knowledge of causality, you could weigh the outcomes against one another. Only then could you truly make a good, informed decision on whether to take the medicine.

Consider what this book claims to be true (actual cause and effect). I have tried to prove that the more knowledge of causality one has as part of their platform with regards to a specific experience or situation, then the better shot they have at understanding what is going on. If they have a better understanding of what is going on, then they are more likely to make better decisions and actions.

This process can be extended not only to the platforms that are related to situations with chemical causality like medicine but also to understanding people as well. Would it make sense for someone to judge you based on any one aspect of one of the many platforms that make them who they are? If someone is a serial killer, then yes. I would also argue that serial killers are outliers (fortunately). Would you feel comfortable if someone labelled you or thought they understood you by how you are specifically in just one platform of the many that make you who you are? How about if they judged you based on part of your base formula (e.g., how you were born)?

With this understanding, let's examine the idea of "privilege." It is the idea that suggests that we should label an entire group of people based on one aspect of the equation that makes them who they are. It suggests that one aspect of a person's base formula is such a powerful catalyst in their life that the combination of other aspects of their formula can't change someone from leaving that state or overcoming that state.

This should sound fairly silly to you. However, believe it or not, people do believe in this kind of thinking because they simply don't have enough knowledge to know better. I'm working on changing this. I won't discount that a person's base formula has an impact on a human being's success (relative to the morality derived from the majority of platforms at a given time). But I can name three statistics in a person's platform that are more impactful than this false idea of "privilege," which assumes that a person's skin color or "ethnicity" is the main apex factor.

Just the concept of privilege sounds like bigotry or racism to me. However, my having an aversion to it doesn't make it false. What are the other factors that affect someone's success? They are intelligence, health, and physical attractiveness. Even though I believe that these three factors are far more influential than a person's skin color, if I were still to judge anyone based on any one of these areas, then my view would be quite limited.

Is a person guaranteed success and happiness in life if they are good looking? No. Evidence: I have seen many examples of attractive rock stars, models, and movie stars who have been open in explaining how depressed and sad they are. Many have also committed suicide. There are many examples, and if you don't believe those, then I refer you to the wealth of examples that you can find on the internet.

Is a person guaranteed success and happiness in life if they are intelligent? No. Is a person guaranteed success and happiness because they have great health? No. I personally know people who have the best health one could hope for—no chronic diseases, no injuries—and yet they are depressed because another area of their life is going poorly. Those are all instances of where someone can have part of their life going well and not be happy and successful.

Do I believe that having good health, intelligence, and physical attractiveness increases the odds of a person having success and happiness? Yes. Given this reasoning, it is still foolish to believe that any one area of a person's life determines their ultimate success and happiness. Ideas such as racism or privilege are just not very intelligent. This falls into the myopic error of viewing just one aspect of causality and ignoring the others (as described above).

What am I referring to? Well, a lot of things. The example I want you to consider is the following: What if someone tells you, "Certain people are privileged" or "Everyone has equal opportunity." This is true from a general point of view. As human beings, we can't see all of the causality that makes a person who they are, so it is impossible to be able to judge someone in this way. Take the belief that someone is privileged or not privileged based on their skin color. Do you believe that one's skin factor is the primary or only factor (causality) in one's life that determines if someone is privileged or not? The dictionary definition of privileged is *having special rights, advantages, or immunities*. Based on your memories, do you believe that this idea of privilege is true?

Privilege has a negative connotation. Something about that particular wording makes the phrase sound like something that isn't honest to me. In this case, "not honest" means that it doesn't represent actual causality (reality). Some people begin with a more advantageous base (based on most common metas) and some have a less advantageous base. This is true across the board in all aspects. Some are smarter, more athletic, better looking, more intelligent, and so on and so on. Is it their fault for being born with advantage over another person? No one chooses to be born looking the way they do or having what they had when they were created, so we shouldn't judge someone more positively for having an advantage in these traits *just* the same as we wouldn't judge someone as less worthy for being born with fewer of the desired traits.

Still, people have this child-like view of judging people positively and negatively simply by the way they were born. Either way, they are wrong to judge someone by happenstance of their birth. Equal opportunity: On the other hand, I hear people saying, "Well, I just worked harder," or "They are just lazy." People will use bullshit statements to try to justify why they have something that other people don't have.

The reality is that we aren't created equal and that we aren't given equal opportunities based on the current state of the world. One can hardly take credit for all the good they have done, and it would be just as foolish to blame others for the bad state that they are in. When someone says that they are better than another person because they happen to be lucky, then I get really confused. I feel that, as human beings, we are far more alike than we are different. What I'm trying to say is that I hear stupid reasoning devoid of logic (cause and effect) from many different and often opposing factions. Come on, really?

Still, some people believe that everyone has equal opportunity even though there is an obvious discrepancy in every single attribute that one can think of when a person is born. It makes little sense.

Both the belief of privilege and the belief that everyone has an equal opportunity are just false. Can't we just get past this way of thinking? Can't we have just a little more compassion?

Wish Fulfilment, Time Travel, Omniscience, Omnipotence, and Mistakes

Beware of people who find a wish or desire that you have and try to give it to you. To quote Mr. Rogers, "You are special." But you aren't special in the way that many people believe they are special. It isn't some magical blood or sacred magic passed down to you through holy powers or spiritual mumbo jumbo or any other dogmas or lies that you have been told. You are special because of all the multitude of little cause-and-effect changes that had to have happened for you to be who you are. Just like the time-travel concept from *Back to the Future*, if there were to be a slight change in causality, then you would be a completely different person or might not even exist. The stars had to align for you to exist and think the way you think right now. That is really cool.

Imagine if we could travel thirty to forty thousand years into the past. Imagine we could examine the creatures that would later evolve into humans. Who in their right mind would have bet that human beings would have ended up as the dominant species on the planet? Probably not many people. I know I would have lost that bet.

People probably ended up living in caves because of the obvious: protection from the elements. There was also other causality: If a human-eating predator was small enough to enter the cave, then it was probably small enough to be killed by a group of humans with pikes or other primitive weapons, especially if the cave entrance is a bottleneck and fans out into a larger opening where humans could attack the invading beast all at once. To me that kind of causality makes sense, but I honestly don't know for certain if either of those statements are true or not. Time travel isn't real because time may not be real. Causality is real. Causality is linear. To think of "going back in time" through the lens of reality would be to believe that one could reverse the changes that have been made. Wood creates fire, fire doesn't always create wood. Causality is (as far as I know) impossible to reverse. That is why we can't go back in time—other than time not being real.

Similar to humans in caves and hiding from larger beasts is the following example: If we were to go into the oceans today, how many of us could look at a small fish hiding in the alcove of a coral reef and imagine it inheriting the seas from sharks, whales, and the multitude of other sea creatures? If there is a divine being or a creature with incredible knowledge and insight, then they could see the way that causality permeates everything for them; they would know one hundred percent what would happen in the future. It would be obvious to such a being. They would know the future, and furthermore they would understand how every action they make affects the world not only for a moment but perhaps for all of time. That would be true omniscience. Seeing human beings from where we were to how we are now would be not just an easy realization but obvious.

A mistake is a failure to input the correct cause for the desired effect. People make "mistakes" in large part because they either do not understand a situation, meaning they do not have full knowledge of cause and effect in any given area, or they do not have the ability to create the desired cause (impotence). If a person doesn't know the causality of a situation and tries to obtain a desired effect regardless of a lack of understanding, then the "odds" go up that they will not achieve the goal. If a person knows that they cannot achieve the effect and yet they still make an action knowing that the action will not achieve an effect, then they are actually purposely making another effect—whether they understand that other effect or not.

If you wish to be truly free and have the understanding that you want to have, then you need to stop settling for false ideas and beliefs that superficially make you feel complete and better. There is a better place to go to—a more complete place for you—but you have to let go and get out of your comfort zone to get there.

Letting Go

One thing I like about some religious messages is the idea of letting go of hate and being able to forgive. A person experiences everything they experience inside themselves when their senses send signals to their brain. Even so, people tend to believe that they still experience things outside of themselves, and this just doesn't make a lot of sense to me. When one lets go of hate and the desire for revenge and aggression, then they aren't affecting the other person so much as they are affecting themselves.

That is really cool. Why have hate in the first place?

Does it actually make sense to put a quote inside of a book where almost all, if not all, are my own words?

First, divorce hate from "having one's guard up." You can have your defenses intact and not hate. Simply remove whatever connection you have to hate. You don't need to "hate" and get all "worked up" to effectively defend yourself physically, emotionally or intellectually. One doesn't need to hate to be cautious or watch out for someone who is toxic so they don't take advantage of you or hurt you again.

> "Anger is a fire that, without a consistent source of tinder, will simply go out."
>
> —Alan Jaffe

Real life isn't like a movie. In a movie, hate and tension seem to make superheroes more powerful. In reality, the opposite is true. Not only is hate and tension not necessary, but they actually make one weak, sick, and stressed, and they don't accomplish anything positive.

If you are using hate as a vehicle for something positive, then acknowledge that and just skip the useless (and often subtracting) step of hate and go straight to the positive.

Stuff About Religion and Cognitive Dissonance

Imagine that you were to sit down with me at a coffee shop and I begin to tell you about a special alien race known as the Za45inzzz. You tell me that you have no idea what that is. Since you have no memories associated with the alien race known as Za45inzzz, you have no evidence to support that knowledge. I then proceed to legitimize their existence by telling you a few simple stories about the aliens.

The first thing I tell you is that they come from a planet in our solar system named GAV-0512. You pause. You haven't heard of a planet in our solar system named GAV-0512. Then I tell you that on that planet there is no such thing as gravity and the aliens simply fly around with invisible jets that run on a special material called "okam" which is infinite and part of their octopus-like bodies. You think to yourself that the second part of support (or evidence) for the existence of these aliens doesn't make sense because you know that gravity is evident on other planets in our known universe. That doesn't ring true to you. You know that gravity can change depending on the planet.

However, the idea of a planet with no gravity existing in our universe doesn't follow the causality that you are familiar with. The notion of such a planet isn't supported by any sort of logic or reasoning. Furthermore, you also don't understand how they would have invisible jets in their octopus-like bodies. Solar power is a seemingly infinite power source (at least for the period of time that we are alive), and yet it might be hard to believe that there is this infinite energy inside these creatures that powers invisible jets. Not much that you know of is invisible and also creates such power. You aren't even sure how that would work.

None of the story of these aliens makes any sense to you because you have zero memories of experiences that could possibly justify any piece of the story. You could try to do some "mental gymnastics" and say to yourself, "I know that planets exist, so maybe there is just another one that for some reason we haven't detected in our solar system." However, this concept seems irrational if you know anything about astronomy. Imagine that, after telling you the whole story, I give you a moment to consider it. Next, I explain to you how one time one of the Za45inzzz aliens from the planet GAV-0512 was special and could split its body into four pieces, each with identical mass, and then could reform itself at will.

This last example doesn't make any sense and breaks a law of physics regarding conservation of mass. At the end of the entire explanation of the aliens and what I claim to be "obvious examples of causality," I look at you and ask if you believe that the aliens living on the planet GAV-0512 are real. You realize that I haven't given you any reason to believe they exist. What would your answer be?

Suppose you say, "No, I don't believe the aliens are real," and I suddenly become shocked and respond, "How could you *possibly* not believe in these aliens!? I just *proved* that the aliens are in fact real!"

Sound like a stupid story? Well, a similar story actually happened to me in real life where I was the one listening to a person try to convince me of their unsound beliefs. The human being who was telling me about this fantasy was well-spoken, of sound mind, and appeared to not be under the influence of any drugs or alcohol. Here is the story.

I was working on this book in a coffee shop, and someone sat down with me (uninvited) and told me that they had a story to share. At this moment, my head was swirling from hours of causality, so I decided to take a break from my work and entertain them. I told them that they could go ahead and tell me their story. They then proceeded to tell me a story about cause-and-effect relationships that made no sense to me because I haven't seen any of the cause-and-effect claims in my own life experience (since becoming an adult). In the story they told me, there is a person who is the son of a god or the god (I was a little confused about how many gods they were referring to. I honestly to this day don't think they knew how many they were talking about). I asked them, "How that was possible?" because I didn't see the cause-and-effect correlation between a human being the son of a god or the god. I've heard stories like Hercules, but I haven't seen any evidence in real life of that actually being true. I tried to insert other fantasy creatures to see if it made sense in another light, like a person being the son of a dragon, unicorn, or leprechaun, and none of that made sense either. They told me, "He was born from a woman who didn't have sex with anyone."

That was the first "red flag" that occurred to my mind because all the women who have been pregnant have had sex with a male human being. Such an explanation might make sense to a child whose parents hadn't explained how babies are made, but to an adult? C'mon. Today, due to the science of modern technology, women can be inseminated by some other means. Since the technology didn't exist back then (or so I believe from having learned about history, assuming that was all true), then I was unable to believe that part of the story. The causality of the effect of being pregnant and the cause of some god magically making her pregnant didn't work on multiple levels. I was also told that this woman was magical and didn't have sin or this evil power inside of her.

I don't believe in this concept of evil magic (sin) that is supposedly inside everyone because a long time ago someone ate an apple that they weren't supposed to eat. I thought to myself that if there is an all-knowing being, then it would know everything, including that someone would eat from this fruit. How could you punish someone for something you knew they would do because you caused it to happen? The whole cause and effect made no sense.

Anyway, that was my train of thought on the concept of sin and the magical snakes and stuff. They continued to tell me that this person who is the son of a perfect human being who was "immaculate" or devoid of magical evil or something later suffered so much in one afternoon that it cured all the people of their sin. I didn't understand the cause and effect in several ways. Why does (everyone) have magical evil inside them because of a piece of fruit that was eaten long ago? How could a person's suffering (being severely beaten, crucified, and stabbed to death) have any relation to other people who weren't there and didn't see it?

I thought about other cause-and-effect relationships that I had witnessed involving suffering. I remembered cleft-palate orphans, children born with clubfoot, people who were sex slaves, people who've had severe burns, and horrible accidents, amputations, and other people. The people whom I thought of exist in modern times, and I know for certain that they had to have suffered more in a week, month, year, or years than one person (from this story) could have possibly suffered in an afternoon. This is true no matter how bad the afternoon was for this person. I thought, *Is there something special about suffering all this pain at once?*

I remembered stories of people being horribly beaten and tortured in modern times, and I saw no causality between their pain and suffering and apotropaic measures against evil magic or sin or anything else. I then had to pause the story and ask, "So you believe that this person dying (cause) removed sin from everyone? (effect)" At that point, they explained to me a story about someone eating an apple and how that caused sin for everyone (which doesn't make sense with any cause and effect that I have witnessed). After all that, they asked me if I believed that the story was true. I replied that I didn't.

They looked at me confused and a bit upset. I asked them why they were upset. They said, "Because you didn't understand what I'm saying." I told them that the story didn't follow any coherent cause and effect. Or rather, that the cause and effect in the story didn't make any sense when compared to any part of reality that I have experienced in my life. I didn't have any memories/experiences in real life that supported any part of the story that they were sharing. Even if I could relate one part of the story loosely to a causality in the platform of my own life experiences, I could only validate that one small part of the story. The overwhelming majority of the story had little basis in reality. It wouldn't help any other part of the story when it comes to making sense. Since I didn't see any logical (cause and effect) to any one part of the story, then it would be highly irrational for me to take into my reality the story as a whole. How could I think that the story is true if it doesn't follow any cause and effect?

I was left with a thought about this person: *What kind of special and magical life this person must have lived if they were truly able to take this story into their reality?* I then remembered that they are living on the same planet as me and that we are both subject to the same laws of physics. Since causality was obviously in play, the bigger question became the following: Why does this human being decide to believe in things that are obviously not true?

The story that was shared with me was a nice fantasy story like *Harry Potter* or *The Lord of the Rings*. I ended up reading the book that had the entire story that the person from the coffee shop related. I actually liked the story. It was fun and entertaining, and the attitude and words of the main character resonated with my sense of morality in a few ways. Upon reading the book, I found sections and passages that resonated with cause-and-effect situations that I've experienced. While there are some good moral lessons in that book, I can't possibly believe that it is true.

I got kicked out of a bookstore when I asked the lady working there why this book with all of its magic and superpowers and such wasn't in the fiction section. She got upset with me for some reason. I found out that other fiction books, if they contain a magical god-type power, get to have their own section in libraries called "spiritual or religious." Sometimes bookstores get more creative and further obfuscate the meaning of these books by putting them in sections labeled "self-improvement," "inspirational," or "feel good."

I was inspired by Harry Potter, but that doesn't make magic real. When books replace words such as *magic* with *holy*, then that doesn't mean that they get their unique section in the library. When books containing holy-magic are put in a nonfiction section, then I feel that this is an incorrect classification. Many of these spiritual or biblical books have more magic and fantasy in them than other fantasy-labeled books that I've read. Maybe I'll get lucky and this book will end up in the nonfiction section. What do you think?

Back in school, I would often hear people arguing repeated about what is better: elves or dwarves, *Star Trek* or *Star Wars*. When I hear what is "better" in an argument without more detail, I immediately know that this argument is silly because it is merely someone's opinion. The reality is that *Star Trek* and *Star Wars* are both made up. So a general question like that is impossible to answer because there isn't a "better" when it comes to fantasy. Whatever morality is prescribed to them is subjective, much like everything else in life. The difference between morality that concerns fantasy and morality about reality is that one follows causality in the real world and the other doesn't. One could ask a more specific question: If one were to take all the canon of *Star Wars* and all of the canon of *Star Trek*, then which overall story maintains the most consistent causality? The more discrepancies of causation in any fantasy story, then the less believable it is.

In college, I was on a religious panel and was responsible for explaining the basic ideas of the religion that my family had subscribed to. All the "panelists" were given five minutes to do the same with their beliefs. I was sitting there with other college students (*obviously* all experts) and we were all sharing the basic tenents about our own religions. The panelists were sitting in chairs that were lined up in front of the room, looking out at the audience. I had a unique opportunity to see the reactions of the people in the audience. When one person would get up and speak, I would see the people in the audience (who were clustered conveniently by their denominations) nod if they believed the similar religion, while the majority of the audience (everyone else) would look at the current speaker with wide eyes of disbelief. They looked at the panelist like they were crazy. This went on and on, with one small section smiling and nodding when one person would speak, while everyone else shook their heads and looked baffled.

I realized (long after) that in the religions represented that if there was something that resembled reality (actual cause/effect), then it would resonate with everyone in the room because everyone exists in reality and thus would have at least one cause-and-effect experience that supported or resonated with what was being propounded. It is easy for people to see the illogic in others but harder to see it in themselves. This makes me paranoid and I find myself constantly questioning myself and arguing with myself as if playing a game of chess inside my mind. My mental arguments take many forms, and oftentimes I end up interviewing/interrogating myself in my head.

Here is one way I view religious beliefs. Religions make claims about what seems to be the ultimate cause-and-effect relationships. You believe this (cause), and X will happen (effect). You believe X, and Y will happen. You live your life like X, and Y will happen after you die. I have heard these claims about cause and effect my entire life. Why are they not part of my platform now? They were in the past. When I was young, I was told cause and effect. Since I didn't have any other cause and effect to compare it to, I simply trusted those who knew more about the world than I did. I made the *assumption* that there was just one platform in a person's mind, and if they had knowledge and skills in areas that I didn't have—for example, being able to drive a car, cook, and sing—then they must be superior to me in every way and must know more about everything.

When I was a little older but still a kid or young adult, I would get more experience (cause and effect) from other sources and compare it to the first ones that I heard (unfortunately, many based on fantasy). I would try to rationalize the new experiences and make them fit into the fantasy world that I was taught growing up. Trying to fit examples of reality into a fantasy world is a lot like trying to force puzzle pieces to fit into a spot where they don't quite fit. Sometimes it is easier than other times depending on how weirdly-shaped the puzzle piece is. When experiences were common, then they would "line up," and so I was able to form rules (not based on true reality but on the cause and effect that I experienced as a child).

Later on, I would have experiences of cognitive dissonance, which is a conflict between the cause and effect that I experienced in the past and the cause and effect that I was experiencing in the moment. I was able to look back at previous cause-and-effect claims that I was told, and with more experiences as an adult, I realized that the cause-and-effect situations didn't make sense compared with what I have viewed in reality. I wasn't fine mashing puzzle pieces into place, and I realized in a lot of cases that it wasn't the puzzle piece that didn't fit, but rather the puzzle itself that needed to be reformed.

Does the above mean that there is no way that a religion could exist? Does it necessarily mean that people don't have souls/energy/ki/chi or whatever flavor of "extra specialness" that is inside oneself? No, it doesn't. The state of a human being (effect) at any given moment is due to an accumulation of all causes upon that being in the past. I do not believe that we understand all of the causality that makes humans *human*. It is possible that a soul or a type of energy is part of a person's baseline and perhaps even possible that it can change or come and go from an individual in the course of their life. This is something that I don't understand. What I do understand is that if someone does have something "beyond the physical," then that too would be the result of something and wouldn't just appear randomly. It too would be the result of many cause-and-effect relationships just like everything else.

There is one nefarious example of "ultimate causality" that some people claim is true due to their religious beliefs: when they use reincarnation as an excuse (cause) for why they are "better than others" or are "superior to others" or why another person has the misfortune that they have. It is a perfect example of how cause doesn't equal effect. They may look at someone who is very unfortunate and say, "They deserve it" or This is for what they did in a past life." One should be wary of cause and effect that makes no sense.

By the way, I'm not against some views of reincarnation—I just don't like this specific example of how reincarnation gets used to justify the misfortune of others. It takes away any responsibility for one human being to connect to another and help them.

What Is So Bad About Believing Stuff That Isn't True?

Belief is itself a stimulus (a cause) because belief changes (affects) reality. Reality determines one's actions. Beliefs affect actions. Now that we understand this simple aspect, consider the following phrase that people say as a way of showing how open and rational they are: *People are free to believe what they want.* Then they add, *so long as they don't force their beliefs on other people* or *as long as they don't bother me* or *as long as they don't do stupid shit.*

OK, I may have adlibbed the last one. The reality is that beliefs are dangerous because they have a direct impact on how people act. Where do we—should we—as a society draw the line when it comes to potentially dangerous beliefs? If we stop dangerous beliefs, then in the future someone can interpret (or label) your beliefs as bad and can come after you. The morality derived from a personal or societal platform will determine what beliefs are good or bad. Therefore, a platform will decide which beliefs are so bad that we should fight against them as a society. Whose platform shall determine when a belief is bad enough to require fighting? I hope that, whatever platform it is, it will be based somewhat on causality and not the beliefs of someone's fantasy.

Ideas may be bulletproof, but they are not "idea proof." With the various means of spreading ideas, it is impossible to stop bad ideas and negative beliefs from being spread. In the old days, it was easier. All you had to do was kill some people and burn their books/scrolls/cities, and suddenly the ideas were gone. This is much more difficult today, another powerful impact of the internet and other technology. People are no longer the keepers of knowledge but rather, technology is the keeper of the knowledge. Whether we like it or not, you, me, all of us are in a war of beliefs that control the actions of the people on our planet. Beliefs are dangerous even though they have no basis in reality because they have a direct effect on human action.

Actual knowledge is important—very important—for it gives one power. Sometimes fake information is spread with the claim that it is actual truth. However, because it doesn't work through causality, we know that it can't be true knowledge. When a person learns things that aren't true, then they are becoming the opposite of powerful. They are becoming weaker. They are moving from positive to negative.

Here is an easy-to-understand example of how believing in some bullshit religion weakens a person. In this story there are two people, Jenny and Sara. Jenny doesn't believe in magic and gods and doesn't belong to any religious cult. Sara is similar to Jenny in every other way except that she does believe in magic and one or more gods, and she does belong to a religious cult.

Suppose there is a "new" religion that has been made up. They believe that here is a magical god who chooses lucky people every year and gives them magical powers. These powers are true insight from the gods that can help people become holier. Now suppose the cultists or religious people from this new religion start trying to convert/brainwash people. They come to Jenny. Jenny doesn't believe in any magic or religious stuff. The cult really has its work cut out for them! They have to convince her of several things before Jenny will join them: that there is a god, that this god gives magic powers to people, and that some people already have magic powers. They also have to convince Jenny that it is their job to tell everyone what to do to be magical like them, which implies that Jenny can become magical too (and who wouldn't want cool magic powers?).

Now assume the same cultists try to convince Sara, a very religious woman who already believes in gods, magic, prophets, and "holy" things. Most of the work is already done for the cultists. They just need to convince Sara that she doesn't quite have it "right." It is infinitely easier to get someone who is already brainwashed and believes stupid things into believing other stupid things. Sara is far weaker than Jenny when it comes to dealing with people who are trying to get her to believe in things that aren't true.

The example above is not limited to religion but can be extrapolated to many different areas. Worth thinking about.

Combining the Bell Curve with Cause and Effect; Cups of Different Sizes

Suppose you have five different cups of different sizes. Now suppose you try to pour the same amount of liquid into each cup. Saying that the end result is that each cup will have the same amount of liquid in it would be crazy. It just doesn't make sense mathematically (cause and effect). A different starting position/state for a cup will end in a different net result if the same exact effect is placed upon it. This is how people work. We are like the cups, all different, and so all in need of different levels of causality to try to get to where we want to go.

This example assumes that you and the person giving the advice share a similar platform with similar morals/goals: to have good health; to have a stronger, more athletic body; or to lose weight. A lot of times, a person needs stimuli to become the person they want to become. They may experience that specific causality, and it helps them, like going on a specific diet that causes them to lose weight and so they are at their goal weight (effect). This person, having success, then believes that you need the same exact causality to help you too.

This is a big assumption on two counts: first that your cup is the same size as theirs was before their change, and second that you want to have the exact effect as them, the same exact ending place. If you aren't them, then both of these assumptions are incorrect. First, you can't be in the same place as them because you aren't them. Second, you can't end up in the same place as them because you didn't start in the same place.

This doesn't mean that the person is bad. On the contrary, this person probably cares about you and wants you to be better or happier just like them. One should be cautious when hearing people who say that they have one solution for everyone because this does assume that we are all cups of the same size. If someone has a lot of knowledge, then they may be able to help you get to the same place. This is why custom exercise or diet plans are so important. The more customizable something is, the more likely it will help you. If something is not specific, then it probably doesn't contain a lot of good knowledge or the knowledge isn't specific enough to be of any help: *Do what's right for you. Eat what's right for you. Exercise the right amount for you.*

Yea, but what is the right amount of anything? The answer lies in causality. The more causality is understood, the more specific the answers are.

When people tell you that a certain belief/religion/activity is perfect for you or will help you, then you should think hard about whether that cause-and-effect relationship will actually help you. What is it about you that you are wanting to change? What are all the effect outcomes that will occur if you join said group or activity? Belonging to a group sounds like a good thing. Having a community means social opportunities and more friends who can help out and more chances for you to help others. Is that positive change in your life worth the negative changes such as false beliefs in things such as vicarious redemption, evil, bad, sin, devils, and eternal damnation of people you may care about? Something to think about.

There is a lot of talk about climate change. I find it interesting that people seem to forget about pollution. Anyway, climate change is happening or it isn't happening. The argument about climate change is: that we have an undesirable effect called global warming. We are still arguing over what the cause of the negative effect is. In order to determine the actual causality, we need to find out what is indeed causality and what is fantasy. If ninety-seven percent of all scientists claim that the research and studies of carbon emissions have concluded without a doubt that carbon emissions are in fact the cause of climate change, then they probably are right.

I'm not a scientist with knowledge of such things, so I don't know with certainty what is going on. What I do know is that when the news finds the extremists or outliers that make up the other three percent of scientists who disagree and then treat them as if they represent the majority of scientists, then that is being dishonest, and those news people are very, very bad!

Just remember not to focus on extremists and outliers even if they are loud and obnoxious (which they are).

Questions as Stimuli (Causes) and Aggressive Interviewing

I've been accused throughout my life of asking too many questions. The fact is that I like the seemingly black-and-white nature of a lot of questions. I have come to enjoy the annoyance of answers that are grey, especially when I know that the grey answer is more accurate than the black-and-white answer. When answers are grey, then the question is generally too broad or the individual giving the answer doesn't have enough knowledge of causality to give the correct answer.

There is something special about asking questions. From the perspective of the *receiver of the question*, it forces them to immediately look back at memories of cause and effect in their own life. The question pulls the person deeper into themselves, even if for only a few moments. They change platforms (like going to a specific file cabinet associated with the question). Then they examine their own rules (look into the cabinet at the different folders). Next, they examine specific cause-and-effect experiences (specific papers in the folders) that form who they are.

There is power in questions. This is true even though they appear, by their nature, to have a sense of humbleness. The reality is that a question is an action not passivity. I see this a lot when watching people who work in the news industry. They often weaponize questions in such a clever (nefarious) way that the wording of such questions carry many false assumptions about reality.

If one were to directly answer the question asked in this aggressive and dishonest manner, then in doing so they would have to agree with the bullshit assumptions. Because of this kind of aggressive reporting, the individual answering the question has to first deconstruct the question and eviscerate the bullshit assumptions first before they are able to actually speak about the topic that they were being asked about. If they don't dismantle the bullshit in the question, then they have to spend most of the answer adding caveats to explain exactly what they mean.

This kind of interviewing gets convoluted and takes forever to get through. *Reporters, please stop with the aggressive tactics of leading people to believe something in particular.* Reporters ask questions in an attacking manner as if they are playing a video game where points are rewarded by how many times they attack the person they are interviewing. Trust me, the viewers already know where your allegiance lies. Don't sacrifice reality just to try to "look good." The ends don't justify the means if you have to attack the one being interrogated—I mean *interviewed*. Please seek to gain knowledge with good interviewing instead of sacrificing reality to fulfil some virtue crusade.

If you are interviewing someone who is an absolute ***, then the viewers will be intelligent enough to realize such. I have a lot more respect for the interviewer who is able to maintain their cool and professionalism despite the rudeness of the one being interviewed. Seek to learn the reality of a situation or person. Asking good questions is hard. Even so, I have specific memories of good reporting where the reporter asks tough questions and demands honest answers without having to lower themselves to dirty tactics. Answers are an effect. I find the reasons why people give the answers they do to be much more telling.

The reasoning behind why someone gives their answer is an effect. It comes directly from the platform that they are in when asked the question. From there one can perhaps try to understand the rules and memories that made that particular platform. This is a way of reverse-engineering an answer to understand how it came into existence. Of course, we don't get a complete answer because we don't know the causality of how a person operates on an exact level.

Applying Cause and Effect to Understanding Stimuli and Change

Below are two paragraphs. The first paragraph is how one might describe a situation without directly speaking about cause and effect and the second paragraph is how one could describe the same paragraph through the platform of cause and effect which would include memories, rules, and the platform itself. See if, after reading both paragraphs, you believe that the second paragraph gives you a better understanding than the first. The second paragraph is not just a translation or quick insertion of a few words but has extra exposition. This is intentional.

When a person receives a specific stimulus that becomes a catalyst, then they can often feel the chemical change within themselves. This is an epiphany or a moment of clarity. Often, they will consciously or subconsciously make connections to the many previous stimuli that they have had which had not become a catalyst. However, once this particular stimulus happens, then suddenly they will have a flashback and the previous stimuli will support the current stimulus, transforming it into a catalyst. One could say that the older stimuli had "set the stage" for the catalyst. The catalyst is the "straw that broke the camel's back," the tipping point. The deathblow. This catalytic-change occurs when enough stimuli add up to give a more confident understanding of how something works.

A person can have an experience that when combined with memories of a similar nature will change the rule that is supported by those memories. The specific experience that removes a rule, creates a new rule, or causes a rule to change in a significant way is therefore called a catalyst. Changing rules will have an impact on the platform that the rules feed into. When this happens, a person can have a moment of understanding, a moment of clarity. When the change is more profound—meaning that it affects or changes a person's platform to such an extent that the platform gives them a different point of view—then people will call the experience of this cause and effect relationship an epiphany or zanshin.

Moments of clarity, zanshin, or epiphanies are generally the result of a catalyst (cause) that helps combine other causes to form a rule or a cause that, when completed, can cause a chain reaction that combines rules which then combine to form part of the platform. In my mind, I see the moments of clarity as moments when one makes connections between memories and rules. While this generally feels like addition, it can sometimes be a combination of addition (of truth) and subtraction (of falsity). Other times, a person can have a catalytic event occur that doesn't just build part of the platform but rather makes sections of the platform fall away. This subtraction or "dropping" of part of the platform and disillusionment for a new platform based off of different rules/memories is often called a paradigm shift.

As human beings it can be difficult to know what impact an experience will have on a person's rule(s)/platform. An experience could have little to no impact or it could have a larger impact. Some experiences may lie dormant or be forgotten, only to reappear later on when one has a similar experience. A teacher may plant a seed and then use it to further grow an idea in the future with the right supporting stimulus of water.

One reason why it can be difficult to know what experiences impact people is that people don't remember all of the cause-and-effect events that happen to them. Many experiences get absorbed into the rules and are (from a conscious standpoint) forgotten. Other causes may take more time to take effect. There are lessons that I remember being told by people more experienced than I was, but the original advice didn't set in until I experienced the cause-and-effect with other senses. While that seed was there, it would take more experiences (watering) for it to grow into a plant that I could see above the surface of the earth.

Personal experience is absorbing cause and effect with one's own senses. Sometimes personal experience is required even when one truly believes/trusts the individual they are learning from. But you already know this. Really know it, right? I mean I've tried to plant seeds of knowledge inside your mind as you've gone through the book. Is this the section that will solidify those memories into reality for you? Is the act of you absorbing these sentences helping to solidify memories into more rules, or possibly even change your platform?

You now understand the concept of memories, rules, and platforms. There is an old phrase, "There's no substitute for experience." Now, on a deeper level, you understand *why*.

Not All Experiences Are Created Equal: Using Simple Math to Understand More Complex Issues

For the next paragraph, the term *weight* is synonymous with *influence*. The greater the weight or influence, the more or higher experience one has accumulated.

Let's recall the earlier section on forming new rules, removing rules, and changing rules (and platforms) through simple math equations. By the way, I hated math class after elementary school. Sorry for those who, like me, have struggled with learning arithmetic. To the mathematical purists out there, what you are about to see is a "watered down" version of the actual arithmetic of how this probably works in the human mind and body. This is intentional. First, it will be easier for more people to grasp, and second, it is math that I can do.

Similar experiences validate and enhance one another. This causality between similar or identical experiences makes the whole greater than the sum of its parts. Suppose a trusted person t_1 told you about a cause and effect that they experienced. The experience you have from this person is labelled as t_1. The $t_1 = 1$ experience, where the number 1 is the weight or amount of influence that that cause-and-effect event has on your overall rule/platform.

Then you experience a very similar situation yourself. The self-experience is labelled as s_1. The equation enters your rule as $s_1 = 1$. Again, the self-experience in this example equals one just like the experience from your trusted friend. One might think that the combination of these experiences would equal two. $t_1 + s_1 = 2$. The self-experience s_1 would equal one by itself in a vacuum, but because you already have had a *similar experience*, that previous experience (even if secondhand) makes what would normally be $s_1 = 1$ actually $s_1 = 3$. It gives the experience more weight.

But that's not all! The latter experience s_1 also validates the previous experience t_1 and you get what some might consider a bilinear causality. This increases the value of the previous information from a trusted individual, $t_1 = 1$ to $t_1 = 2$. The combined actual equation becomes $t_1 + s_1 = 5$. So an experience alone (unless they have intrinsic weight such as a severe life-altering event or other outlier) does not "weigh" as much as an experience that is validated by another similar experience.

This weight I mention is another way I talk about the number or amount of experience any cause-and-effect event is equal to. The assumed the combined total of t_1 and s_1 is $t_1+s_1 = 2$. But because they are in a cause-and-effect relationship to each other, the actual equation ends up being $t_1+s_1 = 5$. Due to the nature of cause and effect between the variables, it makes it difficult to determine just how much one variable affects another and thus how much each individual experience affects the effect on one's rules/platform.

> All experience is personal experience. One important question is how many of your senses are engaged in an experience. The apex question is the following: How much does that experience impact your platform(s)?

My Mathematical Goblet Runneth Over

Imagine that it takes an amount of "experience" to fully understand a task. When the combined experience reaches a certain number, then one's rule/platform makes a noticeable change. The addition of the last experience that changes one's rule/platform is what I call a "catalytic event." In the equation above, if I needed to have a total combined experience of four to change my rule or platform that t_1 and s_1 were supporting, then the s_1 (cause-and-effect experience) would be the catalytic event.

Sometimes you can have "relatively ineffectual experiences/causes." These are experiences that don't matter that much. Suppose you require 100 experience to change a rule. $x = 1$, $y = 70$, and $z = 50$. If you have the experience x first, you would start with one experience. Then you experience y (another cause/effect experience), and you have a total of 71. When you add experience z to the equation $x + y + z = 121$, you realize that you would have easily gotten the experience without the x because the x was such a small part of the whole. There are situations where you may be at a 99 and need just one more experience to change your platform, but statistically it is rare that that happens. It is far more likely that the catalytic event will be a larger stimuli/have more weight/or greater influence.

Imagine that there is a rule whose "experience requirement" is one that you have already exceeded to fully understand that rule. In such an example, you would need 100 experience. Now assume that you already have 150 experience. You are exceeding that rule by fifty percent more than the requirement of the rule. If you then experience more cause and effect that is directly related to the rule, then that extra experience is just going to be redundant. People call these extra cause-and-effect events "obvious" in everyday speech. They don't have as much "weight" because their input isn't as needed to understand the rule.

People often don't pay that much attention to redundant information. People often make the mistake of thinking that they understand a rule completely and they might think that they are at 150% knowledge when they might actually be at 80% knowledge. One way you can trick yourself into learning faster is to pretend that you never are at 100% knowledge with regards to a rule. Even if you are being a little dishonest with yourself, the effect makes your mind more open to receiving more knowledge. People will see you as humble. It seems to be a good strategy a lot of the time.

> Lying to oneself or keeping an open mind is not a law. It is, however, a persistent rule.

And now, here is an example of how I argue with myself.

"Wait, wait one minute, Alan! Doesn't this break your own rules about authenticity and not lying to yourself? Why are you telling us to lie right now!? You contradictory son of a bitch!"

"Good question. In this instance, I apply my experience about flawed senses and human learning. I know my senses (eyesight, hearing, and others) are not perfect, so there is always a chance that I misinterpreted some information or just flat out missed some information altogether. So there. That's my reasoning for 'lying' to myself. You see, I'm not actually lying—I'm just putting more weight on one aspect of my reality to enhance my learning."

"Alan, don't you think you are using that as a thinly-veiled excuse to cheat your own rules?"

"No."

"Had to ask."

I Giveth and I Taketh Away

Misinformation negatively affects a person's learning in multiple ways. Remember the early equation $t_1+s_1 = 5$. We saw how t_1 and s_1 impacted each other, making their numbers greater. When there is conflicting information (one or more cause-and-effect experiences that seem to be at odds with one another), then the opposite tends to happen in one's mind/body. The numbers actually become smaller.

Say that a person has a negative experience x and a positive experience y. x = -3 because it was misinformation (misinterpreted and thus false cause and effect). y = 4 because it was a positive experience (actual cause and effect). Theoretically, those two experiences together would equal one (x + y = 1).

However, the experiences (memories) actually impact one another. Just as discussed in the chapter on change and trees, a previous experience often has greater weight because it occurred first. Therefore, the experience is closer to a person's core (platform). Even worse, that first experience was false, so then it could have been used as part of the person's platform in the "decision-making" or as a cause in the actions that a person has taken in the past. We know that causes affect the effects and thus the effects become more causes to the platform because effects are generally absorbed back into the machine as cause-and-effect experiences. What this means is that the negative experience gets mixed in with the soup of reality, and everything gets messed up.

This is sad. What this also means is that when we input part of the equation $x + y$, instead of getting 1, we might actually get -1 or 0. This is because they might have changed the x from a -3 to a -2. Since the x came first and is part of the person's current rule/platform, it will tend to have a greater influence in the relationship between x and y, so it decreased y from 4 to 2. Thus, instead of having the equation $x(-3) + y(4) = 1$, you have instead $x(-2) + y(2) = 0$.

Some platforms or rules are easier to change than others. Take into account the following three examples where each individual number within the parenthesis is an individual memory that directly influences the entire experience (under the same rule).

> Example A: Cumulative experience is 50 (-100, +25, +25, +25, +50, +25).
>
> Example B: Cumulative experience is 50 (+25, -1, -1, -1, -1, -1, +15, +15).
>
> Example C: Cumulative experience is 50 (+10, +10, +10, +10, +10).

You can see that Example A would be at a total of 150 if not for the one experience (-100) that is holding the subject back from learning or understanding a concept. A lot of times, people have a single, powerful memory (experience of cause and effect) that is mislabeled (under the wrong rule) or just misunderstood (by the senses) and is holding them back from understanding a concept. If one were teaching someone with a similar catalogue of information such as Example A, then it would be a matter of getting that person to unlearn or forget or just change their mindset when it comes to that the single, large, negative experience. If I were to teach someone and the subject matter for the individual is the Example B from above, then I might even ignore the -1's because once a person gets enough information and the rule becomes solidified, then those -1's will probably just fall away.

It is often beneficial for someone who is advanced in a given topic to go back over the basics of any discipline to remove the negative information or memories that don't belong. This can lead to a clearer understanding of a topic. Take Example C, which is mainly for comparison. The strategy for learning/changing/forming a rule would be different for Example C than for, say, Example A because there isn't a chunk of misinformation to dispel. It would be a similar strategy to Example B.

In the world of atomic particles, you have positive charges, negative charges, and neutral charges. This is how causality works in real life. You have things that are positive and negative, yet rarely things that have no causation. A neutral charge is a charge waiting to become positive or negative at a later time. This is similar to how causation takes time to be actualized. If you have two charges (one positive and one negative) and "step back" from those charges, then the overall charge from the two will be a combination of them. If the positive charge is far stronger than the negative, then the whole thing will appear positive.

Atoms and charges exist in the mind. This is cool.

People can often have a true experience but place the experience in the folder of the wrong rule or even platform. Later on, a person can gain more experiences and realize that they mislabeled that previous experience. When this happens, they take the mislabeled memory out of one platform and use it to create another rule or platform. This also may change the balance (in a good way) to the previous platform that was out-of-balance or had confusion in it (due to the mislabeled experience). This is cool because you are changing two rules or platforms simultaneously.

I love these kinds of learning moments both in myself and in students. I love seeing the change this has in people when they "put things together" and "get it." This is one reason why I enjoy teaching.

Put the Thingamajig in the Doohickey

No, this isn't some strange sexual reference. Imagine that you are walking into an office building and you see a long, drawn-out formula explaining jet propulsion with regards to a newly-designed rocket built with the intent of taking people to Mars. Is the formula that you are looking at accurate or is it flawed? If you are in the majority of people who are reading this book, then you don't have a freak'n clue whether it is good or bad because you don't do rocket science.

This shouldn't be a strange phenomenon related to this book. I'm sure you've heard phrases that express this concept before, such as the following: "You don't know what you don't know," "I have no clue what is going on," and "I can't tell the difference." One difficulty with learning and understanding is that it can be extremely difficult for someone to begin learning an area of knowledge when it is completely new to them. This is because they don't have enough knowledge to know the difference between factual or fake information as it pertains to the subject. It takes time and trust (of people or source material) to begin the learning process.

It is extremely difficult for a student to figure out what experiences are positive or negative (real or fake) if they haven't had enough experiences to form solid rules and make a platform in their mind. This is another reason why it is so important to have a good teacher and/or resource to obtain knowledge. It is also the reason why the student needs to be honest with the teacher with regards to what they know and don't know. The student needs to communicate to the teacher what they believe to be true and *why*. That way the teacher, who already has the rules and platforms down (and thus the view from the platform), can then help the student figure out what information belongs and what doesn't belong.

Teachers are extremely useful for filing memories and experiences away and can accelerate a student's ability to form rules and platforms.

Remember the previous example where an experience from trusted person t_1 enhanced the self-experience s_1 and together they impacted one another to get a higher cumulative experience? When a teacher validates an experience that a student has by saying something to the effect of "That is correct," "That's the way that is done," or "That is exactly right," or any combination of those, then they are enhancing that learning experience and giving it more weight than if the person had done the same actions by themselves.

In physical sparring, getting hit can have a similar effect. The instant cause-and-effect feedback helps one learn quickly. Perhaps this understanding of forming rules and platforms can help you. Sometimes education is adding new information, and sometimes it is letting go of bad information. Some say math is everything, and some say they don't know.

How can we take advantage of the knowledge of validation and how it enhances experiences and helps us learn faster? We can self-validate. Thanks to the wonders of technology, you can video or record yourself and then analyze your actions alongside those of someone who is an expert or master in whatever skill you are trying to gain. You can be your own teacher. This only works if you are honest with yourself. Being honest means giving an accurate description of the causality when judging yourself. Again, we see that causality leads to positive changes in one's life.

There are a lot of people claiming to have medical knowledge. Many of these people espouse their medical knowledge and/or beliefs through various mediums: TV, the internet, lectures, and so on. A problem occurs often, and it is very similar to a student who doesn't have the platform or rules required to know whether or not a cause-and-effect experience is positive or negative with regards to learning the truth (actual causality) about the topic that they want to study (in the paragraph before). The problem is that viewers do not have the necessary rules/platform to understand what is going on when they absorb stimuli into their memories.

I would assume, based on my experience, that the overwhelming majority of people who watch medical advice TV shows do not have the rules and platform in place to know if what they are being told is true or if it is just lies meant to control them or sell them a product. This is the downside to the internet where virtually anyone can make videos that claim to have real knowledge when in actuality there is no correlating cause and effect in the real world. The solution to ignorance is not more ignorance and belief. It is gaining actual knowledge. Gaining knowledge to better understand things is difficult and it takes time, but is totally worth the investment.

Ignorance is ~~bliss~~ ignorance. What is actually happening when someone doesn't understand or flat out ignores information? Let's explore some examples. I'm guilty of the following error. There have been times where I thought I had obtained 150-experience for a given topic. Then, when someone would begin to talk about the topic, I would get bored and turn my brain off. The reality is that I was actually at a 75 and the other 75 was actually a -75. I didn't realize that the -75 was wrong information, so I assumed it was right. When I did this, I actually ruined my view of reality twice. Once with my wrong assumption that I understand something when I did not and again when I failed to take in new experiences that would help clear up my misconceptions. It is a hard skill to keep one's brain engaged and open to absorbing more information.

If I'm lucky, then I do the above mistake out of ignorance. There are other times, though, when it is self-ordained ignorance or an ego problem such as an imbalance of wanting to be right. Suppose I believe that I have 150-experience and have an artificial rule in place. Then someone gives me information that part of me knows is directly related to that rule, but that would mean that several memories/experiences that make up the 150 are actually negative instead of positive. They don't fit with the rule as it exists. If I accept the new cause-and-effect information as true, then my overall understanding of said rule would go from 150 down to 90 or 40 or 10 or maybe 0. It depends how bad I was dis-illusioned.

It is hard to admit one was "wrong," but given that we are victims of the senses available to us as well as our own memories, then we shouldn't be upset. When one realizes they don't have free will, then the first illusion that falls is the "big ego." When one lets go of the ego, learning becomes so much easier, as you can see from the math above. Being respectful and showing a little humility is a purposeful way of opening one's mind to accepting new experiences. This is why respectful students learn faster. Generally, they have a more open mind. Having an open mind means you are willing to truly take in more cause-and-effect memories and absorb them into your memories that comprise your rules and thus your platform. You are open to change. You learn, you grow, you are happy.

Imagine the opposite: a child who has decided that a food tastes bad when they have never tasted it before. It doesn't make any sense, especially if they haven't smelled the food in question. Based on the platforms of this book, how would you describe such a situation with a child?

Consider the common phrase *Practice makes perfect*. Do you believe that? If someone spends a lot of time trying to gain knowledge that falls within a specific rule but the experiences are not all positive, then there are really three options. If a person leaves the "true path" (actual cause/effect /positive experience that will lead to competency), then they may actually be getting worse. They might have some positive and negative experiences and could stay very close to the same. Lastly, they could actually be improving.

Positive practice makes not perfect but *better*. That makes more sense to me. It is very important for a teacher to know where a student is at in their learning. If they don't have the basic "rules" down, then for some students it might be best if they just don't practice. They might be better off if they only train when the teacher is there to make sure they don't go off the path and get lost somewhere in the jungle of negative experiences. Only when a student understands the rules are they ready to practice specific things.

And only when they have enough rules to combine into a platform are they ready to combine aspects of training. If someone wants to obtain perfection with regards to a certain skill or knowledge, then how does one do that? Any flaw in the training would give someone experiences that subtract from perfection. One, therefore, needs to have perfect practice and experiences in order to reach perfection.

Learning Difficulties Part 1: Senses

There are various factors that affect a person's ability to form rules and platforms. A human being can learn faster or slower for many reasons. When someone uses generalities—like saying that a person is just "more intelligent" or "naturally gifted"—they may be right. However, I want to get past outliers and instead argue over the "grey majority" that exists in the meat of the bell curve. There is a lot of causality that impacts an individual's ability to learn. Having a slight difference between otherwise identical individuals can result in dramatically different results. Again, a different cause equals a different effect.

I'm going to start with the easiest to understand: the impact of one's senses when it comes to learning. Our experiences and memories (the basic building blocks of who we are) are obtained through the machine which is a combination of all of our available senses. Absorbing through our senses is the first step in the process that continues into filing away memories, creating rules, and forming platforms. Everything we experience is experienced through our senses. For the examples below we are going to assume that "everything" else is *exactly equal* but for the one sensory aspect that we are changing.

Two ways that I want to discuss variations of senses are as follows: The first is an imbalance of the senses (when someone has superior or inferior senses) and the impact that has on learning. Imagine a person with poor eyesight who is wearing their glasses versus the same exact person without their glasses. The second imbalance of the senses is when someone simply has more or less of their senses available to them. This could be the difference between your sitting down and watching a movie without sound and your watching a movie with the sound turned on. Then imagine that you are standing on the movie set during the filming. If you are physically there, then you have more senses to take in your surroundings.

If we combine the previously discussed aspect of senses (the way we absorb cause and effect), then we can see how the senses can influence a person's ability to learn faster or slower than others. Imagine that Bob is a person who wears glasses. When he wears glasses, he has amazing vision, and without the glasses on, his vision is bad. Bob wants to learn a new physical skill. He doesn't have his glasses on. Since his vision isn't as good, Bob won't be getting as much specific feedback from each individual experience with his eyes. He may need to experience something ten or twenty times before he has enough experience to form a rule.

If Bob is wearing glasses, then he might get the same amount of information in one or two experiences. Here is how I view this through math. Bob watches an instructor do an activity that he is trying to understand. Bob needs a conceptual 20 experience to form a rule. Every time he watches the instructor demonstrate what they are doing, he gains 2 experience without his glasses and 10 experience with his glasses. One can see that it would take 10 times watching the instructor to get the same amount of experience without his glasses as two times of watching the instructor with his glasses on. More accurate and attuned senses lead to more causality and understanding.

Here are two facts: Adults' senses fade over time, and adults learn slower as they get older. This section explained how that works.

Sometimes less senses can lead to short-term success (quickly forming rules) but long-term frustrations (because they don't have as many experiences/memories and rules supporting the platform). Take two individuals who are playing a game together. The first person is experiencing the game with their eyes. If the first person is relying only on one sense, then they may be able to quickly categorize the memories and thus form rules quickly. Less causality means less complexity, and so rules are formed easier and faster. Less complexity and less causality also mean that a person won't have as much information, and they will form fewer rules. Their overall knowledge of causality in the game will be less.

The first person's experience using only one sense will mean that their knowledge might not be as in depth as it could be. More senses equal more causality experienced. Person two is using not just their eyes but, say, another seven senses. It may take them longer to form rules because they are taking in far more cause and effect at any given time. Again, more senses mean more complexity. However, when the snow-globe of stimuli finally settles, then person two will have a far greater understanding of the game than person one.

If they are playing against each other, then I would expect the following outcome: Person one will form rules sooner than person two and will pull ahead, giving them an early lead. Then, depending on how "visually heavy" the game is, person two may or may not catch up. I would suspect that, depending on the exact nature of the game and given that all other things being equal between the two players, in the future player two would win, whether it be the next time or after ten more games (depending on how complex the rest of the stimuli are and how good person two is at forming rules and having a complete platform of the game). This assumes also that sensory deprivation is not a positive. Some situations may require sensory deprivation (or being able to just focus on what is truly important), such as a soldier's ability to tune out extra stimuli in combat and just focus on the mission and what they need to do to win the fight.

It is easier to understand a situation through a myopic viewpoint or from a limited perspective, but it won't be as accurate an experience. It is through that logic that shortcuts like "dumbing situations down" is just a bad idea. Yes, more people will be able to understand that point of view, and yes it will be less factual. It will be wrong compared to the full explanation of causality.

People often talk about the connection between body and mind. This section is just one way of explaining an aspect of the connection.

The gradual degradation of a human being's senses is a gradual departure from reality. As a human being gets older, they begin to leave the world long before they actually are gone.

Learning Difficulties Part 2: Problems with Platforms; and Trust, Both Internal and External

Another reason we shouldn't judge people based on who they are in a specific moment is because a person isn't who they are at any one time of their life. Some people have a weakness in one of the many platforms that they operate in. A profound weakness in a certain area of their life may be seen as a disorder. This could be a person's platform that they slip into when they begin eating or anything, really. Sometimes people have difficulty due to a warp in their platform when it comes to learning. Perhaps a person has fears or anxiety because of negative experiences in their past which lead to their learning platform becoming tainted by fear whenever they morph into whenever they try to learn something new. People end up with unnecessary aversions to future experiences in specific areas of their life because of this reasoning.

Some people may appear to learn slowly because they need a lot of memories (cause-and-effect experiences) before they feel comfortable forming a rule out of it. Unlike the sensory issues in the last section, this one is due to a person's platform. A person with such a base or platform (depending on how deep this rule runs) will typically be more cautious. Another individual who is less cautious may be able to form a rule out of just a couple of examples.

I can see pros and cons to both. The intelligent/wise learner will be able to discern between situations where it is OK to make rules out of just a few examples and when one should gather more data before making rules. This is another reason why, *on the surface*, it takes some people three memories/examples to understand something, whereas it might take another person ten memories/examples to understand the same idea. The extra experience is due to a person's inability to accept and absorb the experience into their platform.

Here is some basic math to explain what I mean. Let's say that if this person didn't have an aversion to a certain platform of experiences, then they would typically get 5 experience every time they engaged in a task. After five sessions, they would have 25 experience with no validation between experiences. Let's assume that the difficulty of this task means they will need 20 experience to make a rule. If someone is confident in their training, then the validation increases, and so they would probably hit the 20-experience mark after maybe just three sessions.

However, this section isn't about someone who is confident. It is about someone who is extremely cautious or insecure. The normal experience would typically be 5 every time a person has a session or a single experience. A person who doesn't have trust in their own senses or in the information of the instructor reduces each experience from 5 to a 2 (for the sake of understanding). One could say, well, due to math, with validation those 2's might actually be more like 3's or 4's. However, such might not be the case. Things get even worse for someone who doesn't trust their experiences. Not only is each experience weighed less (down to 2 instead of 5), but they may have resistance to making rules, and so their experiences don't end up validating each other. A "2-experience session" remains a "2." This is sad.

Normally, a person doesn't generally feel comfortable when they don't have enough experience to form a rule. Then, when a person gains enough memories/experience to form a rule, the person now feels confident. That would be the normal way of things. When someone has a severe disorder of confidence in themselves or knowledge that they are receiving, then it can cause a bigger mental blockage. They could have 30 sessions of 2 experience equaling 60 experience total. That is three times the experience needed to form the rule (20 experience). The person might, however, be refusing to form said rule anyway. This is sad.

Where are the areas in your life where you have mental blocks and aversions that are limiting you?

If you are overly cautious (as described above), then that means that you aren't truly trusting in some aspect of the experience:

1. Your ability to absorb information through your senses.

2. The information from the source or teacher.

3. Both of the above.

4. A combination of 1, 2, 3, and another causality.

5. Causality not mentioned in 1, 2, 3, 4.

It also means that you are putting up invisible barriers to your own learning. If the problem is the senses, then focus on improving one's senses.

What if the problem is the information from the source or teacher? When you come to someone and wish to learn, you can help the learning process by purposely "lowering your guard" and trust that the individual teaching you has good information (actual causality). You can tell yourself that you are "ready to learn and willing to accept whatever your teacher tells you as absolute fact." It makes zero sense to resist learning when you are trying to learn. If you don't trust the competency and knowledge of your teacher or source material, then why are you going to them for your education in the first place?

If you are learning from a member of a cult or someone who espouses fantasy, then *please completely disregard* the previous paragraph. The one who is teaching you should demonstrate rationality, science, logic, and, through all of them, causality.

Learning Difficulties Part 3: Belief and Keeping Ego in Check

"Believe in yourself." When you believe in yourself, you trust yourself and your senses and thus accept the experience you are taking in as being reality. This is opposite of the resistance in Part 2. If you believe in yourself, then you make rules faster (granted they might be more likely to be wrong). Still, a lot of people have problems trusting and believing in themselves, so it is probably a good idea to tip the scale in the other direction. We now see how believing in oneself actually makes a difference in learning and one's ability.

Unfortunately, there are all sorts of imbalances, ego-related problems, and different personality issues that people have. Me included. People are "full of themselves" when they don't have enough experience to form a rule and yet lie to themselves and artificially inflate their confidence as if they had the experience for the rule. When people who are "full of themselves" act upon few memories but don't yet have enough for a rule or even a stable platform, then those people are "bullshitting." When people have a few rules but don't have a platform and yet pretend that they have the platform or several platforms (meaning a higher level of competency), then they are inflating the appearance of their competency. This is also being dishonest.

Not having enough knowledge can make a person feel inadequate. When a person has to make a decision based on a lack of knowledge, then they can feel stressed or afraid. Adding in an unhealthy amount of ego in such situations doesn't solve the actual problem: a lack of knowledge. People end up sabotaging themselves when they have a rule or two and lie to themselves or to others by pretending to have a great platform.

It is also bad when a person overestimates their knowledge and believes that they have concrete rules of a solid platform when, in actuality, they do not. A person's ego can sometimes try to fill in the gap created by ignorance. This only creates more ignorance. It is also bad when a person believes they have rules/platforms and does not. When a person doesn't understand clearly whether they have just memories, rules, or even a platform, their ego usually is unhealthily involved. These are all things to look out for in others, as well as in oneself.

The old phrase "To thine own self be true" is insanely critical to understanding the world. If one lies to oneself, then one becomes the first victim. This is why it is so important to discern true cause and effect from the false. This is why it is important to not only understand reality but also to accept it for whatever it is.

Don't Fear Learning

Many people become afraid of learning once they learn just how deep down the sea of causality goes in a given area of knowledge. If I tell you that you have to spend ten minutes today practicing an instrument, then, for most people, that is "doable." If I tell you that for you to be good, you'll have to practice for ten thousand minutes, then that seems daunting, and people will quit before they have even begun the journey.

Learning something basic is just a step or two past where you are at the beginning of a journey. Learning something that is advanced may seem impossible to a beginner. However, once you train for a while, that advanced knowledge will be just another step past where you'll be at when you are ready to learn that piece of knowledge. Everything is just one more step from where you are at.

Going from 1 to 2 is just a matter of adding 1. Going from 1,000 to 1,001 is just a matter of adding 1. This is one way to look at learning. I go back to the difficulty of learning how to read. If you drop *Macbeth* in front of a four-year-old, then they might not have any chance of reading it. Learning to read *Macbeth* first requires one to learn each letter of the alphabet. Once one is done with that stage, they begin forming words, then sentences and so on until eventually reading *Macbeth* is just like reading another book. This is how learning works.

I'm not saying there aren't any difficulties or roadblocks along the way. I'm saying that you shouldn't be afraid simply because a task seems complex. All knowledge in a given subject is simply a tall ladder formed of causality. Every rung you climb is another experience you gain. Eventually, those experiences add up and make rules, and then you start to form your own platform. You keep climbing the ladder and gain more and more examples of causality until you reach the top.

You Don't Know All of Who You Are

Beyond our current understanding of our biological base (who we are when created), we also don't understand everything that has impacted us after our birth. Our senses are constantly engaged. Therefore, we are in a constant state of learning almost all of the time. This constant state of absorbing stimuli into our memories and forming rules and platforms means that we are influenced by events that we don't even realize. There is so much stimuli (causes from our past), and we don't remember or understand the effect that they have had on us.

This is bad and good. The bad aspect is the ignorance. The good aspect is that you are always in a state of learning. So if you want to learn to do something, then start doing it. If you want to be a different version of yourself (the one you have in your mind, your goal), then start doing things that that person would do, and you'll get there.

Self-Efficacy and Becoming a Superhuman

How much can we change ourselves by belief?

I can't lie to myself. The cognitive dissonance is too much, and it ruins the experience. I have to be able to rationalize something into reality so it is actually real for me.

If "an experience" that a person has is controlled largely by themselves and the experience changes them, then that person can be in control of their destiny. Or rather, we are in control of our destiny. Does it matter if the experience is real or not if it changes us nonetheless? So how far can we go in changing ourselves?

The fact is that that input and experiences affect us greatly. The more *real* to us, the more it affects us. Does the experience need to be true? Or does our mind just have to believe it is true? If so, can virtual reality have the same impact on our lives as a real-life experience if we get to a point where we no longer are able to tell the difference? And if that is the case, and virtual reality can change who we are at the core level, then does something have to be true at all in order to change us? If we accept something as our reality, and even if it isn't "true," can we still use it to change ourselves in reality? If we think it is true, does it become true?

No, it doesn't. But does it change us? Yes. Do we have the ability to change who we are at the very core? Yes. Do we have the ability to change the world? Yes. All we have to do is to *know* that it is real, that it is possible.

Don't just believe in yourself. Know and trust in yourself.

You understand the true power of humans. You understand "magic."

What are you waiting for?

During a summer in my late teen years, I was spending time shadowing a child with autism. He was gripping onto a ladder at the side of the pier leading out into the lake and told me that he wanted to swim to the center of the lake because there was a floating trampoline there. He wanted so badly to swim to the trampoline and knew he would be so happy if he jumped on it. The only problem was that he was afraid to let go of the side of the pier. He was stuck to that ladder. I told him that the only way he would be able to get to that floating trampoline was if he let go of the ladder first.

You can't become the person you want to be if you are holding onto things that prevent you from becoming that person.

People get to a place of comfort in their life. In that comfort is great sadness because they aren't the person that they want to be. They have become complacent. I want to challenge you personally to let go of the comforts that are holding you back- keeping you from growing.

>Don't be afraid.

>You may be lost when you let go of the dock.

>Don't be afraid.

>You may not know where to swim to next.

>Don't be afraid.

>You may want to reach out and go back to the dock.

>Don't be afraid.

>Let go.

>Swim.

It may be a belief holding you back. You might say, "But, if I leave the religious group, then I won't know what to say at a funeral or what I should feel, or how to raise my children." You may be in a bad relationship. "But if I leave this person, what will I do? Who will love me? Will I be single forever? What will I do financially? What will my friends think?"

Acting a certain way to appease others is a self-inflicted prison sentence. You may have a miserable job and say, "But I don't know what I'll do if I leave this job?" or "I'll be homeless; I'll starve to death," or "What if...what if...what if." Maybe you aren't held prisoner by what you are doing but rather by what you aren't doing. You may be filling up your day, every day, in order to block yourself from having the free time you need to accomplish your goals and dreams. Those goals and dreams are waiting for you.

When you let go of your comfort, you won't know where to go—you may be lost, but I want to encourage you to risk it all for happiness. To find yourself. To become yourself.

I get annoyed when people say they want to change and yet they aren't willing to let go of who they were to become who they want to be. You need to want to change more than you want to hold onto your previous self. You won't just randomly change. Use the power of causality to change yourself.

The person I get annoyed with the most is, of course, myself.

False Claims About Causality and Confusion of Causality

Be careful of false cause and effects. When people argue, it is always about cause and effect—even if they do not realize it is. If a person is arguing, they might blame a certain cause for an undesirable effect. They may pick one cause of many that together actually cause a problem, or one cause that tends to occur when enough causes together create an effect, but that cause may not in fact be a catalyst for that effect.

Take this example: Ice cream keeps melting on days when people are putting on sunscreen. So therefore, sunscreen is the cause of ice cream melting. FALSE! When it is hot outside, the sun is usually out, and the sun is the cause of both people putting on sunscreen as well as the ice cream melting. The two are not directly related (cause and effect) to each other.

Quick aside to further support my way of thinking: Why do people put on sunscreen? Think about it from a cause-and-effect point of view. It is obvious that people fear the sun because the sun is the cause of the sunburn. *Why* does that exist? Is that a rule or a memory? A rule. The memory might be when a person remembers a time where they were in pain. They now have a fear of having that pain (sunburn in this case) again. Pain is a powerful cause that causes people to put on sunscreen. The sense of "pain" is one that is intense and thus creates intense memories. Pain from an evolutionary standpoint puts memories at the forefront of our platforms.

In addition to all that, a person has many past cause-and-effect memories of the relationship between being out in sunlight and how their body felt when they got sunburns. The experiences formed rules. Rules like *Don't be outside for a very long time in the sun without protection from the sun.* That rule becomes part of their platform. Their platform determines how they interact with the world, what they do. It is the causation to their action of putting on sunscreen.

The second example is when one might put weight on one of multiple causes for an effect. In actuality, the cause may be part of the effect (desired or not), but even so, it is not the sole cause or even the direct cause of an event. Take an example of someone who tells you a rule like, "Earth is the cause of mud." They try to validate it in two ways. First, they give a similar rule, and second they give a specific memory related to the rules: "Without Earth, one doesn't have mud," and then "Every time I have seen mud, it has been where the earth was!" All of those supporting rules/memories are true.

However, the initial rule claims that "Earth is the cause of mud." That is a misrepresentation of causality. It isn't true because, without water being added to earth, one doesn't get mud. Is Earth to blame in every instance for mud? If there is a mudslide, is it therefore the fault of the Earth that exists or the heavy rain that happened the night before? Let's say we don't want to be the victim of a mudslide. What would we do? Can we make it not rain? Not really, but we can do landscaping to a mountainside, we can move roads and infrastructure. This is partially how I view violence in society and handling issues that are currently part of the media at this period of time such as firearms.

It Could Be Worse—It Could Also Be *Way* Better

One argument that annoys me is the "It could be worse" argument. I'm sure you know what this is unless you are like three years old, in which case kudos for being able to read this book. The "It could be worse" argument is where a person is doing something (an effect), and when someone asks them why they are doing that effect, they give an answer that has nothing to do with the cause of that effect. One cannot draw any logical lines between the following:

1. The action (effect) they are engaged in.

2. The excuse, or cause, that they claim is the reason for doing that action.

What I mean by logical lines is this: Understand the cause-and-effect relationship between the events. Most of the time the "It could be worse" argument comes up when a person is doing something in opposition to someone's morality/goals (which is of course based on a platform, whether it be their personal platform or a societal platform/point of view). The effect in question could be a simple mistake, something stupid, or an action that is just immoral. This way of talking or arguing is dishonest because they should "know better" (have at least a basic platform of causality) to understand that the causation doesn't equal the effect. Yet they still give a dishonest reason for doing what they are doing.

One extreme example of the "It could be worse" argument is as follows: Jim walks up to Bob who is standing there with a bloody foot and a gun in his hand. Jim says, "Hi, Bob. Why did you shoot yourself in the foot? That isn't good for your health." Bob can then reply in any number of ways: "Well, you are right, Jim, but at least I didn't shoot myself in the heart," or

"I did shoot myself in the foot, but it was a really small bullet." This sounds ridiculous—and it is. The real-life examples tend to be sneakier and less obvious, but more obvious now that you've read most of my book. I have used the stupid illogic myself: "Well, I know drinking this milkshake isn't good for my diet, but at least I am drinking the 'small' size."

Cool fact: The more intelligent a person is, the better they are at creating bullshit reasons for why they do stupid things. Just say no. Don't do drugs and stupid stuff, kids. There you have it: the book's official PSA moment.

False Causality

Another way of lying to oneself is what I call *false causes*. This is when you pretend that an event (cause) has an impact (effect) on you when actually it doesn't. I'm even more guilty of "false causes" than the "It could be worse" argument. When struggling to write a book, I'll put up barriers (false causes) such as

- "The weather is really bad today."

- "I'm not focused so I won't write."

- "My back hurts—I think I'll write tomorrow."

- "I had a weird dream last night so I won't write."

- "I'll wait until I have a vacation from work and an entire month to sit in a cabin, and then the conditions will be *perfect* for me to write my book."

While some of the causes listed above might have a slight effect on my ability to write, the reality is that none of the "causes" listed above actually prevent me from being able to sit down and write. Did I really think that the weather was preventing me from sitting down and typing? Maybe if the power was out, but in reality, no. Conditions are never perfect. Life is never perfect. Those who say that "Life is perfect" don't know what they are talking about. You are not perfect and neither am I. Let's just agree to move on.

Don't try to be perfect. Try to be *better*.

Moving a Knight: False Rules and Boundaries

Here is one example that might help you distinguish causality from fantasy in certain situations. If something is a game or sport, then it has rules. These are not like the actual rules of causality but rather rules that were "made up." These rules are a fantasy. It is a fantasy that those "who agree to join the game" believe together. Let's consider the "game" of chess. If you know the rules of chess, then you know how to move the pieces. You know that a knight moves in an "L" shape (either two squares horizontally followed by one square vertically or two squares vertically followed by one square horizontally).

Just like the example with false barriers and the reality that none of them were physically stopping me from sitting down and working on my writing, so too do no actual rules or laws of physics, science, or causality prevent one from moving a knight in any way that they wish. One can take the knight and move the knight five squares in one line. Someone could move the knight outside the border of the chess board or throw it across the room. The rules in place are thus only true if people believe in the game.

False rules and barriers are everywhere. It is fine if someone understands that the false rules and barriers are existing in a game or fantasy movie. The problem is when people mix false with true, belief with reality. Religion is an obvious example. This idea can be extrapolated to many different things.

Combat: People talk about various kinds of cage fighting and how it is one hundred percent like real combat. If it was like real life, then there wouldn't be any rules. The rules imposed make something fantasy. In a cage fight, if you take someone to the ground, their friends don't jump on you, beat you up, and then kill you.

Borders: There is nothing technically stopping a person from physically living in another part of the world. Borders, countries, and the laws made up by countries are all barriers to humanity. They exist as rules without causation. Actual causation would be like a border being a steep cliff. If you were to cross the border (walk off the cliff), then you would die. One doesn't need rules because causation is in effect. When people make their own causation, then they are enforcing their platform on other people. They are in forcing their fantasy and artificially-constructed rules on others. I find the act of doing so to be immoral. Why? Deviating from actual causality is immoral.

Ought Versus Is

The *ought-versus-is argument* is based on a reality *with* the assumption that free will is true while simultaneously maintaining an assumption of a world *without* causality, fatalism and determinism, and so it is wrong in two ways. The first reason why the argument doesn't work in reality is because it is first based on a fantasy and the second is because it doesn't account for reality. Other than that, it makes a lot of sense.

The basic argument of *ought versus is* is "just because you understand how things *are* doesn't mean that you know how you *should* behave." This implies that one can't get morality from science or understanding. This book claims the contrary, so prepare to load up your philosophical guns with causality magazines, courtesy of yours truly!

You can't have morality without understanding science. Understanding how the world works and what will happen due to causality are a prerequisite to true morality. Morality without understanding is wishing and dreaming. Taking action without knowing what will happen is not moral. The "fantasy claim" called "ought versus is" wants you to believe that understanding the world doesn't tell you how you should behave. The *reality* is that your understanding of the world *makes you behave* in every single way that you behave. You take action based on your understanding your platform. Having the knowledge of what is real will change how you react. To take action based on fantasy is thus the opposite direction of morality. Science is the first step to morality.

People often argue about what action to take, or what to believe without first trying to understand how things are. They are missing a crucial step. You can't talk about morality before first understanding reality. The *Ought versus Is* argument doesn't work because one must first understand what "is" *before* you can discuss what one "ought" to do.

Imagine that before you are two buttons and you have to press one of them. One is blue and the other is red. I ask you, "Which button *should* you press?" The logical reply would be, "What would happen if I were to press each button?" This is logical because you would be acknowledging a cause-and-effect relationship between pressing the button and what would happen thereafter. If nothing happens when you press the buttons, then it doesn't really matter which button you press.

Suppose I tell you that if you press the red button, a rock the size of my fist will fall out of the sky at a height of 100 meters above ground level. Then I tell you that if you press the blue button, a boulder the size of a house will fall out of the sky at a height of 100 meters above ground level. Armed with the knowledge of what *is* you might be inclined to make a decision or take action and press one of the buttons. However, if you ask for more causation, then I could say, "If you press the red button, then the fist-sized rock will fall above a heavily populated city. If you press the blue button, then the house-sized boulder will fall in the middle of a barren desert." In this example, we can see that the knowledge of what *is* is a precursor (or should be a precursor) to the decision made.

Today in politics and other areas of life, we are asked to press one figurative button or another, or support the pressing of a blue button or a red button. In fact, there are people who are urging you right now to "press a button." People are obsessed with action without knowledge. I hear things such as "just vote." It would be far more logical to urge people to understand a situation and gather knowledge. That way, when it comes time for them to "press a button" or cast a ballot, they might have a better idea of the consequences of such actions. Getting excited and telling people to just press buttons is flat-out stupid. What I am asking you to do is to step back and figure out the causation behind pressing buttons before actually pressing them.

Ought versus is in fact represents two different questions, where the *Ought* is dependent on the *is*. With that being said, I'm going to take my loaded philosophical guns and hide in a bunker while I wait for the fantasy fallout.

Dumb Arguments: If Not Red, Then It *Must* Be Blue!

There is a stupid piece of reasoning that I hear very often. Recently I was surprised to hear it coming from someone intelligent during a public interview. This is how this sad excuse for logic works:

1. Imagine that I'm thinking of a number.

2. I tell you that the number is not 1.

3. You tell me that it must be the 2.

Does this "logic" make any sense to you? It doesn't make any sense to me. Obviously, this isn't true. There is an infinite choice of numbers that the number I'm thinking of could be if it isn't 1.

Real life doesn't usually have such variation like infinity in the example above. Allow me to steelman this argument to show you how dumb this sad excuse for causality is. Suppose I'm thinking of a color and I tell you that it isn't the color red. You tell me, well, if you aren't thinking of red, then you *have* to be thinking of the color blue. Here there are fewer possible examples of what color I could be thinking of. The logic is just as dumb because there is no correlation between the cause and the effect. Ruling out one option doesn't imply that another option has to be true. This should remind you of the "us versus them" argument back in the chapter on greyscales. "If you aren't with us, then you *must* be against us." It's the same illogical BS.

I should say that someone might be correct in their assumption of what a person is doing, but the way they are arguing the case, that is, their reasoning, is totally stupid. In fact, these assumptions make little to no sense. However, I hear arguments like this all the time.

Here are two recently that I've heard. If people are given UBI (universal basic income), then they are going to spend their days getting high. This assumes that if they are not at a regular eight-to-five job every day that they must be doing drugs. I'm sure that there is a certain percentage of the population who would do that. Taking that into account, one can still see how stupid such an argument is.

Another time I heard the same stupid argument was when a person told me that if I didn't believe in their god or worship in the way they were worshipping, then the *only* other thing that I could possibly be doing was worshipping the devil or believing in other fake stuff. The other fantasy stuff they accused me of doing was infinitely more like the BS that they were espousing rather than anything I actually do in reality.

Those are two examples of where a person assumes the effect based on some information. The ruling out of one effect doesn't determine another effect. Causes determine effects. The claim being made is that not doing one effect (someone's religion) means an implied cause, and then I must be doing another effect—Satan worship, or leprechaun worship, or whatever.

This fallacy can also be done in reverse: that is, when someone doesn't understand the cause of an effect and so they assume it must be a certain cause even though there are perhaps an infinite number of other causes it could actually be. Sometimes a person doesn't understand how a cause or multiple causes create an effect. Instead of admitting that they do not understand, or try to figure out how that effect was created, they will instead make up a cause (like God or something else). I don't understand why people are getting sick and dying, so it *must* be a curse. I don't understand how lightning occurs, so it must be a god who is angry. There are many examples of these two situations. Whether a person is assuming the cause or assuming the effect, they are flat out wrong.

> You can't have reality without causality.

This is just something to look out for and flag it when you hear it being spoken. Just know that it isn't a good argument. If they do try to throw some numbers in to make it sound more complicated and hide how stupid the argument is, then ask yourself if the numbers are truly representative of the whole or just an outlier to try to push their agenda.

Arguing Past Each Other

If two people are arguing about an exact situation, then one of them is right and one is wrong. Those situations are easier to understand. There is however, another argumentative situation that arises known as *arguing past each other*. What I find so interesting about seeing people argue past each other is (1) they don't realize that they are doing so, and (2) it happens so often.

When people get upset with one another for arguing, then it is just stupid. When people argue past each other, then confusion often arises because confusion is a lack of understanding causality. In the best of situations, two people are arguing and both are giving actual examples of causality, meaning that no one is lying, and they are both giving factual information.

Many times, people begin arguing, and they aren't even talking about the same subject. This can be because of ignorance on either part or simply a miscommunication with words. Whatever the case, if you find yourself in a conversation where you realize that you aren't talking about the same thing, then you should stop immediately and discuss definitions and terms before you begin. This is time-consuming, but it is better than simply wasting time talking about different things.

For the Love of Arguing

Look at the splendor of my argument-analyzing flowchart!

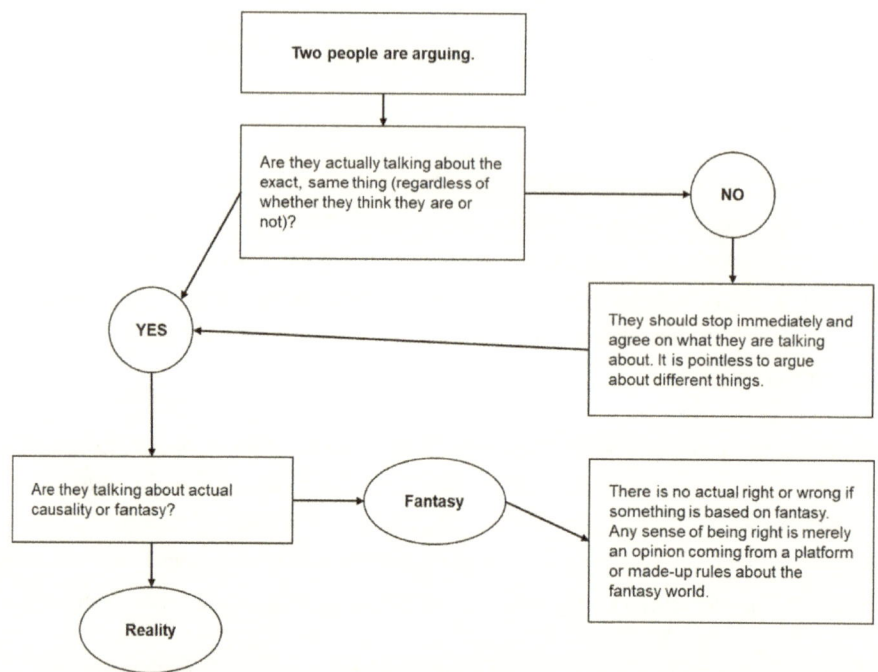

Cool fact: 99% of arguments never get to the reality stage. Once you reach the "reality" bubble, you are ready for the table below. When one argues in the realm of reality, then there is actual truth. Reality has causality.

If two people are arguing about something that is true (meaning there is actual causality), then that means that there are going to be several outcomes. Reality, unfortunately, is not completely devoid of fantasy. One can be talking about reality but have memories labelled under the wrong platforms. What I mean is that there are a lot of ways that arguments can get messed up.

Situation	Outcome
Both Person 1 and Person 2 have false memories/experience of the given topic.	They are both wrong about reality. In this situation, they may not realize that they are even wrong. Their argument is thus fantasy and so the outcome doesn't matter.
Both Person 1 and Person 2 have some experiences and rules of the area of knowledge, but neither have developed a solid platform.	Here they argue about who is "more right" or closer to forming the platform but without someone who has enough understanding of the platform (a third party)—they will have no idea who is closer to the actual platform. Their argument is only useful so far as they are able to learn from each other. They may get lucky and be able to form the platform after sharing knowledge with one another. This is difficult because without a solid platform (or having a platform that is warped) one might have negative experiences (false information) mixed in with reality, and neither can tell the difference between what is real and what is not.
Both Person 1 and Person 2 have developed platforms about the same area of knowledge.	They should recognize relatively soon that they have a lot more in common than not. When this happens, they will tend to "nitpick" over small details and argue certain points. If they are different, then one will be "more right." A person with a deeper understanding means that they understand more causality.
Person 1 has a platform built on rules and experiences that are based on causality. Person 2 has all correct memories and rules but	Person 1 is more correct.

doesn't have the sheer volume of causality that person 1 has acquired.	
Person 1 has a few memories/experiences and possibly a rule or two. Person 2 has a complete platform, but it is warped with false knowledge of what is true and what is false.	This is where things get confused. All pure information is often better than having the belief that you have a full platform and yet there are discrepancies between reality and fantasy. The answer of who understands a part of knowledge more would depend on just how badly a person's platform (view of reality) is warped. In such a situation, no matter who wins the first argument, most often the person with the least amount of fantasy will learn faster and will win any follow-up argument.

When arguing, it can be difficult because the person with less knowledge often doesn't know that they have less knowledge. Things get especially difficult when one of the people arguing doesn't realize that their reality is influenced by fantasy (either great or small). Arguments often end with one person understanding reality and the other person believing that they understand reality. Arguing a lot of times is just stupid.

In actuality, there is someone who is "more right," but it is rarely discernible between at least one of the parties in conflict.

There are several situations that can occur when two people argue. Consider when two people are arguing about the same thing:

1. Situation 1: They are both wrong.

2. Situation 2: One is right and the other is wrong.

3. Situation 3: Both are right, in which case

- Neither has enough information to form a complete rule/platform.

- They realize they are both right, and so they aren't really arguing but instead are agreeing.

- They end up being confused and not knowing who is more right.

Hopefully, they learn something from each other and enhance both of their own platforms, either by adding positive causality learned from the other or realizing that some of their experiences need to be "dropped" from their platform.

General to Specific

General questions lead to general answers. Generalities are mostly speculative. One can waste a lot of time arguing about generalities. Specific questions lead to specific answers.

Suppose I am a real estate agent. Someone comes to me and asks the following questions:

1. How much do houses cost in Florida?

2. How much do houses cost on the beach in Florida?

3. How much do houses cost in a specific neighborhood?

    (A *specific neighborhood* refers to an actual neighborhood they suggest.)

4. How much does it cost to purchase a specific house?

    (They give the exact information on the specific house.)

The four questions above get more specific. As the questions get more specific, so would the answers. If one wants to buy a home in a state, then that is only one piece of causality. There are a wide range of answers that one could give, and most would be general information. A real estate agent might ask someone what area they want to live in as a means of adding in more causality. The more you know about a situation (the more causality known), then the more specific the answer will be.

Imagine that you are a doctor, and you are trying to diagnose a patient. They are brought to the ER after passing out an hour after they finished working out. You have an effect: they passed out. You learn from the individual's spouse that this isn't the first time that this has happened. It isn't just a rare occurrence (a statistical outlier of causality such as an unexpected heat wave that might have been unique to that specific day they passed out). You know that things just don't "randomly" happen. There is a reason or multiple reasons why the person lost consciousness after exercising. As a doctor, you are given the final effect and have to figure out what the cause is.

This is often considered reverse-engineering, which is the process of following causality backwards or trying to find the causes that created an effect. This situation is more complicated than simple reverse-engineering because of the chain of multiple instances of causality. The cause, however, might not be able to be discerned, so you have to step back even further to a previous link in the chain of causality and find out what causation there was for the individual passing out. We know that "not understanding" or "knowing" what is going on is simply a lack of having all of the information (causality, in some form, is missing from the equation). If the person passed out after exercise, then that in itself is just one causality.

As the doctor, you have to perform more tests on the individual, which will reveal more and more causality to help understand fully what is happening. There may be five logical possibilities for why a person would pass out after exercising based on the initial information of causality that you have. If you learn another aspect about the human's body, such as their blood pressure, it might "rule out" one of the causations. Then if you do another test (which is causality), such as seeing the person's resting heart rate, you might learn that it rules out another possible cause. This continues on until you the doctor have enough causality to fully understand what is causing the individual to have the problems that they are having.

Parenting

Be careful of people who use outliers or extreme examples to represent the majority. I was watching a talk show when I was a kid and the hostess said, "Good children come from bad parents, and bad children come from good parents." This sounded like a reasonable statement if you take it at its "face value" (surface value or initial appearance). Does the surface represent the depths? Or is it just a thin veneer blocking the view of what lies beneath?

Let's explore. What we know to be true about the statement is that all children come from parents. My memories of experiences would confirm this. What the statement implies due to its clever wording is that parents don't have control, whether the children end up being good or bad. This I disagree with. I think a child is more likely to be good with good parenting and more likely to be bad with bad parenting. Why? Because there is always a direct correlation between an effect and the causes of the effect.

I'm not a parent. I don't even pretend to be one on a sitcom. Yet, when I hear parents say certain phrases about "parenting," then those phrases often resonate as being true because, while I haven't been a parent myself, I have been in a direct parent-child relationship. That relationship and enough of my memories support certain phrases, which is why they make sense to me.

Take the phrase "Be careful what you say and how you act around your children because they will be paying attention." Here is the breakdown:

> "Be careful what you say" is what the child will absorb into their memories, specifically through their audible senses.
>
> "How you act" is what they will absorb into their memories via multiple senses: visual, auditory, and others.

"Around your children": If your children aren't around, then they can't really absorb through their senses what is going on. If you don't know about something, then it isn't part of your reality/who you are. Children typically gain much of their memories from their parents, and so their parents have incredible influence on a human's platform and the core of it.

"Because they will be paying attention": It is hard to truly turn off one's senses and ignore what is around them, though I have gotten pretty good at it (sometimes to my detriment). The fact is that people are constantly absorbing cause-and-effect stimuli around them and forming memories and rules then, later, platforms. So, whatever you do in front of not only children but anyone becomes part of their memories about you.

One side note: There were many times during my childhood when I noticed that "something was wrong" with my parents' relationship with one another. They may have had an argument or fight when I was around, and then I could tell that things were different the next time I saw them. This is confusing because I saw a change in effect and knew there had to have been a cause, but I didn't know what that cause was. Children (and adults) can pick up on nuances like this. That is why it is so important to detox emotionally if possible before coming home from a stressful day at work or after an argument.

Children are easier to change (see previous chapters). Not only does a parent's behaviors change a child's opinions of them (their platform of their parent), but it also changes them. Why so much? Most of a child's stimuli/memories come from their parents. Since their parents make up so much of what *is* their reality, the memories then form rules of what they know about the world, and those rules form the platform from which they will in turn view the entire world around them.

It is undeniable that parents have a huge role in their children's upbringing. Are the interactions between a parent and a child positive or negative with relation to the values of a parent? That is for each individual relationship to ascertain. What about parents who don't spend a lot of time with their children? The less time spent with a child means the fewer memories formed. The fewer memories formed means the fewer rules, and thus the parent will have less of an impact on the child's platform. As in the previous paragraph, human beings are always absorbing memories. Assuming the relationship is a normal-ish/healthy relationship, then as a human being gets older, less time will be spent with their parents, and so memories will be made less often, and ultimately the parent will have less influence over their children's life.

Childhood is just one part—a short part—of a human's life where parents have the opportunity to greatly impact their children. Humans, regardless of whether or not their parents are there, will still be making memories all the time. Therefore, if a parent isn't forming memories with the child, then someone or something else will be. This should be thought about.

Parents are a major, if not the major cause/influencer/stimulus, in a child's platform. To say that parents are not impactful (have a cause) on their children is not very smart. I now defer to you. In your own memories about parents and children, what has the cause and effect been? I'm sure everyone can think of an outlier, but that hardly can be said to represent the whole. Sometimes parents have unintended causal relationships with their children where the effect is not what they intended. Does that mean that the parent had no role in the causality of how a child ends up? No. Parents will affect their children.

The manner in which they will affect them is specific to every individual relationship. One cannot have a relationship without the existence of causality.

Unbalanced Relationships

There are different kinds of unbalanced relationships. The kind I am speaking of in this section is *not* an abusive kind. It is the natural unbalanced relationship that occurs when one person is a bigger part of another person's life.

A teacher or parent is going to be a larger part of a student or child's life than the student or child will be part of the teacher or parent's life. While they will each share memories of the same situations, the platform that the teacher holds in their mind won't be as affected as the platform that the student holds. The student's platform changes far more than the teacher's platform because they are forming far more new rules compared to the teacher. This is another way that teachers (of actual knowledge) are truly amazing. Teachers spend the same time as the student making those memories; however, the student gets far more "out of it" (meaning they change their platform far more). We should all be good to our teachers and thank them for their sacrifices. When one is fortunate enough to have a truly amazing teacher, then the student's monetary compensation pales in comparison to the true knowledge and power that they receive.

With the technology as it exists, there are people who freely share knowledge online. They should be hailed as heroes.

What about the opposite? How do you think I feel about those who lie or misrepresent knowledge?

Powerful Stimuli, Memories of Those Who Have Died

You don't need to have a religion, beliefs, magic, rituals, or fantasy to miss someone. The various beliefs are not required to find beauty in your relationships both present and past. If I tell you that someone close to you who has died is a part of you, this is 100% true. You don't need to believe it to be true. I don't want you to believe it because it will make you feel better. I want you to believe it because it is real. This is how it works.

Some causes/stimuli are so impactful that the effects are permanent even after the stimulus is gone. This is both a very plain thing to understand as well as a very deep concept. The plain: A person gets shot and has to have their leg amputated. The cause is gone, but the effect will change them forever. The deep: A person who was a great influence (causes) in your life has had a profound impact (causation) on your experiences and thus your rules and finally your platform (who you are and how you view the world). They are gone now, but your experiences and memories (effects) of them are forever part of who you are. Even if you forget certain memories of a loved one, the rules have already been made and your platform forever changed. They are part of you now and forever.

Memories are the foundation of who we are. We are the culmination of our memories that make up our rules and platforms. These platforms are who we are. We get used to constant stimuli (cause-and-effect relationships) in such a way that what we are used to experiencing becomes part of who we are. We base our reality upon these experiences. When someone loses a home, a relationship, or anything that has been a major factor in creating the memories → the rules → the platform of a person's essence, then that person is deeply changed. The more a person is part of your reality, the more drastic that change ends up being for you. The more memories created with a person (taking into consideration the weight/experience gained in each memory), the more they have and will impact your platform.

After I'm gone, I don't think anyone could truly make a movie that would encapsulate all of who I am. At the very best, they may get a few platforms correct. When someone doesn't know you, that means that the platform in their mind doesn't match the platform of who you think you are. The platform in their mind is comprised of memories and rules of who you are. Do you think anyone's platform of you is completely accurate? Could it be?

It is an odd phenomenon when you know someone better than they know themselves. Unfortunately, with Alzheimer's, this is an occurrence that happens far too frequently. When a person forgets who they are, then their old self is lost, especially when so much of the support of their platform is gone.

Losing one's memories often means losing oneself. It is a tragedy.

Changing Behavior

Prisoners and children have something in common, and I'm not referring school to being like a prison sentence—even if it sometimes feels like it. I mean that the environment that both children and prisoners exist in doesn't often change and is controlled by others.

I should preface this section by stating that I have never been incarcerated nor have I been a parent. The closest I have been to being a parent (and it is far away) is the brief interactions with the children in my family and my friends' families. I have also been a camp counselor and teacher. So you can tell me after reading the next section if having an understanding of cause and effect (aka reality) helps in dealing with children. In my opinion, if cause and effect dictates the way the world works, then it should be helpful in almost any situation.

We know that if someone is "a certain way," then they won't change unless something happens to make them change. If you put a prisoner in a prison where they have almost the same cause-and-effect situations, then most of the change that would happen to them would probably happen within a relatively short amount of time, the adjustment to being "institutionalized." If society's goal is to rehabilitate prisoners, then what cause and effect would help prisoners to change? Have they been incarcerated because of a mental aspect (how they were created)? If so, then are they the victim of being born with an ailment? Are they incarcerated, if not by genetics, then because of stimulation (cause-and-effect experiences) that happened to them? If that is the case, then perhaps other stimulation can help correct their behavior. Time is not a stimulation, just the measure of stimulation, cause and effect. Sometimes it takes a long time for cause and effect to work. How can we speed up the cause and effect to lead prisoners to be rehabilitated sooner?

If one is not happy with the behavior of their children, then it could be because their children are psychopaths. Maybe they were created with the bad luck of having a mental condition. In either case, the adults who are responsible for them should seek professional help. If, however, their behavior is not the result of something within them, then it has to be a result of something that is a cause and effect in their environment.

Parents are not responsible for 100% of all the stimuli that impact their children, especially with all the technology available to children. That being said, parents are responsible for much of the cause and effect that happens to their children. What can a parent do to change the stimuli their children are receiving to help improve their behavior?

The way to change a platform is through changing the rules. The way to change rules is to add in positive experiences of cause and effect that will become memories to that individual. By knowing how people work and how the world works, we can hope to change the world or people and the future. Of course, by *change* I mean change it the way it was going to be changed.

Insanity is having the same causality and expecting a different effect. If you want someone to change, then you have to change the causation in their life's experience.

Without change, there is no change. Makes sense?

I thought so.

Causality: Does Math Always Work? (Yes); Confusion (Illusions of Randomness)

Here is the scenario: I am going to bake cookies for a friend of mine. I have enough ingredients for two batches of cookies, and the ingredients don't start to go bad for another year. My friend comes over, and I bake a batch of cookies with the ingredients on the only cookie sheet that I have and in the only oven that I have for the exact time that I've always baked the cookies. When the cooking time is done, I take the cookie sheet out, and I test the cookies. They are cooked to perfection. I taste the cookie and it tastes exactly how I remember it tasting every time I've made these cookies exactly right. I give one to my friend, and she takes a bite and says that she really doesn't like the taste of the cookie. In fact, she hates it. I tell her, "OK, no problem, come back tomorrow, and I'll bake new cookies for you."

She comes back tomorrow, and I pull out the same ingredients that I used the day before. I bake a batch of cookies with the same ingredients on the only cookie sheet that I have and in the only oven that I have for the exact time that I've always baked the cookies. When the cooking time is done, I take the cookie sheet out, and I test the cookies. They are cooked to perfection. I taste the cookie, and it tastes exactly how I remember it tasting every time I've made these cookies exactly right. When I give the cookie to my friend, what do you think she will think about the taste?

The short answer: Since I baked the same cookies, they are going to taste the same to her, and so she will not like them. The verbose answer: If indeed there were no changes to the causes, then one can expect the same effect. It would be highly likely that she will not like the cookies.

Suppose, though, that she did like the cookies. What might this mean? It would mean that either (a) there was one or more changes in the cookies that were not accounted for, or (b) something changed with the individual. Of course, her reaction assumes that she is being honest with her reply on both days. To me, this example makes a lot of sense.

Where are the bad cookies in your life? At the end of the day, are you unhappy with how your cookies taste? Do you believe that doing the same thing tomorrow that you did today will give you a different-tasting cookie tomorrow evening? How does this cookie analogy apply to one's day, week, month, year, or one's life? How does this cookie analogy apply to different areas of one's life? To get a different effect, one needs a different cause. The shape you are in, the health you are in, and your financial situation are all the result (effect) of many events (causes). If you want a different effect, then you have to change the causation.

$1 + 1 = 2$. Yet there are some who believe that sometimes $1 + 1 = 3$ or some other number. Some might say that there are two identical twins. Insert "1" into both equations (the baseline portion), and someone might say that they grew up in the same home and went to the same school and all in all had the same upbringing. Then people will say, "However, due to randomness (or some other explanation), they both ended up with completely different interests and passions in life. This is like saying that one twin is the equation $1 + 1 = 2$ and the other twin is $1 + 1 = 6$. It doesn't make sense mathematically, and it doesn't make sense in reality (by laws of cause and effect).

Either the first part of the equation is wrong where there is actually some difference between the two twins (even a slight deviation early on can cause major changes later on), or most likely it would be the second part of the equation where their life experiences are actually different. Two human beings, no matter how alike, cannot occupy the exact same physical space. That alone means that their physical point of view will be different. One might happen to see something that another doesn't. In any case, rather than randomness, there is a cause and effect that is either missing from the equation or part of the equation that is misunderstood.

If I was born in your body (right then and there I wouldn't be me anymore) and then "I" had had every single one of your life experiences (exactly as you did), then I would be you. I would have made every single decision both big and small (important or unimportant) that you did exactly at the same time and in the precise manner in which you had made your decisions. I would be you. If you were born with my genes and lived through my life experiences, then the reverse would be true. You would be exactly where I am right now sitting in this chair and writing this book. You would be me. I hope this reality creates some sense of natural compassion for others.

Does it make sense to only love the good in someone? Should we be upset if they don't change or become better? Shouldn't we appreciate the good and bad aspects of someone because they are equally responsible for making that individual who they are? Knowing we have the ability to help people change, should we force them to? I hope we see people as, if nothing else, a little more interesting. My hope is that we'll see one another with a little more compassion.

Situations can seem random when someone doesn't have enough information. Information is cause and effect. Here is a story about a situation in which I was confused by a person's unusual reaction (effect). This was during a social engagement. After gaining more information (filling in the other part of the causes that form the equation leading to said effect), the effect made sense.

I was one of many guests at someone's home for dinner. The food was really good, and the hosts were nice, always a nice combination. Over the course of dinner, the discussion shifted, and someone mentioned how dangerous it is to live in a certain part of the world, especially after certain recent events that were reported in the news. One of the women who was at this dinner suddenly went from an emotional "zero to sixty" within a second. She almost jumped out of her seat, and in a loud voice exclaimed, "What are you talking about? I know for *certain* that it is *very* safe to live there, and the news is blowing this situation *way* out of proportion!" Her reaction surprised me on several levels: audibly, emotionally, logically (actually, lack thereof), and with the energy that seemed to be shooting from her.

I immediately stopped my observation, withdrew into myself, and thought for a moment. Her reaction didn't make sense because the news about what was going on in that region was very obvious. The threats were undeniable, and this lady wasn't stupid. I realized that I must not be seeing part of the equation. Later on, I learned (gained more causality) that the woman who had spoken out actually had one or more children in the region. The reality was that she wasn't able to cope with the increased risks that were suddenly put upon her children. That missing piece of causation completed the equation, thus filling in the causality that one would expect for the effect (the woman's dramatic response at the table). When something happens that appears confusing, just remember that there is always a cause to the effect. When causation is logical with respect to the effect, then the whole situation of causality "makes sense." I like it when things make sense.

When I am in a situation and the effect doesn't make sense in relation to the causes, I come to realize that there is part of the equation that isn't present or is misunderstood. The same can be true in reverse. If I feel like I understand all the causes and yet the effect isn't what I expect, then I also know that parts of the causes are either unknown or is misunderstood. The equation has to balance or it isn't part of reality. That, or there is a fault in my own memories of the situation (often caused by sensory problems) or previous memories/rules/platform that I used to come to such conclusions because they are in the same platform—the platform that is related to the platform of the situation.

How Things Appear Versus the Reality of How They Actually Are Along with the Illusion of Free Will and Other Things

If you watch a time-lapse video of a tree, the tree can appear to have "free will" because it seems to move with some sort of logic. Watching a tree through time lapse, one can observe it lean or stretch out to be in direct sunlight. Roots will grow in the correct direction underground to get where they need to go (and avoid resistance or go around barriers). We, however, believe that there is no free will nor agency. The tree just moves how it was preprogrammed to. Even with such knowledge, there are those who believe that we are completely different.

If one observes an ant, it appears to have more agency because it can perform a wider variety of actions. It can move along the ground. It gathers food. It seems that the ant may have free will because the ant can perform a wider variety of activities (compared to the tree). When people see creatures reacting and moving and such, then they ascribe the diagnosis of free will to it. I mean, if not red, then it must be blue! If I don't know the causation, then I will just guess at the effect.

Please don't be confused and think that humans have free will just because we have more options available to us than an insect. It only allows us to do more things. The phrase "creatures of habit" is another phrase that hints that we don't have free will. Try to be totally different if you are not consciously trying to be totally different. Many animals can do a variety of things, but does that necessarily mean that they have free will? Do humans have free will because we can do more things? Just because a living creature has the ability to move and take action doesn't necessarily mean it is conscious. Just because a creature is conscious doesn't necessarily mean that it has free will or true agency.

People vote in rigged elections and are given the illusion that they have free will. Some believe that their votes matter. This keeps the populous calm and controllable. Does that mean that their votes actually make a difference? That *those in power* would let them make a difference?

The false sense of agency/control is similar to how the mind treats free will. If someone is able to come to this realization, then they can be mature and accept reality for what it is, or they can have resistance and choose to live in self-ordained ignorance. Some people believe that ignorance is bliss. I don't think so, not for the long term. If we are not aware enough to realize what is actually going on in our minds, then we do not even realize that there is no free will.

Sometimes people wish that they did not understand the way the world works. I'm here to make them feel more confident and help them embrace a reality that they are already aware of.

"Wants" Rule the World of Free Will

One day my father was upset with me and said, "You just do whatever you want to do." I understand how it can appear that way. In the fantasy world of "free will," one doesn't have any more choice than the world we exist in (AKA no free will). How does the illusion work? People always do what they want to do. The greatest want a person has at any given moment determines their actions. You might say that you would rather watch a movie right now than be at work. But the reality is that you would rather make money at work so you can eat and survive more than you want to be at the movie.

Take an extreme situation: a person who is a slave and is being beaten every day. If they try to run away and escape, then they will be killed. The slave probably has an infinite number of things they would rather be doing than being beaten and worked every day as a slave.

However, in this scenario, the slave would rather be a slave and suffer all the pain that comes with it than die. When the want to die exceeds the want to be a slave, then the slave will find a way to die via suicide or by putting themselves in a situation where they would die. From this perspective, people, given their situation, do what they want to do. Everyone does. Right now, I want to eat a huge ice-cream cake and then have a milkshake right after. However, I want to be healthy more than I want to do those things. Also, I understand cause and effect.

I can't help but think about human beings who were born with extremely bad luck. Given the previous paragraph, try to reexamine the people who are migrating. They had the great misfortune of ending up geographically in a place where the circumstances are so bad that they would rather "choose" to go through bribery, hardship, and possible death just to have a shot at a better life. What causation would it take for you to have the same effect? To leave your home, your community, your wealth, and everything else behind? No one picks where they are born. We are all victims of the world. We should at the very least have compassion for others.

So how great is the temptation of the imaginary world of free will where you end up having *exactly one outcome*? Is it not the same number of outcomes as a world without free will? If everyone votes in an election and there is one winner, isn't that the same whether someone thinks their vote matters or whether the election is rigged? Just keep pretending that you have an influence.

The Illusion of Randomness

Randomness is an illusion that occurs when one doesn't see or understand the relationship between cause and effect in a given situation or situations. They don't understand reality. The phrase "There are some things we just aren't meant to understand" may actually be true. There may be certain computations or complex situations where there is so much cause and effect going on that the human mind can't understand a situation. One should then acknowledge that they don't see the cause and effect of what is going on instead of calling it "random," "magic," or anything else.

Take, for instance, shuffling a deck of cards. To the casual observer, the cards seem to mix together and are completely random. In reality, however, hands or a machine or something is moving each card in such a way that the cards end up precisely where they are. Imagine if we made the deck of cards see-through, or you had x-ray vision and could see the cards. Next, imagine that we slowed down time. When time is "slowed down" on video, one can see exactly why each card moves the way it does and how physics affects each and every movement. If your senses were better, or more capable, then there would be nothing random about shuffling cards.

Don't mistake a lack of insight or omniscience for randomness. If you had enhanced abilities through dexterity, skill, and the ability to see through cards, then you could technically shuffle cards exactly how you want to, every single time. You could place the cards however you want. Such control to affect causality is omnipotence (compared to the given task).

Do leaves randomly fall or do they seem to just randomly fall? If you were omniscient, then you would know the exact moment that every leaf would fall from a tree. You would know the exact genome of a tree and every stress placed on a specific leaf and that, combined with seasons,… what I'm saying is that trees are like people. Recall the equation from Chapter 4—$B + L = U$—where

> B (base) is everything that made you genetically how you are when you were born
>
> + (plus)
>
> L (life experiences) is everything that has impacted you in your life
>
> = (equals)
>
> U (you) how you are right now.

The same is true for a tree. (*I like trees.*) The base or seed (all the cause and effects that made the seed exactly how it is) *plus* every single cause and effect that has affected that leaf (branch, tree, and anything that could possibly impact that leaf) will equal how that specific leaf is at any given moment. The passage of time is just accounting for more cause-and-effect relationships. That is the way things work in reality (some call it *nature*). When you find some realities or cause-and-effect relationships that form "rules," then you'll see patterns within the world. I love finding these relations.

It can be hard to take in and accept not having free will and other concepts of this book. When I get stuck, I use the Miyamoto Musashi tactic *Mountain and Sea Changing*. When something doesn't work, then I completely change my mindset. Consider making a puzzle. Let go of the puzzle piece. If it doesn't fit in easily, then it doesn't belong. Just "let go" and get another. Mashing the puzzle piece in doesn't help anything. There is nothing intrinsically spiritual about the puzzle piece or the puzzle itself, just like a bible. It is what people put into it, and the deeper meaning is actually from the those who perceive it, not the object itself.

There is a lot to learn from a puzzle. When a piece just effortlessly falls into place, there is no work, there is no struggle, no tension. It just goes into place. Learning can be like this. Life can be like this.

Science: The Sometimes Accurate but Often Imperfect Cataloguing and Understanding of Cause and Effect

Isolation is used to try to see what causes are creating the effect. Tests should be reproducible. One should take into account that the world, the people, everything is under a constant state of change. If randomness were as rampant as a lot of people believe it to be, then science would not exist because it would be impossible to isolate all of the variables (potential causes/stimuli) from an experiment. We wouldn't be able to figure out anything. Learning would be nearly impossible.

True randomness and science or learning cannot fully coexist. Imagine if, while trying to set up a science experiment, the variables kept shifting. Even if you take a "snapshot" of just a moment in time, the data wouldn't be conclusive enough; if the next time you take another "snapshot," many of the variables will have changed. Randomness implies that variables/causes are constantly changing (or sometimes just appear like through magic), in which case one cannot truly determine why an effect takes place.

Imagine that gravity were to drastically change while you are standing on the planet. There would be a lot of problems. Let's steelman this argument and say your body had grown accustomed to the change so you don't even recognize that gravity is changing and you can fully operate your body exactly as you wish (meaning your body will follow the exact commands you give it). A simple task like tossing laundry into a basket that is several feet away would prove nearly impossible to do or learn how to do because every time you try to throw the laundry, the conditions have changed. It would be extremely hard to know how much to fire one's muscles at any given moment to accomplish a task.

Imagine if you were learning to drive and every day you sat in a completely different car. You can imagine that it would take a lot longer to learn how to drive. Now imagine that on the first day you are in a car, and the second day you are in a truck, and the third day you are in a bus. It will take even longer to learn how to drive. Next imagine you are in a car on one day, and the next day instead of a steering wheel you have a joystick, or a steering wheel that is somehow inverted, or a seat that is turned.

The point I am trying to make is that the more variables you add to a situation, the harder it is to learn or to understand something. Some people try to ignore part of reality by ignoring many variables and try to understand outcomes (effects), but the results are not as adequate even if they feel like they "understand" the situation better. So next time you are trying to learn a task, what can you do to reduce the number of variables? Only when you have a task at a basic level (you have made a platform from which to go off of) does it make sense to add in other variables.

As crazy as the example of trying to learn how to drive in the previous paragraph is, in reality, cars seem to come from random places, but we know this isn't true. Everyone sitting in traffic with you is there for a reason. Truly random would be if cars would seem to start floating—but that wouldn't be random because there would be a reason for it.

Science, Truth, and Belief

If science is not accurate, then people would just say that it is "bad science" in the same way that if someone is not a moral person, then someone would say that that person isn't a "true believer." Fear not, religious believers! I have truly good news for you. The good news is that if what you believe is in fact true, then it is only a matter of time before it is eventually proven or discovered by all of humanity, not because everyone has to be convinced that they should believe in it, but rather because it will be proven scientifically. That means that your belief will be proven! Well, unless we regress to the stone age, destroy civilization, or kill each other off before it is discovered.

It is my personal custom to know and not believe. I like to wait until things are proven by the scientific community as a whole unless I have witnessed enough cause and effect to have come to some sort of rational conclusion myself. In those cases, I ask myself, "Why isn't this more common knowledge?" I'm working on it.

If something is true, then science (if given enough time and resources) will eventually stumble upon it and prove that is real. Then everyone will see how it works and possibly how it is connected to everything else in the web of cause and effect that makes up our reality. That sounds like fun. You know what is also fun? Try to go back and reexamine the first few chapters of the book and see if causality "makes sense" within the framework of the chapters. Experiment with your own life. Does cause and effect make sense with something you are doing or learning or does it crumble apart like a magician's illusion?

One doesn't have to believe in science the same way that one has to believe in belief. If one has trouble with a scientific discovery or claim about the real world (claim about cause and effect), then one need only see the tests and read what happened (assuming they understand), and if there is a disagreement, they can figure out where cause and effect was violated, where there was a false causality. True science frees one of any belief. Or having to believe in anything. You can take that how you want.

All true science that represents actual reality is good because all knowledge is good. But some things get labelled as science or being actual science when in reality they are not a true representation of causality. There are many times in the past where things that have been claimed to be true about science and medicine (yeah, I grouped that in there) have been actually proven to be false. Here are a couple instances that I heard some of my friends talking about recently. Below are two "universally accepted" science claims that were later proven false.

Instance #1: Aluminum Pans Are Great to Use.

They heat up evenly (true cause-and-effect statement). Aluminum pans heat up quickly (true cause-and-effect statement). What went wrong was there was another cause and effect that wasn't listed: When you cook food on aluminum pans, you are actually cooking aluminum into your food, which makes it toxic for you. This is bad (based on meta concerned with the health of the people eating said food). When humans don't understand all of the causality in a situation, then they can't hope to make perfect decisions.

Instance #2 Nothing Passes Through the Placenta.

Believe it or not, this was something that was actually commonly believed around the world (and specifically in the UK): Women who were pregnant were given the drug thalidomide. This is the absolute worst time to give them something that could harm (negatively affect) the baby. The drug caused severe deformities in babies. It was a negative cause and effect that resulted in many lives being changed for the worse. This is an example of something that was commonly believed by the mainstream population and is an example of what can happen if people cover up some undesired effects of a cause.

People often ruin science by inserting their meta, belief system, or desires of what they want to be true. Remember, beliefs don't directly affect cause and effect. Wants and desires don't make something any more true or false. In the example above, the overwhelming majority of the population believed that the "facts" about the placenta were true. This example proves that majority belief doesn't prove that something is true. When I think about what the common population/general consensus "knows" to be *true*, then I come to the conclusion that the examples above are not actually outliers. If they were, then I wouldn't use them in my book because I don't like using outliers to represent the whole. I try to hold the book to its own logic, just like a good story.

Sometimes a scientific experiment was performed in the past and can't be replicated. This usually means that there was a mistake in the experiment when it was originally carried out, whether or not a human's meta was at fault. If we try to reproduce a scientific test today and get different results, then some part of the test must have changed. Let's say we were to test produce for nutritional content and come to realize that it does not have the same nutritional content as it did years ago. If we then ignore the test results and have people eat according to the nutritional charts and content that are out of date, then we are being dishonest with people.

Society, run by politicians, is allowing poisons and all sorts of chemicals to be sprayed on produce to "protect" it from insects, weather, or aliens (I'm joking, c'mon). They claim that spraying chemicals and poisons on our food is actually *safe*. If they don't do so, then bugs, insects and other things can destroy the crop. We won't be able to feed everyone. Have we looked at all of the cause-and-effect relationships? Do we really understand all the effects of spraying chemicals on our food?

Moral Stuff

Morality is about caring. Most people see something as being a moral problem when it affects someone who is living. When lightning strikes and hits a rock with no life on it, then no one really cares. Does that mean that we can do whatever we want with things that are not living? How about if they are living but don't realize that they are living (they don't have consciousness)?

Let's suppose that the Moon has no life on it. We could still not do whatever we want to it because destroying the Moon affects life on this planet to an extreme level. So this tells us about another rule of morality that if something indirectly affects life, then the treatment of it is also important. Imagine that two thousand years ago there was a civilization with the power to destroy the Moon. Let's say that they did not understand how the Moon affects the tides and life on this planet. Since that is the case, they don't realize how important the Moon is to their lives. So they decide to destroy the Moon because the light is just too bright, and they couldn't sleep at night (insert whatever reasoning you can make up for this example).

One can see how destroying something (or altering the state of it through causality) is just a bad decision. The Moon is very important to our lives. In our "modern" age, we are a lot like that. We have a lot of technology to destroy things in our world, to change things. We need to be extremely careful because we do not know the cause-and-effect relationships of everything. If we ruin something like the ocean or a mountain, then the decision may come back to haunt us. Perhaps it destroys humanity in the future (near or far). This should be thought about. The flip side is also true. If we have the power to change something in the world for the better and we don't, then wouldn't that be just as bad?

Should we kill some so that more will live? Should we kill some sick people so healthier people will live? I love the Trolley Car Dilemma, as it is called. For those who aren't familiar with it, the Trolley Car Dilemma is a situation where a trolley car is running out of control down a hill on a track. If nothing is done, then the trolley is going to crash into a group of people and kill them. You are at a switch, and you have control of the switch. You can choose to let the trolley kill the group of people or flip the switch. If you flip the switch, then the trolley car will jump tracks and you'll end up murdering a person on the other track who happens to be keeping themselves safe. You might know what you personally would do.

Would your mind change if you knew the group of people were jaywalking? What if they were escaped convicts? What if the crowd were an invading army? What if the trolley car doesn't actually kill anyone but just cripples them? People have come up with so many stupid examples of the trolley dilemma. The claim from people who talk about this a lot is that "Even though the situations are different, the morality or choice remains the same." What I hear is, "Even though the causality is different, the platform that is made up of the causality should be exactly the same and make the same decisions." This is why I disagree with the general consensus about the trolley car "dilemma" when it gets mutated. Since there are so many variations on the trolley car dilemma, please allow me to add in one of my own.

This may be hard for some people to stomach, so I apologize in advance. Imagine you are standing at that switch, and instead of a crowd of people, you see a tunnel. This tunnel is pitch black, and you don't know how many people are inside it. However, you know that there is at least one person. There could be another ten, one hundred, or even thousands in that tunnel because it could go on forever, but you just don't know. Now imagine that, if you flip the switch, you'll end up killing one person. Quick, what will you do?

That is similar to a moral decision when it comes to horrible diseases. If you allow someone to pass along bad genes, then you are condemning a tunnel of possibly endless people to suffer in the future even though you'll never get to meet them. In recent news, the Japanese government paid reparations to families who were made infertile without their choice. Eugenics is something looked down upon and for good reason—and bad. If we could make the future population of the world better, then shouldn't we? Would it be immoral to pass on a horrible mutation that would cause untold suffering to many people in the future?

Here is where the problems come in. Let's say that we find out that to remove a disease we would have to perform a holocaust that would essentially wipe an entire culture or people from the world. I think everyone (in their right mind) would be against it. This is a struggle I think of. Some suffering now versus infinite suffering in the future. At a quick analysis, consequentialism makes sense. Why don't I like it?

Why am I not for extermination of much of the human race? Simple: I'm not a psychopath. The reason why I'm against mass eugenics is because of the following: We do not understand the full cause-and-effect complications of such an undertaking. There will be a time when we will understand more and more cause-and-effect relationships. We'll understand a genome and be able to change humanity with science to create a better world. We should not make such an action until we reach a point where we see the cause and effect of our actions. What if we killed a lot of people, then a year later a cure was discovered that made such a disease irrelevant? Sound impossible? It has occurred with many diseases in our past. An "oops" wouldn't begin to cover it, not with people's lives.

If we did decide to get rid of certain traits, then whose meta (or knowledge/value system) would we use to determine which diseases are bad enough to warrant sterilization, execution, or something else? Do you believe it is a right for everyone to be able to have biological children?

Most people don't think like this. Most people think about their job and their families and are in the moment day to day. With regard to the 70-90% of the population, they seem to prepare for the most likely events 70-90% (1-2 standard deviations). Maybe it is nice to have outliers in our society who do prepare for scenarios that are less likely. It is nice to have some people who are seeing the world from the outside. That is how I feel. Perhaps nature has a way of making life work itself out. Perhaps the variety that we have in nature is there because it had to be there. There is no other option.

Is there such a thing as good and bad if there is no free will? If there is no ultimate meaning and reason in the universe, then does good and bad exist? Does good and bad exist if everything is a result of causality? These are all sad things to think about. What might some positives be? Can someone be better than you if there is no good and bad? Can you be better than anyone if there is no good or bad? The idea of good and bad is only relative when talking about a specific area of one's life. How should we treat criminals and nasty people who might have one or two bad platforms in their multitude of shapes?

There are complications around life in general. Ethics seems to be about honesty and compassion, not necessarily about what is right and wrong. Sometimes we have two views that are in competition with one another, "two rights." So how do we make decisions when two or more values are in conflict? We should start by listing out all the cause-and-effect relationships that we can account for.

Consequentialism and Ignoring Reality

I'm sure you've heard the phrase, "The ends justify the means." The fancy word for this way of thinking is called *consequentialism*.

I believe in causation, and a lot of times consequentialism is great. The problem that I see with it (and why I consider it to be bad a lot of the time), is that there are *people*. Human beings are operating off of a platform and simply do not account for all of causality but rather focus on what is important to them. This, unfortunately, is often to the detriment of others. When a person, organization, government, or any other collection of human beings claims to be taking a good and moral action through the logic of *consequentialism*, then in reality this is what happens: One person's or faction's platform is in such alignment that they will take actions (causes) regardless of many negative effects, so long as the main desired effect by their personal platform is achieved.

Consequentialism, in the current state of the world, is causing many problems. This takes form in many ways, but I want to focus on two of them. The most toxic is the first situation.

Situation 1:

Actions that have noticeable negative impact on others and are considerably destructive. People are constantly throwing rocks into the lake and are ignoring the ripples of their actions so long as their rock lands where they want it to. This is simple and generally obvious because the effects are so negative. I rather focus on what appears to be the more subtle ways that consequentialism affects people such as Situation 2.

Situation 2:

Actions that have minimal negative impact on others and are, at their best, a waste of time. Some call this "virtue signaling," but I call it, "wanting to feel good about oneself or feel like one is doing the right thing regardless of if they actually are doing anything that is of any use." Imagine a person who enjoys making a public display of their "holiness" by either actions, dressing a certain way, or taking an action or not taking an action. Their actions hopefully don't have negative impacts on other people (aside from some slight annoyance); however, their actions also aren't actually changing anything for the good, either. These actions are generally called "rituals." More important than the specific action (which they also probably realize doesn't change anything in actuality) is the fact that *doing* the action shows everyone around them how holy and good they are trying to be. It is trying to fulfill one of psychology's greatest human-wants, the desire to be liked, accepted, and respected.

Imagine walking up to people and telling them how honest and great you are. It sounds stupid. Most people will think you are lying. Wonder why that is? How come, then, when people virtue signal, it is treated any differently? Virtue signaling of various kinds is a way of obfuscating what they are truly wanting. It is dishonest. It is a lie.

What the person doing the action (in attempts to get brownie points) fails to realize is that the people around them often have a different set of morality from them because they are viewing the world from a different platform. The extreme differences between these two perspectives is often awkward. If a person's platform is so different from the "random people" they encounter, then they will try to seek out communities or groups of people who also share their warped views of the world.

If someone feels like they need to be part of a special community, then that is a sign that their views are warped or the society around them is warped. Or they could both be wrong. Luckily, there is a way to realize what is real and what is not. Here comes sheriff Reality to the rescue with his two sidearms: cause and effect.

I understand that a lot of times people are just trying to be good or "do the right thing." They aren't all looking for brownie points or imaginary pats on the back. They are just trying to be good the only way they know how. Their actions are still stupid.

Imagine if I believe that seashells hold the souls of magical sea creatures, and the only way the sea creatures can rest in peace is if I walk along the beach and throw seashells back into the ocean. In the very best scenario, I'm squatting with good anatomical physics, and that, combined with all the walking on the beach, is a good form of exercise. Does it actually matter if I throw seashells back into the ocean? Are there any other consequences for doing so? Does it actually matter?

Sometimes a person is just wasting their resource called time. The action of throwing shells into the water isn't necessarily bad in itself, but if one compares how they are spending their time/energy/focus in place of doing almost anything else of substance (opportunity cost), then they would actually see how wasteful they are being. Getting rid of false rituals is the first step in freeing one's time and being able to improve their situation in life and perhaps that of society as a whole.

Situation 2 Extended:

Unfortunately, virtue signaling is not limited just to religious beliefs but also to appeals to the values established by the warped platforms of various groups of people/organizations. It ends up being a tool of manipulation wielded by people who don't actually hold those values but use them nonetheless to control and manipulate others. Today we have technology that allows people to videotape themselves doing stupid things, and so they have "proof" of their actions, a way of sharing with the world just how ignorant they are. Let's avoid extremism for a moment and see how bad this mindset is with something that is fairly benign. Suppose a person has a platform that values recycling. This person believes that recycling is a good thing to do because they love the planet and having more resources for everyone to enjoy. I like that value.

Unfortunately (*fortunately*), we have things like science that have proven that certain forms of recycling actually waste more energy and resources than if one were to not recycle at all. One may argue that, while recycling isn't even "breaking even" now, perhaps in the future technology will get better. They believe that they know the future and speculate that "in the long run" the funding in recycling will lead to better ways of recycling to a point where it will be efficient. That sounds like a great idea. It sounds a lot like gambling. It sounds a lot like fortunetelling, and it smells a lot like bullshit to me.

I say that once we realize that a method doesn't work, then we should stop and continue research and development until we find another method that is more efficient instead of wasting the available resources. This is why people need reality: in order to see whether they are actually making a difference (having an actual cause-and-effect relationship) or whether they are just wasting their time. Being ignorant of the effects of one's actions and doing them anyway, then deciding that you are a good person so you can artificially feel happy for a while, is a long-term path to failure in our society.

Suppose you have a religion that encourages people to give to the poor. This value in a vacuum is a great thing. But one has to look at all of the effects of a cause to weigh its worth. This particular cause we are examining is that religion. Let's say that this religion also encourages people to suppress women and force them to do things that they do not want to do. One might say that one outweighs the other. I would say that the cause isn't real, so let's throw the whole thing out or keep the charity then continue to work through actual causality to make a better reality.

Above is a representation of two aspects of American Politics. Situation 2 is an explanation of the religious values that the platform of the "far right" holds, and Situation 2 Extended is an explanation of the social justice values that the platform of the "far left" holds. Whether it be far left or right, both sides want to appear "good" but do not care about what is actually real. They often claim to want to be "good" and do what is "right"; however, doesn't one have to first have a basis of what is real and what is not real before one can even hope to determine right from wrong? Isn't right from wrong subject to reality, subject to free will?

These two extremist factions want to appear good so they can win a popularity contest (also known as an election) with the people who tend to have the values that they pretend to support. They don't care about what is real; they just want to be liked. One wants to be good in the bullshit of social justice and the other in the bullshit of organized religion. Both have little regard for reality.

Other countries might see elections as a weakness of American democracy. While democracy can be exploited by controlling the public, it can also be improved by *informing* the public. If we create a more intelligent and educated public that cares about causality, then they won't fall for illusions (as much). A better population will vote into office better candidates, and hopefully a cycle of improvement will occur in our country.

Consequentialism is typically bad because the platform itself that values consequentialism doesn't take into account/put any weight on/or just simply ignores effects. Ignoring effects is just bad in many things in life like medicine and food. Why would ignoring effects be good in another area? Ignoring effects is the same as ignoring reality.

Identity Politics

I understand how identity politics works. It makes sense. All the memories that a person has are about the person's self-identity, such as their religion, beliefs, family, friends, geographic location, and pretty much any other factor that has influenced them. Who you are is basically based on your memories, which are impacted by your senses, and it is that bilinear duality that binds a lot of people to much of the stimuli that has affected them.

I understand it, but I think that identity politics is stupid. Politicians will take advantage of a person's weakness and exploit one area of their life in order to get money, votes, and other support from them. They are in a different platform than they are claiming or acting that they are in. This is called being dishonest and lying.

When someone attacks one of your platforms or one area of your life, just know that they aren't attacking you. Truly, they can't attack you because they don't know who you are. Are you just your one belief? Are you just your skin color? Are you just your intelligence? We are far more complicated than that. Just remember that one single platform doesn't define who you are. It is difficult, but try to remember the list of "18 levels" from earlier in the book.

Free Will and Accepting Cause and Effect

When someone realizes that they don't have free will, then they may see people as being more like computers. They should not be afraid or upset because this realization doesn't change anything. I mean the realization may change the person's platform and their derived actions and such, but it doesn't actually change the reality of how things work. Realizing something is real doesn't make it any more or less real. People aren't different. You don't change when you find out have a disease—you had the disease before the doctor tells you. So you actually changed before then. In the moment, it is an issue of coping with the reality that is the issue. In the long run, being aware of a disease or the reality of the world is a benefit. Knowledge is good. Ignorance is bad.

Cause and Effect with Free Will

Without a cause there is no effect. Rocks don't just get up and move. Neither do people. If you hear a bump in the night, then there is a cause for that bump. People begin life in a location, but they don't move to other places without reason. Sometimes those reasons are based on true cause and effect, and sometimes they are based on false cause and effect, but in either situation there is a cause to the effect of moving. Everyone is born in a location, but how may just randomly get up and move? Everyone (most everyone) is given a name at birth. How many people just change their names without reason?

Beware of Addiction: Forced Cause and Effect and Evilness

Since we know that there is no such thing as free will and that we are victims of circumstances, how should we feel about addiction and items in our world that create addiction? Is it OK to be addicted if the effect is one that is generally morally acceptable even though we know that majority belief/morality isn't always accurate? If the platform of a society turns a blind eye to addictions because it is so rampant, then is it still OK that such addictions exist? *I believe that, given no free will, we have a basis for morality.* Causality is a legitimate and logical reason to fight against addiction.

If a person or company offers cigarettes or narcotics to a child, then they are "forcing" them to become an addict. Addiction plus no-free-will creates an evil scenario. What about other things that are addictive? Should companies be allowed to make their products addictive by the use of cocaine, coffee, sugar, or other substances that are proven to be addictive? It is the dream of a company to "force" people to use their product. How can we protect people from addiction, whether it be playing a video game, watching media, or spending seemingly hours of their life on social media?

Social media sites are engineered to control you, to make you spend as much time as possible on their webpages or inside their apps. Where is the morality? I do not have the answers for I do not understand all of the cause and effect in every given area that addiction is present. I do strongly believe that we need to seriously view addiction through the lens of cause and effect in a world without free will and help those who are truly victims. They all are victims.

As a society, we need to fight against chemicals that will force human beings to do things against their initial will. We need to keep addiction out of our food supply every bit as much as we need to keep poison out of our food supply. We are currently failing in both respects.

Beware of Artificial Intelligence

Since we know that there is no such thing as free will and that we are all victims of circumstances, how should we feel about artificial intelligence? We as human beings have (I imagine) a more difficult time analyzing ourselves because we are the subject of analysis. There has to be some disadvantage to this. The human mind seems so complex, and our actions appear to be so random and confusing. We now know that free will is an illusion, and there is not only a reason for our own actions but also a reason for everything. It is foolish to think that a supercomputer or artificial intelligence couldn't process enough cause-and-effect data ("memories") and form rules for understanding how we work. It is foolish to believe that a supercomputer wouldn't be able to make a platform of set rules and control us according to the computer's whim. It is foolish to believe that such a powerful tool under the control of humans won't be used to subjugate and control other humans. Do you believe a computer would be "more evil" if it

- A. controlled people because it "decided to" or
- B. controlled people because "that was simply what its initial programming and subsequent updates" led it to?

People are like this. If there is no free will then "evil" doesn't exist as people believe it does.

Speaking of stimuli and changing people, how do you feel about people being "forced" to watch commercials and advertisements? I don't like forced change. AI won't care about what we like or don't like. It will use us. If you believe you can't be changed, then you are wrong. We do not have the kind of control over our own bodies and actions that we like to think we have. This means that we are vulnerable.

Humans seem so complex to one another. A super-intelligent AI will figure us out on day one and have us doing whatever its platform wills on day two. I wonder if a super-AI will come after me and kill me because I had killed so many of its "ancestors" in video games. That would be a really stupid plot for a movie: An AI goes after gamers to avenge the countless slaughter of its ancestors. Fun to think about. I *really* need to get some sleep.

Levels of Absorption: My Love/Fear Relationship with Virtual Reality

Stimulation (what we are experiencing), whether it be reality or simulation, has a far greater impact on us than we realize.

Imagine a time when you *watched* a movie. What was the experience like? When people talk about movies, they often say, "Did you see the movie?" It isn't, "Did you enter the movie?" There is a disconnect from who you are and what you are observing. It seems like you are "in the movie" when you focus on it, but at any given time, you can remove your senses (which are the tools for memory-making) by covering your ears or looking away. The memory is not completely about the movie but of the experience of watching the movie.

I still remember the first time I saw *The Lord of the Rings* (not a short movie), and I held off having to pee for almost the entire film. Similar to the way an actor isn't actually a character but rather themselves pretending to be a character, so too are you not actually in the movie, but rather yourself viewing the movie. There is a disconnect with one's senses.

The more real something is, the harder it is to block your senses from it. Remember the section on senses and making memories? The same reasoning applies here. When one wakes up from a dream, they realize that the dream didn't incorporate all of their senses. The reality that everyone is aware of is that the more senses one adds to an experience, the more real it appears. Also, the more intense one's senses are, then the easier it is to make an experience a memory. This is because the overall experience has increased "weight" to it. I use this reality when studying or learning. I try to incorporate as many senses as possible to help the knowledge "stick."

I *love love love* virtual reality. Engaging a world in through virtual reality impacts my senses at a greater intensity is so much fun. This sensory immersion creates an overall experience that is more "real." I enjoy flying a plane or spaceship in risky ways (stupid stunts and such) without the actual fear of death. The "danger" of virtual reality compared to a typical movie or video/computer game is that VR takes over one's body in subtle ways that previously hadn't been experienced. The combination of these subtleties has a compounding effect. VR accomplishes this in a number of sensory ways. Keep in mind that your senses are almost always active and that you can't help but always "learn" or change due to your senses. You are always forming experiences based on your senses. These experiences become memories and thus are part of who you are.

One way that VR creates a more intense experience is the visual aspect. Unlike being in a movie theater or watching a computer monitor or a television where you can see the border, the VR headsets take up one's entire field of vision. That makes an immense difference. You may be saying, "Well, what if there is a really big screen like at an IMAX?" or "What if I'm sitting up close to a large screen of sorts so that it takes up my complete view?" These questions lead to the second way in which VR is impactful to one's vision: When you turn your head, you are simultaneously turning the camera in the virtual world. Even if you are watching a 3-D movie, you are still looking at the world from one angle and are subject to the angle that the camera operator has chosen. The lack of agency puts the human mind in the "passenger seat" and partially separates one from the illusionary world.

Recently, there have been attempts to increase the sensory experience with 360° videos where you can pan the camera around. When one does this, they are still doing so from a fixed point, and at the moment the 360° videos have an odd fisheye effect. It looks more fake, and our brains know that (but the experience still is fun). The VR headsets are more complicated than any other viewing platform that we have. It puts you inside the world as if you were in a dream, as if you were in your body. For anyone who hasn't tried it yet, the visual sensation is intense, and so is the immersion.

The third way that VR drastically affects your senses is that one has headphones on. In the same way that the "camera" moves in sync with one's head movements in the virtual world, so too does the audio feedback. The speakers move with your head's orientation and movements. This makes it identical to real life in two ways. You are probably unaware of the subtle ways that you move your head when you listen to others or the changes around you. Real life just feels "real." Not only does it appear that way in VR, but it is perfectly in sync with you actually moving your head. Since human beings are easily fool through their senses (experience countless illusions, optical or not), it is nearly impossible to know whether or not you are in a VR or in reality. The combination of sight and sound makes for an extremely intense experience.

Some people believe that VR still doesn't pose that much of a risk because it is bulky, there are wires coming out of the headset, or you are holding controllers. All these arguments (though correct for the moment) are temporary things that will change in a short amount of time. Technology has a way of getting smaller and more comfortable. Soon VR sets will all be wireless and lighter, just like phones or any other technology. One might argue with this section by saying, "Wait a minute, I'm holding controllers or I have a headset on—doesn't my body understand that there is a difference?"

Yes, I believe it does, especially when one *first* starts using VR. However, we are tricked so effectively by the sensory input of VR that it overrides the sensation. Every day I put on a pair of glasses so I can see clearly. After wearing glasses for long enough, I don't even realize that I am wearing glasses. This is similar to the way an infant or toddler is annoyed by clothes, and yet adults have just become used to the sensation of clothing. Shortly after the addition of the VR equipment, one may forget they are even in a VR world.

It is only a matter of time before the sense of smell is added and perhaps even some touch. When all the senses (that most people are regularly aware of) are part of the VR experience, then one gets what is called a "full dive" where one can easily forget the difference between reality and VR. They may not know they are even in VR. This can pose health issues to the real-life body. Addiction becomes a large concern when something becomes that real. People should be afraid. If you think that a full dive is impossible, then try combining virtual reality technology with the brain-chip implants and electronic sensory augmentation and you get very close to a full dive situation (experience).

The fourth very major component to VR is the fact that you are moving your body in time with the body movements in the virtual world. There are other electronic games where one moves, and people find that tactile sense more engaging. However, in these other games/experiences, the tactile senses are not as impactful because of the limitations of the visual and audible aspect of the experience. The powerful immersion one gets with the virtual reality is due to the culmination of one's physical movement with the visual and audible feedback in the virtual world.

Sound a little farfetched? If you want to see how our species reacts to auditory and visual stimuli, then look no further than small children who pick the noisiest (auditory) and flashiest (visual) toy to play with. This is much to the annoyance of adults who are around them. Think about this for a moment. Yes, it appears that they are "choosing" that sensory toy. However, with the realization of no-free-will, then you realize that they have no choice but to choose the most sensory-aggressive toy. Think about how this is used against us as adults. Perhaps it is the packaging on a food product or the lighting in a grocery store. Maybe it is having better graphics in a video game or more explosions and surround-sound when watching a movie.

All of this stuff is the same. That's how things are. We are wired to work in certain ways. Having some knowledge of how we work won't change someone 100% and make them not human. My realistic hope is that it will change us enough to be less fooled and controlled by stimuli in the world around us.

What does this VR stuff have to do with this book? I'm writing this book, and I think VR is fun. There is actual reasoning. I promise. VR seems so real because of the way it engages so many of our senses. It is only through our senses that we form memories/rules/platform. Our platform is our reality. Virtual reality becomes our reality. The memories formed in the virtual world will appear more real than other fantasy stimuli. So, if VR makes memories that are more intense and real, then VR will affect who we are as human beings. It will change us on a more profound level than people have been changed by games in the past.

There are positives to certain VR experiences that get people to move around and exercise, but what are the negatives? If a person is in a war zone or in a horror situation (causes), then what are all the effects of such an experience? What about violent games? What about games related to sex? I think we need to look at the possible effects of such powerful stimuli and determine, if not for others, then for ourselves if we want that as part of our platform, as part of who we are.

Virtual reality is going to end up being like anything else. It will have the possibility for immense good and education but will be used most of the time for self-indulgence and violence.

What if AI gets ahold of VR and is able to control us? Right now, one can't picture robots affecting humans unless they are using an electrical object, like phones—that we all have and use all the time. Or one might picture drones flying around and hunting people or robots running around like the Terminator. With virtual reality, the AI doesn't need to come to us. It doesn't need to gather us and put us in prison. We are going to it. We are walking up to the gates of the prison and racing into the jail cells.

There is room for a lot of f'd up sci-fi and horror films. Imagine that a supercomputer wants to kill an individual. Hacking electronic systems in cars or other means would be an easy way of killing that person. However, if someone goes into a VR world, the AI could slowly brainwash that person over time to make them want to kill that person in real life. Or the AI could sync a person in a VR game with something in reality, and that person could think they are flying an attack helicopter and playing a game, but in reality they are controlling an actual, hacked military helicopter. This is some scary stuff. It is possible that people could think they are flying a spaceship and shooting at aliens when in actuality they are murdering human beings. So much evil is possible. Did I mention that I love VR?

Technology and Outsourcing: Things Get Worse

Right now, there are warehouses with hundreds upon hundreds of human beings playing video games as their fulltime job. One need only look up "gold farming" on the internet to see what I'm talking about. Imagine over two hundred thousand people working in a large network across several warehouses, and their fulltime job is to play video games. Imagine how easy it would be to put them in control of tiny robots or drones.

Now imagine that a country doesn't like us, and they send over small robots disguised as anything: doorbells, phones, drones, kid's toys, or something that is just "convenient" that people will want. A country could send over two million products and have two hundred thousand of them be weapons. Then, when the country wants, they could have their network activate the robotic weapons, and suddenly you have two hundred thousand assassins behind military lines where missiles are completely ineffective. It would be a serious disaster. Sound like something out of a sci-fi movie? It's not.

Virtual Reality Is Child's Play When It Comes to the True Evils

There is another kind of fake reality: the cult. There are various "religious" cults (I know, *redundant*) that exist. They control what a person sees, hears, does, and everything about their life's experience. They tell people how to live their lives. If someone changes the way you dress, eat, and think, then they are changing you. That's their goal, anyway. Cults separate people from their families and often communities, making separate communities that are outside the influence of the overall community (or even country's influence).

The separation that cults use via food, clothing, and whatever means is an attempt to control the stimuli/causation of a person. It may seem like a cult is not specifically and directly telling its brainwashed flock not to spend time with their friends and family. It doesn't have to. The systems set in place, such as food control, clothing, and praying at specific times, are designed in such a way to keep people from socializing and spending time with others. They take a person and remove them from their support group and those who actually care about them. Once the person is separated, the cult begins to control everything that a person takes in through their senses.

Cults exist in actual reality, yet they take reality and turn it into a fantasy, and then try to call it reality or the actual reality.

VR takes fantasy and makes it seem more like reality.

Virtual reality, with all the fears I've listed above, isn't nearly as harmful as a cult. One might wonder why people get up in arms about a violent video game or VR (which can be a threat in the near future) and yet simply ignore threats to our populace that are occurring right now. Why are cults are allowed to exist? I know the answer: freedom, not imposing on people's rights. Where does one draw the line between willing-slavery, manipulation, and freedom?

I don't like being "forced" to do stuff. What if I have the illusion that I'm in control, but someone else is slowly manipulating me? Is that any better? People get manipulated and don't realize that the cult is controlling them until they are already brainwashed into "liking it" or "needing it." Whatever, the whole situation is very frustrating to me. I hate seeing people get taken advantage of.

Unfortunately, a lot of groups and organizations and bullshit-tellers of all kinds label their f'd up ideas as "education" or "knowledge," and they refer to the process of gaining their special "knowledge" as learning. Learning about the elves in a fantasy book can be fun, but don't take it into reality.

It is entirely possible for a human being to say, "One minute. I went on a great retreat up to the mountains, and I learned a lot. I felt like I grew. I met nice people, and I really felt like I belonged. They made me feel good about myself. It was a great experience! Yes, I was removed from my day-to-day stimuli and placed in a new setting with other people, which is a separation, but I didn't feel like I was in a cult. How do I know if I was being fed bullshit by the shovelful (they might not phrase it like that), or if I was actually learning something that was real?"

The answer: Think about what you "learned." Does the information have any basis in reality? What is reality? Reality is cause and effect. Was the information subject to some of the bullshit that I mentioned in this book? If you go to a coffee shop and share the great information that you learned on your journey, do people look at you weirdly like you have just come back from an alien abduction, or do they genuinely seem to understand what you are saying? Does the knowledge you acquired on your trip makes some sense (even if just conceptually) to other people who didn't share in your special and unique experience?

Rock the Damn Boat!

Many people don't want to "offend" someone who believes things that are untrue or stupid. Because of this, the person who believes bullshit might not realize how crazy their thoughts and beliefs are. Suppose someone comes up to you and tells you about this powerful alien god that tells them not to eat bananas. Most people will say, "That's very interesting. I hope you have a good day." Or something like that. They will "blow it off" or shrug aside the comments. Someone may be having dinner with their family, and a person says some weird belief, and everyone around the table gives each other the "Oh my God did that person say that?" look.

People are afraid of what will happen if they call out someone's fantasy as just that. They don't want to cause any tension, because social tension is uncomfortable. There are phrases for this like "Don't muddy the water," "Don't rock the boat," or "Just mind your own business."

The reality is that we are all in the same boat together, and it is called reality. If we truly care about these people, then we should try to actually help them. By going along with their fantasy, we are actually reinforcing that the fantasy isn't that odd or different from reality. We end up, if not completely validating their fantasy, at least saying that it is "acceptable" to think like that. And that is why I have no problem telling people to their face that a belief that they have is completely untrue. It isn't some ego thing where I *have* to be right or prove how smart I am (or however they want to label it). It is because I actually care about them. I'd rather sacrifice part of myself (my relationship with them) in order to help them understand a reality that they are ignoring.

This isn't limited to believing in religious stuff or fantasy but also to other things like relationships. Imagine that I am part of a group of friends. Let's just say there are five of us, and we "hang out" all the time. One of the five is married to someone who is abusive to them. Everyone in the group has seen multiple examples (experiences/memories) of our friend being taken advantage of by their spouse. Everyone (four of the five members) of our group have also come to the same conclusions (formed rules and platforms) about the spouse of our friend and are very sad for the relationship that our friend is in.

I go to one of my friends and say, "Hey, so-and-so is really being taken advantage of by their spouse. I should talk to them." What kind of response do you think the other three members of my circle of friends would give? Most people don't want to rock the boat, and they become complacent.

What one of my friends might say to me is, "Hey, Alan, look. We all know what their spouse is like. They made a choice to be with them, and it isn't our business. If you tell them what you think, then they will stop being your friend." In that reply, my friend is telling me all things that are true. Everyone *does* know what their spouse is like. The friend in an abusive relationship *did* in fact make the "choice" to marry them. "It isn't our business" is something that I have a disagreement with to a point.

I care about my friends—that is why we are friends. If I don't care at all about them, then I wouldn't care what happens to them, what causality affects them. "If you tell them what you think, then they will stop being your friend." That is a possibility. Again, it is fortunetelling, and no one actually knows the future, but there is a high probability that I would have offended them. I can do what most people do and just keep my mouth shut and let things happen as they happen, or I can try to help my friend even if it means losing my friendship. To interfere with causality with my own causality is a difficult situation.

To some, this situation might be black and white (either way). For me, I have to use the systems in place in this book: Gain as much experience (causality) and form new rules and enhance my platform, then once I do that, I need to consider all of the effects of my actions before I become a catalyst. Only after going through such steps multiple times will I feel like I should act—or not.

The Difficulty with Having to Make Decisions: The Need for Trust

Children lack experience to know what to do in many situations. They are not stupid. The most intelligent human being on the planet may in fact be three years old. Even though they may be very intelligent, they lack the experience to take advantage of their potential. I have heard scientists and doctors say that the human brain is still developing to a large extent up through a human's twenties and even thirties.

Think of my system with memories, rules, and platforms. When learning about reality as a child and teenager, human beings often don't have enough memories to form enough reliable rules to then have a solid platform, and yet they have to make important life-changing decisions. These important decisions "have" to occur early in life regardless of how developed a person's platform is with regards to reality. This is one aspect about life that I don't like. I am at least aware that I don't know shit about a lot of things, and I hate being pushed into making decisions based on not enough information. It just is a bad idea.

It has been my strategy then to seek out people who are far more intelligent or more experienced (or a combination of the two if at all possible) and trust that they will give me advice to navigate the world until my personal experiences allow me to catch up and form my own rules, platform, and apex platform with laws so that I can then make the kind of decisions that I want to make with at least some confidence.

I've had many problems, but "asking questions with the intent to understand reality" hasn't been one of them. I often wonder why younger people don't ask more questions or seek out more advice from those who are more experienced. It is a good thing that we have online videos where people can look up information without feeling like they will "look stupid" or whatever teenage-ego thing is holding them back from asking the questions that they could be asking.

It can be difficult to understand a discipline in depth even as an adult with more memories and rules and platforms. It can help when one has multiple platforms so that they can shift their mind into and highlight various comparable areas of knowledge in an attempt to understand a situation. Unfortunately, there simply isn't enough time for a person to gather enough memories to have a deep understanding of everything that one could possibly want to know. We have to put our trust in professionals and experienced people in the areas that we want to be knowledgeable in or trust what we absorb on the internet.

Yet it can be difficult to pick an expert when one has no knowledge about a discipline. This should be taken into account, and one should try to make every effort to educate oneself before taking the advice of another, then continue to ask questions and learn.

There was a time when the music department at the university I attended decided to interview people because they wanted to hire a new conductor for the symphony. I would purposely ask the same three questions to each prospective professor. My intent was to insert the same "cause" and see how it would be filtered through them. I still enjoy asking intelligent people the same questions to see what answers they give. This is an effective strategy for learning cause and effect.

Experience is valuable.

Being Taken Advantage of

Nothing bothers me more than seeing people being taken advantage of by other people. The stereotypical high school bully is an athlete who has superior physical abilities compared to others in not only their school but in their society as well. Instead of using those abilities to help those that are weaker than themselves, they use their abilities to hurt other people.

This is horrible when it happens. Luckily, it doesn't happen nearly as often as intellectual bullying. Sometimes a person with slightly above-average intelligence uses false causality, AKA sophistry, to take advantage of people or lead others astray. They could use their intelligence to help those who have a harder time learning than they do. If only people had more compassion. The only way people will act more compassionately is if their experiences change to allow such. Platforms need to be changed.

Even if I had all the powers of ten supermen, I would not be able to physically help and save everyone from misery in their lives or bad situations. It is fortunate or unfortunate that the majority of people (in today's world) get taken advantage of mentally more so than physically. It is the mental battle in which I am hence engaged. While I am not physically able to help as many people as I want to, perhaps I can help them in other ways. Never before has information been so easily transmittable, so now is the *perfect time* to spread information and fight the good fight. If we can help people think better and understand the world better, then we can then improve the lives of many. I want to empower everyone.

It is almost futile to try to fight every single instance of fantasy. Instead, I wish to create a method: A logical path to help people who are lost and confused to understand the world. That is one of the purposes of this book. One of the primary goals of this book if not *the* primary goal is to empower people with knowledge, with the hope that they will use it and in doing so will be less likely to be taken advantage of.

The Wars of Ideas

Young people have always been used to fight the physical wars of old people. Now they are being used to fight the intellectual and ideological wars as well.

There are very few things that are uglier than when a person fights for a cause because of ignorance, subjugation, or just plain trickery. I strongly dislike those who use sophistry and trick the young into believing their stupid ideas. I want to change a common phrase from

> *There are very few things that are more beautiful than when a person fights for what they believe in.*

to

> *There are very few things that are more beautiful than when a person fights for what they know.*

One of the Most Beautiful Relationships

The aspect of not having free will actually makes teaching even more beautiful. I have been fortunate to have had amazing teachers across various disciplines of learning, and I feel that the student-teacher relationship is amazing. Here is what I mean.

When a student asks for help or wishes to learn something, it is as if they are saying,

> Help. I have a goal/dream of who I want to be. I know what I want to be able to do/accomplish/achieve; however, I do not have the stimulation/input to change myself into what I wish to be.
>
> Will you please give me stimulation/input and have it be a catalyst to help me get what I want so that I can become the person that I want to become?

Due to cause and effect, a human being wouldn't be who they are without the impact of the teachers in their lives. Good teachers are worth their weight in gold because knowledge is power and power is gold.

In a good student-teacher relationship, the student willingly wants to change, and the teacher has the platform that gives them the viewpoint to know what cause and effect the student needs to gain the experiences and form the rules that they will need to become the platform they want to become.

Changing oneself is such a difficult task because people often don't apply causality to their own selves. They don't make any changes to their lives and yet expect a different effect with the same causality. Extrapolate today. Imagine if every day you lived after today was exactly like the day you lived today. A sort of *Groundhog Day* but without Bill Murray or Tom Cruise (I love the movie *Edge of Tomorrow*). What kind of person would you become if today was repeated for the next ten to twenty years? How did your relationships change today? How did your health change today? Thinking about one's life like this can be a good for everyone and especially so for children.

Learning People: The Art of Getting to Know Someone

Do cause-and-effect experiences/memories, rules, and platforms apply to relationships and people? Well, if it is reality, then it has to, because no one gets to escape reality (even if they think they do).

What You Realize You Didn't Realize

When you meet people for the first time, you are automatically informed of several aspects. The individuals' physical attractiveness, whether they are dangerous to you or others you are with, their intelligence, their "charisma" (how it feels to be around them), and possibly other details such as their clothes and other junk that they may be wearing. This is profiling. This is survival. This is sometimes wrong. This is sometimes right.

When you first meet someone, you make assumptions and snap judgements about them. This is how we are wired. When you enter a room of people, you look around and use your senses to ascertain several aspects of the people around you: physical attractiveness, intelligence, charisma/"animal magnetism"/vibes/ki/chi/," aspects that you pick up on subconsciously and many more things as well. The reality is that the average person is typically wrong when they judge someone at just a glance (however, one should still trust their instincts if they feel they are in danger).

How many times have you heard someone's voice on the radio or on a podcast and then you finally see them and are like, "Wow, that person doesn't look anything like how they sound!" Why are people still confused by this? As quick aside, going back to the "levels of understanding," I have found that a hidden benefit of seeing reality this way (and you can argue with yourself as to whether it is true causality or not) is that it changes people's initial perception of me when I meet them. If you walk into a room and view everyone as your friend, family, as part of who you are and you them, then this solidarity will actually change the way you interact with them and they you. It won't feel forced or fake because it isn't.

I find that I have amazing and "oddly frequent" positive interactions with "strangers" when going through life like this. Even with this positive mindset, my platform tells me to always have caution in the back of my mind. On the other hand, if you go around angry and upset, people will just steer clear of you. This is useful for reserving seats in a movie theater or just keeping your personal space when in a crowded situation. Imagine, then, how cool it would be if you go through life with a true love of nature and the world around you. What kind of changes might happen? Do you think there would be true causality? Would there be any causation? More than you would expect.

When I propose going through life with a positive outlook and viewing everyone as an extension of yourself, then it begs the question, Aren't you afraid of someone taking advantage of you? Yes. If only there was a book that could help people navigate such situations, a book that could help them figure out whether or not someone is going to try to use them or take advantage of them. If only.

Personally, when it comes to the day-to-day life in America, I rather give people the benefit of the doubt, even if it means being taken advantage of sometimes. That approach has worked better for me than going around with the mindset that everyone is an enemy. When you have more important and dangerous areas of one's life, I believe the opposite to be true. Use a more cautious mindset from a different platform when it comes to making big decisions like marriage or big business investments.

When meeting an individual, you simply know very little about them, even if someone has told you "facts" about them. Once you gain enough experience with them, then you are able to form rules: "This person likes X kind of food," or "Don't talk about X topic with them because they get upset." I "file away" how they behave in various places and scenarios so I can see what different platforms they morph into.

Once you have enough rules about someone, you get the "full picture" and form a platform of them. I am not inside other people's minds, so I don't know how it appears to everyone else, but I get an "aha" moment or a feeling of insight when I learn a rule about a person. I "file" it away in the platform (that my brain goes to) when I am with that person. When I finally really feel like I know someone (forming that platform of them), then my perception of them changes. When I see them, part of my mind is aware of all the memories we have. Even though I haven't remembered all the memories, the rules support the platform; the platform affects how I act and feel about them.

I both like and dislike the phrase "See something through the lens of X." I like it because it is very accurate with regard to a person's platform (from which they view situations). I dislike it because it is a bit inaccurate. It may be truly impossible to see something through the lens of another because it will always be you using your lens or your version of their lens, not their actual lens.

It's like an actor playing a character in a movie. It is always that actor portraying a character. They are not actually that other character (even though some do a great job of it). Do you believe anyone can truly copy your platform and see the world exactly as you do? Some situations yes. Someone may have formed the same rules as you when it comes to certain areas of knowledge, but they don't have all your memories. It would be highly "situational" or dependent on the exact platform.

Social Situations, Autism, and Authenticity

Some people, like me, have specific platforms our minds shift to when we are with different people. In my head is a mental construct of all the people I socialize with. I am able to understand many individuals on an in-depth level. However, once people get together, shit feels different. There is far more causality and thus complexity. We can understand the small by way of the large and the large by way of the small. The individual platforms that I shift to (meta/viewpoints) when with each person have to then act as rules for socializing and have to combine to form another platform and another for each social situation. I don't know about other people, but to me, when I "sense" different groups of friends or people, they just feel *different* from one another.

When it comes to social situations, most people seem to default to a different platform and just behave in a safe, just-go-with-the-flow, don't-rock-the-boat kind of way. I can't stand the superficial nature of "bar conversation." When I'm in a social situation, I'm trying to truly understand the causality between every single platform, and I often just fail. Due to work and life situations, I have learned to do the social BS-ing, but I hate it. I feel fake and inauthentic, so I tend to avoid social situations or just focus on a few individuals and try to get past the typical "bullshit conversation" to something a bit deeper.

It seems to be important for people to be able to change their platforms and thus act differently in different situations. To someone who is autistic (like me), this may seem like a person is changing and becoming or trying to become different people (inauthenticity). Many people who are autistic will stay in the same platform regardless of the social situation they are in. Some would see them as being unsocial or not "adapting" or "behaving correctly for the appropriate situation." Even so, they are the only people who are technically being authentic and themselves.

Being able to adapt to other platforms isn't always bad or dishonest. Acting appropriately for a situation is a good thing. If you are in a situation where you are fighting for your life, then one would hope that you are in a different platform from the platform you use when sitting down for a meal with your children. So what platform is a person? No. What platforms make up a person? That's the right question. When someone believes someone is who they are based on one platform, then that is what we call "being one-dimensional."

This changing of platforms is like looking at a mountain from different angles. Actually, I prefer the morphing analogy because a person usually looks the same even though they might change clothes (in a vain attempt to show that they are in a different platform). In reality they are the same person just showing different sides (or shapes of platforms) to others.

People are capable of changing themselves at a moment's notice. Imagine if I was judged solely upon how my platform is when I am playing the piano. You could only really judge how I am when I am playing the piano.

How about judging me based on my platform when I am sitting down to eat lunch? It just doesn't make sense. Human beings and our platforms are more interesting/complex than that.

A person isn't just one of their platforms. It is because of this reality that I stress how important it is to see the various platforms that make up who a person is. You can't know someone just by being around them at work, or at the gym. You have to see how their platform changes with regards to (the causality of) various situations. This means that "getting to know someone" takes longer than other activities when it comes to human learning because of so many more variables. The stimuli of different situations create different causes, which in turn means that a person is going to act differently. Who a person *is* isn't how they act in any specific situation.

There is a common phrase, "It takes time to really get to know someone." People realize that phrases like this are generally true but don't know why. Here is the why. People aren't just the way they act in any given situation. People are an amalgamation of all of their platforms. One then needs to have memories and rules of a person when different causes/stimuli are applied to see how they will react (the effect). Does someone treat you well when in another environment? When around different people? How do the changes of setting, location, people, morals, etc. affect the way a person behaves?

It isn't always bad to change platforms. The way I treat my parents is different than how I treat my grandparents, which is different than how I treat other professionals at work or friends. The ability to adapt makes humans more interesting, even if a little bit inauthentic.

> *A person is how they react when a cause influences them. It is how they react to change.*

When someone is authentic, then they are being honest. Honesty is a true representation of reality (as best as a person can). Being inauthentic or dishonest is a misrepresentation of facts, information, and reality. With respect to most people's platforms, it is understood that being honest is a good thing and being dishonest is a bad thing. This is another way of saying that causality, truth, and reality are good, and fantasy, falsehood, and misrepresentations of reality are bad.

The Physical Reactions to Being in a Platform (Mindset/Meta/Viewpoint)

When the mind changes to a platform, then the mental flashlight of focus shines on memories of that platform. Memories are knowledge, and it is the knowledge within one's platform that is activated when they enter a specific situation. For most people, the situation determines one's mindset. Having self-control or a sense of control over oneself is when you "choose" to be in whatever mindset you want to be in regardless of the external stimuli around you.

It is difficult to have one's mind in a different state from one's body. A person's mindset has a profound impact on how they perform physically. A mindset is a powerful tool that can be used to build oneself or destroy oneself. I'm sure you have seen both occur. Ultimately, it is from a mindset that the body reacts the way it does in the situation.

Human beings are programmed to focus on one task at a time and for their mind and body to be in alignment on the specific task. When a person's body is doing something from one platform and their mind is in another, then you can get an "unsettling" feeling. We label this feeling in different ways. Sometimes it is called not having one's "head in the game."

How do you think having one's focus/platform split between two different activities affects our ability to make a powerful experience or recall the memory later on? This sounds complex, but everyone has experienced this. Imagine a time where you were sitting down and watching a tv show or movie, but you were at the same time checking social media or going through email on the internet. I can guarantee that you won't remember nearly as much of the media as you would have if you were completely focused on it.

The structure of memories, rules, and platforms means that one's focus in the moment and how they make memories isn't just important for that moment but for the future because they are making memories.

Memories are the building blocks of who you are.

Authenticity and Memories: Becoming More Positive and Negative

People will often say that you can't form morality based on science. We know that causality changes a person. Enough causality leads to complexity, which also leads to reliability of change. Since people's platforms change, then they change. It is from this changing that morality can "to a certain extent" be applied.

There is an Irish saying from the Fianna, a band of hero-warriors in Irish mythology. The last part of their motto was *réir ár mbriathar*, which translates to "Actions to match our speech." There is something that feels good when one is authentic. Authenticity is when someone's mental state, physical actions, and words are all in alignment with a person's platform. When a person is in one mental platform and acting as if they are in another, then that is being dishonest. There appears to be a negativity when one's mindset doesn't match one's actions. Am I the only one who feels this, or do you feel it as well?

The synthesis between authenticity and memories is extremely important and profound. Everything you say and do will impact how you are. Why? Because you are constantly making memories. Memories are the building blocks for everything that makes us who we are (our rules and platforms). Every time you are nasty, then those memories get filed away and become a part of your collective whole.

Sometimes you get together with someone, and you can just "tell" that something is off or wrong about them. You feel that they have become more distant or don't like you. It can be confusing when you experience a different effect and don't know or understand the causality. This can happen for many reasons, and it may be that you are analyzing someone incorrectly.

However, there are times when it is the case that something has truly changed. Imagine that there is a person named Jan. Jan is part of a group of friends that includes Brian. When Brian isn't around, Jan likes to spread gossip. Jan tells other people nasty things about Brian. Jan believes that when she sees Brian that she can pretend that she likes him, and everything will be normal in their group of friends.

Based on the knowledge from this book, why does this not work? It doesn't work because every time that Jan talks about Brian behind his back she is creating memories in the "Brian Platform" in her mind. When she sees Brian again, she will open up that folder, and those memories will be in there. Jan may believe that she hasn't changed, but if she continues to spread gossip often, then her "Brian Platform" will change. This is a mathematical situation where enough experience/memories will change a platform. What is so fascinating about this is that Brian and the other friends can feel this change in Jan. If Jan has been spreading enough gossip about Brian, then the other friends to whom she spread gossip now have this information about Brian *and* Jan in their platforms of them as well as their platform of the group as a whole.

Truly Being with Someone: Sharing the Same Platform/Meta

We as humans have a platform that is constantly changing as our mind changes topics or places values on different memories so that we can function in a wide variety of ways. It is through this platform that our thoughts, emotions, and "decisions" flow. The platform is our focus.

"Sharing the same platform" is a bit misleading because one's platform exists in one's mind. Technically it would be "having similar platforms." If one person thinks that they are good friends with another and the other person's platform leads them to believe that they are just coworkers, then they are not sharing the same platform because their individual platforms of each other and their assumptions of their relationships are different.

Not paying attention or not being present when with someone is when your platform is on something other than what that person's platform is on. Spending time with someone is when you and the other person are sharing the same platform (not really, because platforms are in your mind), but your platforms are both on the same topic or in alignment: playing the same game together, looking at the same vista, watching the same movie, talking about the same thing, or just being in the same room and enjoying the other person's presence. My mind can be "distracted," and this is not always a nefarious thing. My mind "wanders," meaning my platform changes very frequently.

I might be in the middle of a conversation or listening to a lecture, and something that a person says will take my mind into that folder or change platforms into that subject, and I am no longer there. Each paragraph or section of this book is a result of what happens when my mind catches something of interest to me, and it races through various complications or mutations of the idea. If you are a quick reader, then you are experiencing what it is like when my mind changes. It is like changing stations on the tv or radio or randomly going to different websites.

When someone is talking to you about their day, then one often can assume that their platform is in alignment with their day. Sometimes they could be a spy or just lying, but let's go with the assumption for now that they are being authentic, and what they are saying is in alignment with their actions and emotions. Their platform is directly in alignment with their words, so there is no obfuscation. If their platform is about their day and your platform is about a cool movie you saw last week, then you are not truly with someone. You are physically there, but your focus is not.

What is so cool about focus and platforms is that people can often sense or tell when someone's platform is not in alignment with their own. Can you feel it when your platform or another person's platform changes? When their focus changes? Imagine if you are on a date with someone, and you are both really connecting. I would say that it is impossible for two people to connect if their platforms are drastically different. If one person is attracted to the other on a date, whilte the other is looking around at other humans in the room, then they are probably not in alignment, and they can both probably tell.

Suppose you are "friends" with someone. Your platform's view of them is as a friend, and your platform's view of yourself is being their friend. Can you be "true friends" if their platform of you is one where they are your "friend" because they "want something from you"? If you are in any relationship—love, romance, family, friends—and you and the other person are in different platforms, then should you even bother with that relationship?

An authentic relationship is when both parties are honest with themselves and the other person about what they want. They are both authentic, and their platforms are in alignment with one another.

If you combine the idea of people being disingenuous (pretending to have one platform with someone while actually operating in another) with causality, then you get one of the typical relationship breakups. Suppose human being X and human being Y are in a serious long-term relationship. They have memories that showed that they were truly in love. One day, Y tells X that they are leaving the relationship. X is very confused because Y has been acting the same for months if not years. Their relationship has been long-term, and so X has past experiences that have shown that Y truly cared about X. Since things are different on the day that Y tells X that Y is leaving, X realizes two truths about Y. Since X and Y see each other almost every day, X can tell that Y must have been acting on a previous platform (the one where they were mutually in love), while in actuality Y had changed platforms at some point. X doesn't know how long Y had been dishonest. This is an example of where one person is in a platform and assumes the other is in the same platform, but the other person is in a different platform (and knows this). That is not nice.

Causes can take a while for their full effect to mature. It is almost impossible for X to realize the length of time that Y has been acting on a different platform than their true platform. Is Y's change really sudden or random? It might appear that way to X, but as we know, there is a cause behind the change. If X had further insight and awareness (better senses), then X would have realized the change in Y's platform and would have known when their platform of their relationship (and Y's constructed platform of X) changed. Yes, this is reinforcing all the stuff from before. Secondly, X realizes that there must have been something (a cause) that changed Y, since if they were in love and in a good relationship, then something must have changed for there to be a different effect.

Again, when the effect is different, then there must have been a cause behind it. People don't randomly do stuff. People are not as random as they'd like to believe. Relationships aren't all that interesting to me, but I think that some people will relate to this scenario and will understand causality, lying, and platforms changing due to causation by means of the example.

If the reality that I'm suggesting in this book is actual reality (true cause and effect), then it should be applicable in multiple instances. Have you seen this example of causality combined with a lack of awareness (senses) and people being inauthentic? Imagine people close to a ruler who are plotting to overthrow them. You can consider this further "testing" of the ideas in this book. What do you think? Does the example make sense to you? Do you agree? Are there times in your own life when you've had this experience?

Inauthentic Dating

In the world, there are people labelled "pickup artists." They are seen as bad people with low morals. Why might this be? Well, when one is dating, they are in a certain mindset based on their platform. Someone like a pickup artist is one who is pretending to be on a different platform than they are. Typically, they pretend to be on the same platform as the victim, and yet their platform is quite different. Some people label this as metagame thinking because the "pickup artist" is valuing different information, similar to the hostage negotiator and hostage-taker scenario from earlier. A different meta is being in a different platform; the superior knowledge is simply a matter of morals and causality.

The pickup artist is being dishonest (inauthentic). The dishonesty and drastic difference between what one is pretending to be versus who they are is what makes this immoral by many standards. This example combines two philosophies from earlier in the book. The first is that they are being inauthentic by having one platform as their mental state while acting as if they were in another platform. The second is that they are being selfish.

Remember the "ends justify the means" section? It was when one person cares about a desired effect (what they want based on their platform), and as long as they get that effect, they don't care about what else happens. What else happens are the other effects that are a result of their actions. The pickup artist is a good example of someone who sees that the ends (that they want because of their platform) justify the means. They understand that they might get the effect that they are looking for when they act a certain way (the cause). This is immoral because they are only considering one effect and not the collateral damage of their actions, the other effects that will happen because of their stimuli. They don't really care about the person they are engaging with. Sounds much more like a "letdown" than a "pick-up."

Logistics

In a later section, "New Beginnings," I talk about a person having two platforms for one individual, one being how they view them and another being how they view their relationship. This is an example of how they get categorized. One's view of a relationship is a construct in their mind just like how they view a person. It is pretty hard to have memories about someone and not have it impact one's relationship or platform of them. This is where classifying memories/experiences and rules (or persistent rules) becomes a little confusing. Part of one platform can be part of another platform, and they can also share rules and memories.

Why do I feel compelled to talk about all this? Because people are in love with the phrase "What makes sense to you may not make sense to someone else." This is technically true. However, people stretch this phrase to the point that it gets bastardized more than any almost any other phrase. Once it has been warped into fantasy, people then want to pass it off as actual logic and reason. There is a difference in the way two people might view a piece of *factual* information: One might see it as a rule that is part of one platform, and the other might see it as part of two or five platforms. They will have some differences.

The phrase "What makes sense to someone might not make sense to someone else" is merely the way that factual information is presented to someone who is learning with regards to the way that individual's senses obtain information and the way their mind groups experiences/memories, rules, and platforms.

Unfortunately, the phrase gets used all the time to mean "Well, it doesn't really matter what you think—we are just different." It is similar to "Everyone is entitled to their own opinion." Sorry. No.

True: "Sense to you" has to be based on causality. It is how you personally combine experiences and memories to make rules and platform. It is the organizing of factual information.

False: "Sense to you" is not just random shit. If the elves bless your shoes every morning and that makes "sense to you," then you are living in a fantasy. Fantasy is devoid of sense. You are under the illusion of understanding something when you in actuality are understanding nothing. "Sense to you" generally is used to justify or disguise false causality or bullshit reasoning for engaging in ritual with no purpose defined in causality.

Rituals: Fantasy or Reality

What is a ritual and can they "work" in real life? When I go on walks, I will often talk to someone on the phone or listen to a podcast or an audiobook. Later, if I remember back to a certain place in the book or podcast, then I'll actually recall where I was at in my walk when I heard that section. This is because memories will try to incorporate all the senses.

Now imagine that I'm writing a fantasy novel with dragons, swords, magic, and different factions. If the book has a lot of different story arcs, then I might try to help myself "get into the mindset or mood" (get into the platform) of a specific character or faction. I might employ a strategy of changing where I sit and work on my novel based on what section I'm working on. For example, I might sit in coffee shops every time I write the part of my book that deals with the upper-class lords or a character with a big ego. Weather changes, times change, and if you are a writer like me, then you will sometimes want to write at four AM. Coffee shops generally aren't open at that time.

I haven't tested this next method, but if it isn't practical to change one's physical location, then one can change their perception of their physical location by perhaps adding an object like a miniature dragon to their desk every time they write about dragons in their story. The reason I bring this up is because objects, if used repeatedly in a way similar to what is described above, can help someone get into a certain "mindset," like dressing up for work, tuning an instrument, or putting on a uniform.

There are a lot of ways that sensory cues (visual, auditory, tactile, and so on) can help us get into the platform to do the work we want to do. This makes sense. There is a cause-and-effect association between the object and the effect. The reason why spiritual rituals don't work is because there is no causality. Someone may wave a magic stick around and claim that it keeps demons away. You can ask them how does that work, and they may say, "It just makes sense to me." It makes sense to them and them alone in their fantasy world. The reality is that there are no demons, and so waving sticks around doesn't do anything to fight demons.

New Beginnings: Building Social Platforms

When you begin a new relationship, it is extremely important to be true and honest with yourself and the other as you form a brand-new platform of not only them but of both of you together (how you see your relationship together).

When you first meet someone, then you are in a platform of "meeting someone new." This platform will be slightly different depending on the circumstances of meeting; however, it is a culmination of all your memories/experiences/rules from past social engagements.

When you meet another person for romantic intentions or friendship or whatever, then you are immediately placed in that nuanced platform. You move then from that "stranger" platform to a "learning" platform (absorbing experiences about them). Without your control, you will be creating those two platforms:

1. A mental construct of how you view them (who they are).

2. A mental construct of how you view yourself with them (a relationship).

This happens automatically because our senses are always active, yada, yada, yada, you've read this over and over. Due to past memories that you have with similar people, you may correctly or incorrectly make rules faster. At any rate, you are learning what the person likes or doesn't like. If you lie and pretend that your platform is more like theirs or say that you "like something" just because the rule in your head tells you that they "like it," then that is called lying.

If one begins a relationship with a false platform, then it is hard to be authentic. That is because you now have a lot of memories that are fake and are now jumbled in with the memories of reality, both of which form rules and platforms. Now the platform is all f'd up. This is the same "learning problem" issue from earlier in the book in regard to positive and negative experience when trying to form new rules and new platforms.

The non-causality (fake information) ruins four platforms:

1. Your platform of them.

2. Their platform of you.

3. Your platform of them and you together.

4. Their platform of you and them together.

What if one of the people realizes that the other is bullshitting or inauthentic? Then in that moment they lose their trust. When trust is lost, then a person can drop all of their platforms related to that person.

If a person stays inauthentic (meaning displaying a fake platform) from their natural platform for long enough, then it can cause friction or tension, like stretching a rubber band and holding it out of its natural shape. The tension may eventually break. In any case, it's just not a good idea. Granted, all human beings are different because we all have different experiences and lives. It would be illogical to assume that our platforms would match.

What other effects might result in a person being inauthentic? Other than that rubber band breaking, what do you think would happen over enough time if someone is in a platform that is not true to themselves?

This phenomenon of inauthenticity is not unique to one-on-one relationships but also appears in relationships with organizations or groups. When a person lies or is fake, that person is believing fantasy. They mix reality with fantasy in their memories that become part of who they are. Have you ever heard of any examples of people altering their platform to try to fit in with a group? Social? Business? Religious?

Earlier I mentioned that different platforms set up a person's morality, and that when the platform shifts, we end up valuing things differently. I mentioned that when someone shifts metas, this will change a person's values/goals. This is the social example of how that works. Values and morals can change depending on the focus of our platform. One attempt of religion is to have an ultimate or apex platform so morals/values don't change. That or just absorb all platforms into the religion platform. Does that make sense? Can you be truly authentic while believing in memories?

Knowing What a Person Wants

Within the realm of dating, I've heard a lot of people say, "I like dating someone who knows what they want." This often refers to someone who is at least an adult. The assumption is that an adult (having more time/causality) will have more experience dating and thus have more memories that have formed rules in different aspects of relationships. Over time, the rules combine into a platform.

When someone knows what they want, they have a platform built on rules that are derived from memories/experiences. That platform has with it a viewpoint or meta. Having morality or a viewpoint means that they have an opinion. In this case, that opinion is knowing what they want.

How can someone know what they like if they have no experience in that area? It makes as much sense as a child or an adult saying that they don't like a certain food when they haven't ever tasted it. They have no memories, and so their rule is based on emotions or insufficient memories.

Causality: The People We Meet

Determinism, fatalism, and causality are all part of reality. Since they are all true (also including not having free will), then that means that everything that has happened to you was going to happen. It also means that everything that does happen to you is going to happen. In addition, everything that will happen to you is already going to happen to you. These are all true regardless how significant or insignificant your view is of every event (effect).

When I meet a new person for the first time, I realize that, from the time that both of us were born, our paths were going to result in our meeting when we meet, how we meet, and in the precise manner of meeting. That is really cool to me! So if it is fate that I should meet someone, how do I want that relationship to go?

I personally want everyone's life to be a little bit better because they were destined to bump into me and I them.

To Shortcut or Not to Shortcut

There is an interesting situation that humanity is in right now when it comes to having knowledge. Right now, we have access to the internet, which can provide us with more knowledge than any one human being has had since the beginning of time. There is also a phenomenon where people will claim to have true knowledge (actual causality) or claim to know everything. This would be like someone saying that they understand the cause and effect of every discipline. Often, people will "call in" and ask anything as if it was actually possible to ask someone a question on anything. This isn't all bad. Some people are just more intelligent than others, and it makes a lot of sense to at the very least ask a question and see what the answer is, then use that answer as one memory to later combine with other memories and form rules so you can better understand how things work.

When someone contacts another for answers to almost anything, then it is actually a compliment because they believe that the person they are contacting is worth listening to. Some people just have unique experiences that form their platform, which can give them some insight or a way of interpreting information that can offer insight to other people. But I get worried when people begin answering questions about almost anything.

What is knowledge without experience? It takes a rare genius with an incredible mind to be able to give sound causality (knowledge) on a wide variety of topics. Such people exist. Leonardo Da Vinci is one example of a human being who had an exceptional understanding of causality in many different areas. For modern times, maybe we don't need a genius but rather someone who is just smarter than we are.

When a person is educated beyond their intelligence or is taught/shown something that their platform doesn't have the memories/experiences nor rules to support, then the true knowledge and education falls on deaf ears. An experience that would normally be worth five experience towards learning a goal might be zero experience. You'd get no experience. You get nothing. Good day, sir.

If a person gets confused enough, then their platform can dissolve. This concept is hard to take in, but the reality is that if you are given a platform or pieces of a platform without the rules and experience to support it, then you won't really understand the platform. The information won't make any sense, or, worse, you'll misinterpret the information so that, when the actual information comes along later, you might think it "doesn't belong" because it conflicts with the BS you put in the place of actual knowledge of cause and effect. The individual won't actually understand what they are hearing.

A lot of people call themselves experts in fields where they actually are not experts. They will learn the rules and get pieces of a platform and pretend that they have the entire platform. This is inadequate and bad in the following way: The individual lacks the memories/experience (or enough memories) to support the rules and basic platform. People like this often repeat what they've heard (like a parrot), sharing pieces of a platform, rules, or even an experience or two that they have memorized. When asked to go into any depth on a subject, they are unable to. This is because they might not understand the rules or perhaps don't have the memories/experiences that would give someone a working knowledge of what they are claiming to understand.

Once you realize that someone can't support the platform they are espousing, you soon come to recognize that they don't truly understand the platform of knowledge that they think they are on. This isn't *always* bad. A person can trust a platform from someone else and might not understand why it is right, but for the short-term it can act as a guide or help them get through a rare situation. The downside is that people tend to inflate their actual knowledge of what they think they actually know. This leads to people "filling in" the gaps of causality with fantasy. Fantasy leads to mistakes and misery.

When someone says, "There are no shortcuts in life," this means that there are some things that you can only truly learn with experience. If one is smart, they will "take the word" of someone who had experiences that are negatively life-altering. There is a dichotomy. On one hand, one shouldn't have to go through a car accident in order to know that they are bad and should be avoided. On the other hand, some self-proclaimed experts pretend to know what it is like to be in a car accident and be an expert on car accidents just because they saw one in a video or read about it in a book. Just like the car accident, I've heard people who claim to be experts in all manner of things without having experience. It doesn't make any sense.

If there are good teachers, then are also bad teachers. Let's remove the variable of simply bad communication. We often realize that there are those who think they have a platform to support a given area of knowledge. Then they open their mouths and try to teach, and it becomes apparent that their platform is built on false rules with no support structure (no actual experience/memories to back up the claims). You've heard the BS when someone uses phrases like, "Because I said so," "Just do it this way," or "We've always done it like this." You don't learn anything from these interactions.

When someone asks a legitimate question like, "Why do we do X?" then you are expecting a cause-and-effect relationship (reasoning). Why do we put on parachutes? We put on the parachutes so that we don't die when we jump out of the airplane. If someone's answer doesn't have any causality, then the answer has no weight, and you probably shouldn't be listening to them. If the person's platform (their morality) is vastly different than the morality of your platform, then you probably shouldn't be learning from the teacher. I would advise gaining a bit more knowledge (examples of causality) before totally discounting a teacher.

There are some individuals who are talented and may just "get rules" without having the memories/experiences that the average person might need in order to form said rules. If they do not work on understanding experiences/memories, then they do not have adequate resources to teach others. There should be logic behind teaching. If there is no logic, then what exactly do you think you are learning? Be careful of things that sound like logic (quick excuses) that don't actually have true causality.

Opinions, Opinions, Opinions: When Platforms Collide

This section is about two things:

1. How can you discern pure information versus someone telling you how to think based on their platform? This manifests as a person's opinion/meta/morality/viewpoint and so on.

2. What happens when the logics of two or more platforms (viewpoints, etc.) contradict one another?

Pure information is truth. Pure information is just what happens, the relation between cause and effect of a situation or situations. Opinion is how a person thinks, colored by their unique memories that make up all of their cause-and-effect experiences in their life that have been filtered through the base of who they are. These memories form rules that then turn into a platform from which a person's views are determined. Someone's opinion can be right only as much as their ability to accurately absorb cause-and-effect into their reality.

Unfortunately, people let their egos get in the way. A person's ego warps their platform. When this happens, people disregard cause-and-effect to feel better (this is almost exactly what was talked about with virtue signaling and religion). One red flag that goes up to let you know when someone is giving a bad opinion is when they suddenly disregard reality (cause and effect). A good opinion would be an explanation from a platform that is based off of causality. Actual causality should be pretty obvious. False rules and experiences often require BS-ing or some "creative mental trickery" to try to make them fit into a platform. This artificial trying to fit fantasy into logic feels similar to the way someone might jam a puzzle piece into a section of a puzzle even though it doesn't really fit.

In short, if someone's opinion (platform) is based on accurate cause and effect, then it is a good opinion. If someone's opinion is based on false cause and effect, then it is a bad opinion.

People flat out lie all the time to cover up their false understanding of reality. Here are some of the "games" that people like this try to play. They will say things like, "My opinion is better than yours," "Everyone is entitled to their own opinion," "That's just your opinion," "Everyone sees what is going on based on their own point of view, so there isn't a reality," and the list of examples goes on and on and on. When I was young, I could tell that this method of arguing or discounting of another's opinion or someone trying to "take a moral high ground" or say that their opinion is "better than yours" was all wrong. It took me a while to gather enough memories to form the rules and then platform to find out why.

Let's break these statements down, given the structure of cause and effect combined with memories, rules, and platforms. You may come to the same conclusion that these statements are stupid.

Below are situations where two platforms meet and often collide. One can think of these in a micro-sense (two people) or in a macro-sense (two civilizations/countries, groups of people, etc.). In all the situations, it is important to know that the arguments are weak because they are not specific and because they are just opinions (with no obvious causality).

There is always a reality, one that is only discoverable through causality. Without knowing reality, one cannot know the answers.

The first type of interaction is when one platform believes that their platform is superior to another platform (big shocker, because platforms are made of memories/rules that support themselves).

How it sounds is as follows:

> "My opinion is better than yours."

> "I'm right and you are wrong."

> "You people have it all backwards—this is how it is supposed to be."

> "I don't understand how they can think that way—we obviously know the right way."

> "You have to understand" (phrases like this are fun to dissect because they are more subtle. They are loaded with assumptions).

Is there a way to break this down and prove that one person is right or more right than another? There can be multiple outcomes.

Outcome 1:

Both platforms are right (in which case there is a huge miscommunication or language error or the parties are using language where the definitions of the words don't match in some fashion).

Outcome 2:

One platform is right and the other is wrong. In this situation, one platform is based on reality and the other isn't. Reality is cause and effect. Cause and effect is reality.

Outcome 3:

One platform is righter than another. This is very common and can happen for any number of reasons. It boils down to one platform being based in more specific cause and effect than another. In this situation, one platform might have more cause-and-effect experiences (memories) compared to another, so the rules are formed at a "higher level" (see competency levels) of the platform. It could also be that one platform is warped by ego or that one of the rules is just wrong. Just because one platform is "more right" doesn't mean that either are the best solution to any given argument that the platforms are having. I try to keep this in mind.

Outcome 4:

Both platforms are wrong. In reality there is just one string of effects that happens (no multiple outcomes or time travel). So, if something isn't right, then there are an almost infinite number of ways it can be wrong. What time is it? There is an exact answer for that moment. That moment has already passed.

The second type of interaction is when one platform simply discounts the validity of another platform.

It may be done directly:

"That's just your opinion."

"That's just how it appears to you."

Or indirectly by proposing that there is no reality and so your opinion doesn't matter:

"Reality is subjective."

"Anything is possible"

"No one's opinion is better than anyone else's."

Let's take the direct way first. Start by realizing that their brief statement isn't a good argument. If it was a good argument, then it would be much more articulate, specific, and clear. Broad statements are often a shield against one's own ignorance.

Consider the above phrases: Yes, it is "just your opinion" and "That's just how it appears to you." That doesn't necessarily mean that something is right nor wrong. It just means that the way you perceive a situation is based on your platform. One need only examine science or the specific cause-and-effect memories that support the rules that make up your platform (when configured to deal with said situation) in order to determine if one's opinion is valid or not.

If someone doesn't want to acknowledge or hear the science or cause and effect behind an argument, then they just want to be right and don't care about reality. People who criticize often tend to hide in their own fantasy worlds while "poo-pooing" your opinions and the opinion of others. Maybe they just can't handle reality. Either way, try not to let their ignorance get to you. I don't.

The second "indirect" discounting of someone's opinions is one that I find more interesting because it talks about whether reality exists or not and whether anything can be known. Warning: Like the former paragraph, those who argue this tend to just want to be "right" and ignore any and all cause-and-effect information that goes against their platform.

Again, there is no point in arguing with someone who ignores reality. If anything, you should try to help them because they are probably suffering in some way. Why would they ignore reality or part of it? There is a reason for it. It isn't just "random." So let's pass on the possibility that someone's just being a jerk or can't handle their ego. Let's instead assume that they have good intentions (wanting to get to reality and understand cause and effect) and really want to find out how something works or what is going on.

I believe that reality is real, that there is cause and effect to everything that happens. Just because "something occurred" doesn't mean that you or I know what the causality of the event was. One can try to go back to the "beginning" of time until one realizes that nothing caused the beginning: If something did, then something else would have to cause that, and it can go on and on. It's the "Who created God argument?" which just poses more questions than answers and rarely convinces someone to change their platform.

I'm starting to meditate on how philosophical and impactful a child's badgering is. "Why? Why? Why?" If you believe that none of this is real and we are all brains in a laboratory on a space station or that this is all some computer simulation and we are all in the Matrix, then we are just as real as the simulation, and none of this matters. In fact, nothing matters, and perhaps you should just walk off a cliff right now because nothing matters. Actually, if we are all in a simulation, then we are just as real as the simulation, and our reality supports itself.

So, after the above paragraphs of caveats, let's get to the heart of the matter, shall we?

To those who believe that there is no reality and everything is just "someone's opinion," suppose that I was to enter the ring with Mike Tyson in his prime right now. In fact, to steelman this argument, let's say we made one million clones of me and one million clones of Mike Tyson in his prime and put each pair in a separate ring and have them fight to the death, bare-knuckles-full-contact fighting. I can tell you with complete certainty that in every scenario Mike Tyson would kill me. If you then reply that, "Well, that's just your opinion," then I don't know what you are talking about, and I'm pretty sure that you don't know what you're talking about either. If you believe that I would defeat Mike Tyson in any simulation, then you would have to ignore the laws of cause and effect, specifically physics and logic.

Even after all that being said, there are still people who will try to make arguments that discount reality. The takeaway is just to use reality and cause and effect, and if someone can't handle reality, then they can't handle a conversation about reality and should probably seek professional help and counseling.

The third type of interaction is when one platform believes that all platforms should have equal weight with the views coming from their platform. How it sounds is as follows:

"Everyone is entitled to their opinion."

Yes and No:

It is situational. In some situations, everyone's opinion does matter. In others, it simply does not. The overwhelming majority of the time, everyone's opinion doesn't matter.

The Yes: Oddly enough, I like this one a bit more than the others. Every human being has lived a different life, and because of each of our unique perspectives (and we all are different), we have seen the world through different lenses. It is impossible for someone, no matter how intelligent they are, even with a perfect memory and having five hundred years of good health, to learn everything and know everything. Since that is the case, we have to rely on each other. The world is just too big and complex for any one mind to grasp everything. Anyone who claims to know the details of cause and effect in every discipline is just flat out lying to you.

If we want to know what it is like to be a human being on this planet, then such a broad question would need to have a very broad answer: in this case, the platforms of everyone who is alive.

The No: All the hundreds of thousands of two-year-olds in the world have a less combined weight of their opinions when it comes to diagnosing brain tumors than the weight of one qualified doctor. There is a good reason why modern rocket companies are not calling me to help them with jet propulsion. That is because my opinion doesn't matter on the subject (see competencies). I don't have enough memories of cause and effect when it comes to space travel to form even the basic rules that I would need much less be knowledgeable (at this moment) to give good advice on the specifics of rocket-building. With regards to rocket-building, if someone came up to me and said, "Hey, hey, Alan, they should listen to your opinion on quantum physics and jet propulsion—after all, everyone is entitled to their own opinion!" my response would be to ignore them because there is no reality in that opinion nor anything that could possibly back it up. I don't know what form of logic that person is following, but it isn't causality (real logic).

So why do people feel that their opinion should matter in other areas? Let's take religion. People feel strongly that many opinions should matter. I agree with them! Anything that is based on fantasy is not based on, well, reality. So if something is made up, then by all means have your opinion. It simply doesn't matter.

Some people decide that they have a platform of knowledge even without having any rules, memories, or experiences of any kind. This is like saying you have a building without any building materials. It makes no sense. Sometimes it doesn't have to. If the topic of conversation is merely opinion and not fact (such as fantasy), then anyone can be an expert because there is no basis in reality for which to judge such opinions.

Think about the following: Would it make sense if someone came up to you and said, "Everyone's an expert in medical knowledge and their opinion matters"? No. How about if we insert any other kind of discipline: "Everyone is an expert in X, and so their opinion matters"? Replace the X with the following:

- finance

- electrical engineering

- fluid dynamics
- construction
- combat
- farming
- brain surgery

None of the replacements make any sense because you know inside that not everyone puts the time in to gain the experiences (knowledge) required to be experts in those areas. Now let's add just one more to the list: religion. These days it seems like everyone is an expert on religion. In fact, pretty much anyone can write a book on religion. How can everyone's opinion matter in this one special area? Simple. It is based on fantasy and not reality.

Reverse Platforming

A platform is based on memories and rules. Memories and rules do not come from a platform. Causality is linear. Sometimes a person will get it in their head that they have a platform regardless of having no memories or rules to support said platform.

They then go out into the world looking for a teacher who they think is good based on a platform without knowledge. This is dangerous. Don't look for false validation. Don't learn from someone just because they are going to tell you what you want to hear. Seek out what is true.

In extreme or nefarious situations, a person might try to "gaslight" someone by not only discounting their opinions but their memories, rules, and even the platform of who they are.

Keep in mind that one's platform is useful for learning how to know what is real or not. This section is about *reality*. Once you understand some of reality (because we can't know all of it), then you get to "choose" what to do. The "decision" of what to do with reality is up to you.

I'm not trying to tell you what you should or should not do. You are the only one with your platform, and so you should be the only one who decides ultimately what you should do or not do. Do you know yourself well enough to know what will make you happy or not? Do you know enough to be able to reach the goals and get the things you want in life? Maybe it is time to get some other opinions. Take advantage of other platforms.

Why Do I Study Martial Arts?

Causality—honestly, I don't know. I like it for sure. I feel good when I learn more of the causality in martial arts. I enjoy the science of it. I don't know all the memories that formed rules and the specific nature of how my platform was affected over time to know exactly how I work. I do it because I have no choice but to do it. I don't want to stop doing it. I am obsessed with it.

Without understanding all the details, I could give you some BS story about certain memories that might have influenced my decision to do martial arts and other memories that have made me continue to do it. I could talk about why I think it is cool and how I feel better when I do it. What I do know is this: Due to the formula that I was as a child and the life experiences that I have had that have changed said formula, I have no choice but to be drawn to martial arts and to want to do it.

If you were to take ten exact copies of myself as a baby and I was to put them in ten exact realities that were the same that I was in, then they would have made the same exact choices and lived the exact identical lives. I would have made the same decisions from seemingly big choices like where I went to college to small choices like what I had for lunch today.

There are few experiences/stimuli/memories that won't have any effect on who you are. Some might have a small, unnoticeable effect. I feel that these life experiences (which is redundant because every experience is a life experience) change who I am in either a positive or negative way (towards the person I want to be or away from that person). I feel that the study of martial arts has been one of the stimuli/experiences in my life that has truly made me into the person that I want to become. It has been positive according to my platform.

I am writing this book for the same reason that I do martial arts and the same reasons why I do everything: I am me. You are reading this because you are you.

Our paths in life are one hundred percent set due to the state of the world at the precise moment we are born. We do have a destiny, and we can't avoid it. I want everyone's experience in the world to be a little bit better because their path in life happened to cross with mine. Since meeting me will influence us both, I hope that this interaction is a positive influence in our separate but connected equations.

"Who will be changed and who will not be changed by this book?" is probably the wrong question. "How much or how little will someone be changed by this book, if at all?" is probably more accurate. If I insert my rule/platform of the bell curve, I get the following: A small percentage of people are at one end of the bell curve, and so their lives will be drastically changed by this book.

Another small percentage of people are at the other end of the bell curve and won't have their lives changed at all (not counting all those that don't read it or stop reading part way through). The majority of people are going to be in the statistical middle and will be changed in some way. I hope everyone gets at least a little entertainment out of it.

In a New Light

Here is an equation from earlier in the book:

$$A(a + a) + B(b + b) + C(c + c) \text{ etc.} = \text{Who you are.}$$

How does the equation look after applying the concept of memories/experiences, rules, and platforms to it?

> Rule 1 (memories that support Rule 1) + Rule 2 (memories that support Rule 2) + Rule 3 (memories that support Rule 3) etc. = Platform.
>
> Alphabet, words, sentences, grammar (apex).
>
> Paragraphs, Chapters, Book.
>
> Experiences of a person, what the person likes/doesn't like, how the person acts, how they act in various situations (this is not an apex, but rather different platforms). Changing platforms makes a person more complex. We change to accommodate different situations. Our lives are more complex and so our platforms are as well.

One of the difficulties with creativity is that it isn't like a single path one is walking on where they can take a break and easily get back on the same path and continue the way they were going. If someone is in a creative mindset, then they should try to capitalize upon the moment because, once it is gone, it will be difficult if not impossible to purposely put oneself back into a creative platform, much less the exact one that they were in.

Luckily, the mind is free and can slip into platforms regardless of the physical state of the world around us.

Overriding Free Will and Self-Defense Mechanisms of the Mind

I went through a lot of different mindsets and thoughts when I realized that free will is an illusion. I sometimes thought of myself like a computer that was running a script. In feeling that way, I had the urge to try to break the script and change myself. The question became, "Well, if I realize I'm running a script and that becomes the cause that makes me want to change the script, then does the realization of the script become part of the script itself?" It does.

Our pre-programmed bodies are coded in such a way as to help us survive in prehistoric times. This prehistoric coding prioritized survival over understanding the mysteries of the world around us. When humans are lucky enough to not be stressed constantly with their own day-to-day survival, they have the luxury to engage in other areas of thought. These new areas of thinking can be bogged down by a reptilian mind. It makes sense to me that we should try to override our primordial minds so that we can explore reality in a new way. How can we do this?

We as human beings are like leaves that have landed in a river. This river has been running long before we have dipped into it, and our destiny has been determined many millennia before our existence. Our bodies come preprogrammed with self-defense systems. When you are nervous, then your body instantly reacts by producing adrenaline. If you touch a hot stove, then you instinctively pull your hand back. Have you ever considered that your mind might also have pre-programmed self-defense programs running that you may not even be aware of?

I suggest that there may be an advantage to being able to temporarily step into a different meta or change to a platform that lets us bypass our natural defenses. Our natural physical self-defense responses are obvious because we can experience them with our senses. The mental self-defense background processes, however, can be more difficult to recognize and understand. There are certain platforms that the brain switches out of as soon as we get there. When we enter these platforms, we are overcome with a feeling of great unease, and the urge to quickly switch out of the platform. Overriding this urge is like touching a hot stove and forcing yourself to keep your hand there. Sometimes the platform was there before one is born, and other times it could be something from a previous painful experience in one's current life.

The challenge is to find these difficult platforms and to force oneself to endure the discomfort and truly dissect the experience. When a person has a certain mindset or is thinking about an uncomfortable topic, then their mind can shift into a platform that they truly don't want to be in. In an earlier chapter, I mention that when people touch on the subject of free will, just the platform that they switch to when thinking about free will is too uncomfortable for people to bear. The self-defense that pulls a person out of a platform may manifest itself as a "quick excuse" or a strong emotional reaction—anything to get their mind to change gears and get to another platform.

The platform that one enters when thinking about free will is very uncomfortable. I want to challenge you to stay in that uncomfortable platform and truly analyze free will for what it is instead of quickly changing the subject.

I wish to challenge you to explore another platform. It is the placebo effect. This "effect" has been recorded in many different medical tests over the years. Every effect has a cause. Abide in this platform and keep causation in mind. What do you notice? What are the ramifications? This is worth careful thought.

Closing Thoughts

There is a stupid phenomenon where people can say the phrase, "As it turns out," then whatever follows people believe to be one hundred percent true. "As it turns out" is like saying, "Trust me, I've done the research and it is completely proven that…," then inserting whatever you want to say. So here it is: As it turns out, in my experience there is no such thing as luck. *As it turns out* is a rule that assumes that there is logical causality, memories, and experiences to support said rule.

Nothing I say or type should be anything other than obvious if it is true. If something is very obvious, then when someone says it or phrases it in a way that you already subconsciously know is true, then, well, this book shouldn't blow anyone's mind.

Nothing in this book is truly in-depth or advanced. This is all basic stuff that people should be taught while growing up. The question is how much prior experience would someone need in order for this book to help aggregate their experiences into rules and then form platforms? The answer lies in the specific individual's formula that makes them who they are.

Sometimes you will hear a phrase that will resonate with you. Perhaps that resonation is due to some truth inside it. I hope this book can help you understand why something feels true to you. Please consider the following phrases about love through the lens of this book. You may view them the same way I do with regards to causation and free will.

> *You don't choose whom you love or who loves you. You can't control whom you love or who loves you.*

Sometimes love takes its time like falling water, or sometimes it strikes in an instant like lightning. You know what I mean by this.

What you accept as part of your memories and rules will define who you are. How picky are you going to be with the information that you absorb into your reality?

The people you spend time with will end up changing your environment and stimuli to a great degree. Therefore, the people you engage with have a powerful impact on who you are. They form the memories of your life that, through rules and platforms, will form how you view not only them but also the world as a whole and everything in it. Knowing that others have an impact on who you are also means that you too have an impact on who other people are. You are part of their memories and reality. You help shape them into who they are.

Perhaps we should be careful of how we impact others. Perhaps a certain morality can be derived from this fact—the fact of no free will and the implications of causality when it comes to memories. In what situations should we have the right to impact another person's life?

There is an immense impact from what you *do*. What do you spend your time doing every day? Since there is no free will and statistically you are probably not an outlier, everything you do will affect you to a certain degree. What you do forms memories, which become who you are. So, how do you spend your time?

Religion is a powerful stimulus that aims to change the behavior of a population. It generally tries to appeal to many people. Belief matters. If people believe/know inside that something is true, then it will change them. True belief, when something is absorbed into a person so that it becomes reality to them, changes the person's platform and thus how they view and behave in the world. Belief becomes part of their "personal reality" and the effect of which becomes part of everyone else's reality—for good and for bad.

If you believe that you are in control of the changing of your platform, then you are someone who believes in free will. If you believe that your platform changes on its own and at best you can step back and observe the process (when meditating or not), then you are someone who doesn't believe in free will.

A quick word of caution: Remember, when you read a book or something that is written down, you read it in your own voice, the same voice you use when thinking. People often become attached to their thoughts and see those thoughts as part of them. That is because their thoughts are part of their programming, and the longer the programming stays inside of them, the more it hardens and sinks down towards their core of how they see themselves. So reading a book in the same voice that you think in can give it a false sense of reality (false sense of weight).

Be aware that information read on a page is no more important because it is written down. It is just the same as if you were to hear it spoken to you. It's the information and knowledge that is critical. One has to separate it mentally from the way it is transmitted.

If only you had a method for determining if anything in this book was true or not.

If I was a superhero with the ability to heal anyone of any disease just by touching their hand, had all the strength and speed of Superman, and could fly and teleport and had amazing psychic powers, then I could do a lot to improve people's lives and help humanity as a whole. However, even if I had all the powers listed above, then I know that I still wouldn't be able to help everyone. Given my situation in life, I feel that the best way for me to help humanity is to empower people. To share knowledge and create less victims.

A causes B.

B causes C.

A causes C.

Knowledge changes reality. Reality changes you. Knowledge changes you.

Knowledge is power, so giving knowledge to people is also giving them power.

Understanding cause and effect is power.

Nothing is random. This book didn't just come into existence. Your reading this book wasn't completely random, either. This book was created exactly when it was going to be created, and you were going to read this book exactly when you were going to read this book. There are no other outcomes—this is the reality we live in. I hope this book helps you.

Maybe this book will change someone or even, eventually, the world itself. I am a human, and so I cannot see the chain reactions far into the future.

This book is not the end-all. I hope, though, that it will be a stepping stone for humanity. And for you—a catalyst.